Carissa Phelps is CEO of Runaway Girl, and guides local community efforts to protect and care for youth by making available resources and networking options. Runaway Girl training programs improve responses to youth in crisis while offering employment and career development opportunities to survivor-leaders.

Phelps is admitted to practice law in California. She lives on the Central Coast of California, where she creates and contributes to worthy businesses as a social entrepreneur. She is passionate about inspiring others to see the potential in themselves and others. For more information and to book a training, visit RunawayGirl.org.

Larkin Warren's essays and articles have appeared in the *New York Times*, *Esquire*, *Glamour*, *More*, and *Good Housekeeping*. Among her recent book collaborations are Mary Forsberg Weiland's *Fall to Pieces* and Elyn R. Saks's bestselling *The Center Cannot Hold*.

■ ■ ■

Praise for *Runaway Girl*
A *School Library Journal* Best Adult Book for Teens
A Joan F. Kaywell Award Finalist from the Florida Council of Teachers of English

"This devastatingly honest memoir is not for the fainthearted. . . . Kafka famously wrote, 'A book must be the ax for the frozen sea within us.' *Runaway Girl* just might become such a book. [Phelps] gives the reader valuable insight into a problem that is larger than most people realize." —*San Francisco Chronicle*

"Carissa Phelps's story illustrates the power each of us has to speak the words that are the difference between life and death, freedom and imprisonment, success and failure. Carissa is brilliant. She's changing our world for the better, not despite what she's been through, but specifically because of it." —Rhonda Sciortino, radio host of *Crack the Code* and author of *Succeed Because of What You've Been Through*

"Riveting . . . A genuinely important book that casts the problem of sex trafficking in America into stunning, heartbreaking relief." —*Kirkus Reviews*

"*Runaway Girl* may break your heart but I promise it will ultimately awe and inspire you. No child should have to endure what Carissa did, but thousands do. Her story is a testimony to the resilience of these children and the difference a caring individual can make in their lives. If you have any doubts whether one person can make a difference in the life of a traumatized, 'delinquent' young person, *Runaway Girl* should put them to rest."

—Dr. Howard Zehr, professor of restorative justice, Eastern Mennonite University's Center for Justice and Peacebuilding, and author of *What Will Happen to Me?*

"*Runaway Girl* demonstrates a great amount of insight and maturity. Crisp writing and perfectly chosen events highlight the story of what happens to the majority of twelve-year-olds on the street."

—*School Library Journal*, selected as a Best Adult Book for Teens of the Year

"As a captivating account of the triumph of a battered heart, *Runaway Girl* is truly a modern profile in courage, a spiritual odyssey, and a riveting read. Any child who experienced the trauma that Carissa Phelps so poignantly portrays will gain comfort, encouragement, and hope in reading this book."

—Paul Freese, Public Counsel Law Center

"A brave memoir."   —*Publishers Weekly*

"What happens to the thousands of kids every year in the United States who are forced to leave home? Many of them find themselves in the same situation Carissa Phelps did: fallen between the cracks in foster care and forced by a vicious exploiter to walk the streets. With courage, insight, and unflinching honesty, Carissa reveals the truth about her life as a runaway, bringing to light the many issues facing homeless youth while providing them with a beacon of hope to follow. I want everyone who cares about our country's young people to read this book."   —Janice Erlbaum, author of *Girlbomb*

"This book is provocative in the best sense of the word: it incites readers to *help*. . . . *Runaway Girl* is an effective, socially aware book that offers unique insight into one woman's personal experiences with trauma and recovery and her journey to find herself in a difficult, frightening, and ultimately supportive world."   —Katie Shaeffer, *Bookshelf Bombshells*

"With not a trace of victimhood or unplaced drama, this is a terrific read."

—Amy Cheney, *The Rumpus*

"*Runaway Girl* should be required reading for anyone with kids, especially girls, in their lives."   —Jesaka Long, jesakalong.tumblr.com

"*Runaway Girl* is both a cautionary tale about the realities of sex-trafficking in the U.S. and an inspirational story of the change that is possible with the help of others. A very important read for both parents and teenagers."

—Vera Pereskokova, *SheKnows*

To God goes the glory!
To Pat goes the thanks!

RUNAWAY GIRL

GIRL

Escaping Life on the Streets

Carissa Phelps

with Larkin Warren

PENGUIN BOOKS

PENGUIN BOOKS
Published by the Penguin Group
Penguin Group (USA) Inc., 375 Hudson Street,
New York, New York 10014, USA

USA | Canada | UK | Ireland | Australia | New Zealand | India | South Africa | China
Penguin Books Ltd, Registered Offices: 80 Strand, London WC2R 0RL, England
For more information about the Penguin Group visit penguin.com

First published in the United States of America by Viking Penguin,
a member of Penguin Group (USA) Inc., 2012
Published in Penguin Books 2013

Photograph: Carissa, age six, outside the home of a family friend, ca. 1982. By permission of Tim Macleod.

THE LIBRARY OF CONGRESS HAS CATALOGED THE HARDCOVER EDITION AS FOLLOWS:
Phelps, Carissa.
Runaway girl : escaping life on the streets, one helping hand at a time / Carissa Phelps with Larkin Warren.
p. cm.
Includes bibliographical references.
ISBN 978-0-670-02372-1 (hc.)
ISBN 978-0-14-312333-0 (pbk.)
1. Phelps, Carissa.   2. Runaway children—California—Biography.   3. Sexually abused children—
California—Biography.   4. Prostitution—California.   I. Warren, Larkin.   II. Title.
HV883.C2P49 2012
362.74—dc23
[B]
2011038441

Printed in the United States of America
5   7   9   10   8   6   4

Set in Dante MT Std
Designed by Alissa Amell

CONTENTS

Part I

· BELONGING TO SOMEBODY ·

CHAPTER ONE

∎

But for many, love is their primary unmet need.

—LARRY K. BRENDTRO, MARTIN BROKENLEG, AND STEVE
VAN BOCKREN, *RECLAIMING YOUTH AT RISK*

Early one bright, hot August morning, during the first week of second grade, my stepfather picked me up and tossed me out the front door. I hit the ground hard, instinctively protecting my face, breaking my fall with my hand.

As I struggled to catch my breath, I realized two things: I was hurt, and the kids on the school bus out in front of my house were watching me. All those eyes were aimed right at me.

I looked at my mother, standing slightly behind my stepfather. She just stared calmly, her arms crossed over her pregnant belly. She said nothing, did not move, acting as though nothing had happened.

"Mom?" I said, waiting for the comfort and dust-me-off that didn't come.

"Get up and go to school!" Steve barked. I got the message: This was all my fault. I had it coming. I should not have caused problems. "Get up!"

I staggered to my feet and made my way to the bus. As the bus door wheezed shut, I saw Marcy, a girl who lived up the street, standing in the aisle waiting for me. She was one of those junior-high girls a second grader dreams of becoming. Almost a teenager, she wore makeup, had a cool backpack, and didn't talk to me like I was a stupid little kid. Marcy led me into the empty seat beside her while I squinched my face tight, determined not to cry. To show weakness would have been like putting a target on my back. I was concentrating so fiercely on toughing it out that Marcy noticed before I did that my hand was bloody.

At school, we headed to the girls' restroom, where Marcy helped me rinse off the blood in the sink, gently patting my hand with dampened brown paper towels. "Your stepdad's an asshole," she said. I nodded. I wanted to hate him, but I was half sorry that Marcy and every other kid on that bus knew how he treated us.

As we were leaving, Marcy asked, "Are you going to be all right?"

"Yeah," I said. "Thanks for staying with me." I knew she would be late for her first class.

"Okay," she said. "I'll see you later."

Standing in line outside my classroom door, I wished that this could be any other day. My heart thumped as the teacher began to call attendance. "Carissa." She said my name so softly, as she always did, and she looked straight at me. I'd managed to not cry yet, but when I saw her concerned look, the tears started to pour. Then she glanced down at my hand, clutching a bunch of wet and bloody paper towels. Minutes later, I was in the principal's office.

Not long after that, two serious-looking men in suits and ties arrived in the office. They were there, they said, "just to ask a few questions about the morning." I didn't know how to answer them. I didn't want to tell them the whole thing was my fault. That I was late for the bus because I wanted my mother to find the piece of paper my teacher had sent home for her to sign. My emergency card. I couldn't tell them how I panicked and dug in my heels, insisting to Mom that I couldn't go to school without the card, because the teacher said it was required or else I would not be allowed back at school. My stomach turned upside down. Was I going to be in more trouble than I already was? *Maybe I had it coming.* Maybe these guys in suits would blame me for what happened. I couldn't take that risk. Quickly, I told another story: My mother was pregnant; the baby was coming soon. "I thought she needed me, I didn't want to leave her, and that's why I didn't want to catch the bus."

"And then what happened?" they asked, as if they didn't already know.

"My stepdad, he picked me up and threw me out. My hand . . . It's bleeding from the cement." I knew even as I spoke that I was only making things worse. I kept looking down at my hand, still wrapped in the messy paper towels. I was pretty sure I was going to have a scar.

After I left the office, the school nurse bandaged my hand and sent me back to class. My teacher treated me really nice the rest of the day. She didn't even seem to care that I didn't have my emergency card.

The yelling started the moment I got home. Someone had called them. The men in suits. "Why would you lie like that?" my mom asked.

"About what, Mom?"

"About needing to be home. About me being ready to have the

baby. I'm not due for six weeks, and I sure don't need you here. That makes you a liar."

I was a liar. I felt horrible. Mom didn't ask about my hand. She didn't seem to care that it was bandaged or that I would probably have a scar. My brothers and sisters called me names, saying I was a tattletale, a big baby, a snitch. And it was pretty clear Steve was mad. I recognized that look and I knew what was coming.

Steve didn't care whether we called him Dad or Steve. But he had a rule—once you crossed over and called him Dad, you couldn't switch back. It was disrespectful. For that reason, I always did my best to not call him Dad. "Steve" was a good enough name for him. And Steve was what I'd called him when I told the story to the men in suits. I wondered if they knew who he was. If they were afraid of him too.

■ ■ ■

As far back as I can remember, I imagined being in a life that wasn't the one I was actually living. I knew I didn't really belong to this family. I was different from my brothers and sisters, I was sure of it, and all I ever wanted was to get away.

We were ten kids, soon to be eleven, in a noisy, crowded house where the competition for space, food, and attention never stopped. From the time I was five, Steve was the boss, the enforcer. A red-faced, red-bearded man, he was sometimes sweet and generous but more often angry as a bear roused from hibernation. One day he'd be hugging us, taking us to the movies, or treating us to Pink Panther ice cream bars at the swap meet. The next day everything flipped upside down, with huge explosions and fists flying and shouting, always shouting—he even shouted when he was telling us to be quiet. I never knew which mood he'd be in or how fast it would turn. What I did know—what we all knew, in the way that animals know—was that he had the final word. There was no second-guessing or negotiating. Mom was the soft one, the gentle one, the more reasonable one, and even my stepsiblings tried their best to work out their problems with her before anything got to Steve. Once he was involved, it was too late.

Nothing made Steve angrier than Mom being upset or hurt by one of us kids. He didn't care if the house was cluttered and chaotic, with wallpaper torn down and never replaced, broken appliances or wrecked bikes in the yard, just as long as none of it got in his way. He worked long hours to feed and clothe us; he didn't have the time or energy to care about household messes. But if Mom told him one of us had crossed the line with her—talking back, telling a lie, not respecting her—that was it. *Do what you're told!* Those words echoed through the house almost every weeknight after six. Yelling, he'd grab the belt with one hand and the offending kid with the other. If any of us dared to scream, his calmest reaction was to line us up in the hallway—his cue that he was going to be giving us all the belt.

We'd plead with Mom and with him: "It wasn't me. It was Richie. He started it."

Mom was hard to upset; it usually took a lot to push her into anger. But Steve was always ready to boil over. Anything from chewing too loudly to disturbing his favorite TV show might lead to a chase, swinging fists, broken furniture, or just a solid kick. "These are the rules," he would shout. "If you don't like them, go somewhere else."

Before I was born, Mom became a Jehovah's Witness. Her faith found her when she responded to a stranger's knock on the door. Very soon, Witness beliefs were the center of our family's life. My sisters and brothers never seemed to talk about kid things. Instead, they talked about the end of the world—Armageddon and the paradise on earth that would come after, with the wolf and the lamb lying down together and the fierce lion changing his lion ways, no longer eating flesh. Over ground-beef patties drenched in ketchup, we imagined that someday we would be able to sit close to that lion too.

As I see it, my mom encountered everyone—her children, her friends at Kingdom Hall, even strangers—with an open heart. She approached the world with a childlike curiosity. To me she seemed like the most reasonable grown-up ever, with big, soft eyes, a quiet voice, and an endless supply of gigantic hugs for all of her kids. Mom was five years old when her own parents abandoned her and her four siblings, leaving them to be raised by a combination of family, in-laws, agencies, and adopted parents. In many ways she stayed frozen in that moment, as if she were still five and waiting for her mother and her father to return so that she could trust the world again.

Mom ran away with Richard Phelps, my biological father, when she was fourteen and married him when she was sixteen. He was eighteen and joined the navy to support his new wife and expected child. In less than a year they had a healthy, dark-haired, blue-eyed baby girl, Emily. My father declared that "Robert" would be the name of his next child, after his adopted father. Instead he got Sophie. He tried again for his Robert, and this time got Roberta (later Robin, Bobbee, and finally Sky—as if the whole matter of her name were to remain up in the air). My older brother Richie was born unable to breathe. He nearly died before my father had the chance to name him.

By the time I was born, Dad had already left the navy, trading the adventure of different posts around the world for stability back in his and Mom's hometown of Coalinga. Dad set out to start his own business, a lumberyard. When that failed, my parents' fragile marriage began to collapse as well. Mom and Dad would fight, yell, break up, and get back together, then stay together just long enough to make another baby. I was born and after me, Jacob, who also barely made it into this world. My oldest sister, Emily, soon felt the stress of the growing family and the on-and-off nature of our parents' relationship. She'd become the default caretaker and begged our mother to stop having children. But Dad stepped in and said that we were Emily's responsibility and that she needed to stay home from school and help with Jacob, because he was sick.

Mom breast-fed each of us, and one of my sisters was always around if I was hungry or had a tummy ache. Mom provided comfort if we fell down, but she could never sense when we needed encouragement to start back up again. She was my source for everything; she gave me food, a kind of love, and bits of affection, like letting me go back to bed with her on days when I stayed home sick. There, Mom would instruct me on her relaxation tricks. Lying in bed on our backs we'd prop our feet up on the wall at the head of the bed. "When I waitressed I had to do this every night, it's good to get the blood flowing when you're on your feet all day—otherwise you'll get varicose veins," Mom said, as we both checked our thighs for any unwanted signs of blue or green.

She had a gleam in her eye every time a new baby came along—it seemed to spark something deep inside her, and her energy became almost totally focused on the new arrival. But Jacob's birth was a breaking point for Emily. At fifteen, she was no longer willing or able to be the second mom, constantly caring for her younger siblings and afraid that the situation might force her to drop out of high school. Determined to live her own life and get her education, she petitioned the court for legal emancipation. With Mom's support, and despite Dad's protests, Emily's freedom was granted. She stayed in constant touch with each of us, but her departure, and her absence, was a loss and an example. There was a place for all of us outside our family, and one way or another, we would each have to find it.

■ ■ ■

At Kingdom Hall we learned that in heaven children would be happy. Eternal life meant forever and ever. Luckily, everyone we saw in the pictures of paradise seemed to be resurrected at one of their best moments. Children had their brightest eyes and even the elders were wrinkle free. They'd left all traces of illness or sadness behind. We didn't celebrate birthdays or Christmas or Easter—we simply lived out our lives in unmarked time, waiting for death and the new beginning. I never worried about the future, because it was taken care of. Instead, I soaked up the present world—playing in the sprinklers, riding my bike, naming my dolls, and if my parents weren't home, dancing with my older sisters to any record that wouldn't skip.

My father did not participate in meetings or go to the Kingdom Hall or consider himself a Jehovah's Witness. He thought the whole thing was brainwashing—first Mom, then his kids—and he made no secret of not liking it. Mom did not try to convince him to convert; maybe she knew he wouldn't budge. But the strain and tension around religion grew more obvious every day. Mom felt that being a Jehovah's Witness made her better than Dad—better than lots of people—and he believed that the religion was taking away his family.

I was five when my parents separated for the last time, and we moved far away from Coalinga to stay with our "uncle" Steve in Southern California.

During the separation, Mom and Steve became close, and we soon learned they were going to have a baby together. A divorce, a remarriage, another baby coming, plus the six of us kids and Steve's four (three boys and a girl), and everything upside down and backward. My big sisters were mad and embarrassed. My new roommate—my soon-to-be stepsister, Sara—was six, totally confused, and mourning her own mom, who had died not long before. I was five, my dad was gone, and so was all my stuff.

I didn't have many toys or clothes of my own and quickly discovered that Sara had plenty. "Those are mine!" she screamed one day when she found me playing with her Strawberry Shortcake dolls. "Grandma, she's playing with my dolls!" Her reaction was more than I could handle, and I threw the dolls at her.

I wanted my stuff back. I wanted my dad back. I wanted my old room back with my brothers, and in a weird way (because, after all, she was right there every day), I wanted my mother back too.

As I grew older, Mom began to fade out, like a radio signal that occasionally came through but couldn't stick. She'd held small jobs in the past—one of them, doing data entry for the IRS during tax season, got us access to an Easter party with chocolate eggs and a huge bunny. I guessed the bunny was a dressed-up person, but I didn't care if the Easter Bunny was real or not—I was getting candy. But as Mom's world shrank, so did ours. For many years there would be no more office parties, no more jobs.

Steve did not like bosses, so he never submitted to one. When odd jobs weren't enough to pay the bills and swap meets couldn't keep our band of growing kids clothed, his mother Elaine helped him buy his own auto repair shop in Coalinga.

We kids knew that every month there was trouble paying bills, "keeping the lights on," and having enough food to eat. Yet every month, Steve somehow provided, even if it was only potatoes and cheese for dinner. Suspicious of agencies and paperwork, he would not allow Mom to apply for welfare or food stamps or even low-income health-care benefits. He didn't want to answer to anyone, ever. He was the sole authority on anything having to do with how we survived, except for religion, which Grandma Elaine bargained to control.

In exchange for any loans Grandma gave Steve, especially the big one to open the shop, he pledged to her that all the children would go to church regularly. For my brothers and sisters that meant attending Kingdom Hall on Sundays and on Wednesdays. For Steve's kids it meant the local Mormon church. Ethan (only a toddler) could choose either. Mom, however, stopped attending any church or meeting. She told us that although she still believed in Jehovah, she had been judged by the members of the Kingdom Hall for being married to a nonbeliever. But her disfellowship did not stop her from supporting us in our religious studies or talking about paradise at the kitchen table.

I loved the energy generated at the huge Jehovah's Witness stadium events, which felt less like church and more like a baseball game. I liked being part of something that seemed to hold our family together, the one thing we had in common from before Steve and his children came. I diligently memorized and could recite at Kingdom Hall the names of the books of the Bible—the five that Moses wrote, plus Joshua, Judges, Ruth, and all the rest in the Old Testament, the Gospels and Epistles in the New Testament, and everything up to and including Revelation, which scared the heck out of me, even though Mom assured me that it would all be beautiful after the end. I believed in Jehovah; I believed he had a son named Jesus who had suffered for my soul. And most of all, I believed that the Jehovah's Witness beliefs that my family shared kept us a family—it was the only real tradition that we had, even after my parents' divorce and my mother's remarriage. I said my prayers every night in bed, lying flat on my tummy, putting my hands together, crossing my legs at the ankles, and resting my head on my knuckles. I knew some kids prayed out loud and on their knees next to their beds. But I always shared a bedroom and didn't want to share my praying too. I prayed silently in the dark, my eyes closed, being private with Jesus. Through Jesus I could tell Jehovah all my troubles and ask Him to please watch over my family, my sisters, brothers, and parents, and everyone in the world, asking that they be safe and free from pain and suffering. Near the end of every prayer, I imagined a blanket of God's love covering the earth. *In Jesus' name I pray, amen.* I knew I was always heard.

■ ■ ■

After Emily left the house, we were a family of twelve, but we were frequently even more, because the house was often a pit stop for wayward aunts, uncles, or cousins or Steve's down-on-their-luck buddies. Someone was always camped on the couch, making a sandwich, or opening a can of something. There was constant cleaning going on, and as hard as my sisters scrubbed, the cockroaches still took over the kitchen. Mom insisted she couldn't keep the house clean because of us kids. Her solution was to send us outside as much as possible. The alternative was being sent to our rooms until Steve got home. She never had to ask me twice—I had my bike and loved riding until I was lost, leaving the chaos far behind me.

On weekends I was often out the door before anyone woke up, going to my friend Kristie's house, the only two-story in the freshly baked development across the street. If Kristie was still asleep, her mom let me come in and watch cartoons. I felt a little lonely waiting sometimes as long as an hour, but once Kristie was awake, it was worth it. We started the morning by practicing cartwheels on her impossibly green lawn. When my bare feet touched the soft blades, everything seemed to make sense. Kristie wasn't allowed to come to my house to play because of my rowdy brothers, but that was okay—I liked being at her house better, eating my favorite cereal in her kitchen, making up dance routines to our favorite songs. I wished, I prayed, that when we moved the next time, we could have a two-story house with that kind of grass, the kind I could turn cartwheels on.

■ ■ ■

My new stepfamily celebrated Christmas, and at eight years old I was going to see my very first Christmas tree inside my living room. We'd never had much money for gifts, which didn't matter when we weren't celebrating, but now, in an effort to put something under that tree, Mom decided to try something special for us.

"I have a surprise for you girls," she said. We were in the station wagon, and my stepsister Sara was with us. "You're going to Kmart on Saturday morning, and it's going to be a special morning there, just for you and a bunch of other kids."

"Will Santa be there?" Sara asked. She was nine but still believed in that sort of stuff. Mom had already ordered me not to tell anyone that Santa didn't exist, so I went along with it, knowing very well that if Santa was at Kmart, he was really a person in a costume, just like the Easter Bunny.

"You both won a contest," Mom said, "and it's twenty dollars to spend on a shopping spree!"

All week long, I couldn't stop telling my friends at school about the money I'd won from a contest that I hadn't even entered. Finally one of them, annoyed by my blabbering, said, "You didn't win anything—they're just giving it to your family because you're poor!"

What? It was because I was poor? How did Kmart know that? I was crushed. The sting disappeared when we showed up for the shopping spree early on Saturday, before Kmart opened to the public. I had my picture taken with the man in the Santa suit and met some very nice firefighters, who gave each of us our gift cards and took us around the store. "This is your money," they said. "You can spend it any way you want."

I went to the toy aisle first with the rest of the kids. The shelves were filled with amazing things. Maybe I could buy a Barbie and the Rockers doll, the one with the pink hair and the shiny, metallic skirt. That was tempting. But something inside stopped me from wanting to spend all the money on myself. I thought instead about getting a gift for Kristie's mom, something to say thanks for always opening the door for me early on Saturday mornings. I couldn't find anything nice enough in the five-dollar range, so I picked out a ten-dollar gift set of soap, perfume, and lotion in a baby-blue box that said "baby powder scent." The box was so pretty, I wouldn't even have to wrap it. As soon as we got home, I jumped out of the car and ran across the street to Kristie's, too excited to wait for Christmas day and not wanting to take the treasure into my own house, where it might be lost or stolen. When Kristie's mom answered the door, I handed her the box. "This is for you! I mean, the whole family."

"This is very sweet, Carissa," she said. I beamed.

Maybe I didn't have a new Barbie like Sara did, but that was okay. I didn't want to be poor, and for a brief moment in Kmart, I wasn't— I was generous and open. I had been given a gift, and I gave it to someone else. I liked the way that felt.

■ ■ ■

When I was ten, we left Southern California and returned once again to Coalinga, where Steve bought a house. It was two stories, but not like Kristie's, the kind I'd always dreamed of. It had a big, burned-grass yard. He made the deal without considering what Mom might think. She held back tears as she walked through the house for the first time, the day we were supposed to move in. We didn't know how many people had lived in the house before us, but it looked like nobody had ever taken good care of it. None of us wanted to be there, so when Mom said we were staying at Nana's, no one disagreed with her. Steve promised that if we moved in, he would have everything up to Mom's standards as soon as he could get away from the shop. He never did.

In the move to the house, we lost some things. One suitcase came off the top of the car on the freeway—Mom was so embarrassed about her underwear somewhere out there on Interstate 5. And me, I lost my friend Kristie, now nearly four hours away. At our age it might as well have been the distance between the earth and the moon.

Coalinga is little more than an hour's drive southwest of Fresno, in the Central Valley. Once a stagecoach stop between the Sierra Nevada and the coast, Fresno and the land around it were transformed when the pioneers figured out how to reroute nature, building miles of irrigation canals that harnessed the rivers that flowed down from the mountains, primarily the San Joaquin. Water transformed the valley into what became the richest agricultural area in the United States. "Coalinga" might sound like many of the other musical, vaguely Spanish-sounding names that dot California's history. But it is not. Coalinga, a stop on the freight-train line, was originally "Coaling Station A." Not much music in that. It was hot, dry, and often brown. On any given day, truckloads of cantaloupes, cotton, lettuce, and tomatoes went through town on their way to someplace else, leaving lettuce leaves and tomato skins for flies to nibble on in the heat. All through the valley there were oil rigs, their drills endlessly bobbing up and down like big steel birds pecking the ground, searching for pockets of black gold, not knowing where it would be found or when.

During harvest season, migrant farmworkers stayed in every Coalinga motel, including the one right behind our new house. "Damn wetbacks!" Steve would say when a group of men gathered in the alleyway.

"Steven, that's awful language," Mom would reply.

"What?" Steve would say, chuckling at seeing my mom get upset.

Then my stepbrother would chime in, "They need to go back to their own country."

This kind of talk went on regularly and left us kids feeling uneasy about our own Mexican heritage, which no one ever discussed or acknowledged. Our father was half Mexican—his family was from Guadalajara. To me that meant we were somewhat Mexican, and every time Steve or one of my stepbrothers complained about "those people," I wanted to run away. My mom had Jewish roots, but that was fine. Steve's family was Scots-Irish—white. That too was okay. Mexican was associated with everything bad, but not in my eyes. Some days, I wished I could take the whiteness out and fill it with this other part of me.

It took less than a week in Coalinga for my brothers to get into trouble at school. Fights, detention, phone calls home from the office, with suspension or even expulsion coming next. Steve was angry that nobody seemed to be adjusting to the move. At the time, I felt overwhelmed by all the change and tension; looking back, Steve was probably the most overwhelmed by all of it, and by all of us.

I stayed out of the way and out of the house. I rode my bike for hours, wheeling around until the streetlights came on. Not far from our house was a small field where people kept a few goats. They were small and gentle, chewing on grass, walking cautiously up to the fence when I spoke to them. "Hey, goats," I said. They looked up as though they were about to say something. Sometimes they chased each other through the grass, rolling and tumbling, but mostly they were calm, busy with eating, busy with just being. They were watchful, with soft brown eyes, and they were quick—I imagined that they wouldn't bother running away until the very moment a predator appeared, and then they'd fly. Maybe it wasn't so smart to wait that long. Or maybe they were saving their energy for the race. Dusk was my favorite time of day to be there, when the air was cooler, the day coming to an end and the light turning soft.

Sometimes I rode my bike to Nana's. Mom was always there because she hated the new house. She and Nana played Scrabble, and if I arrived at the right time, I could play too. I learned to spell things like "qintar," which was some kind of foreign money, and "qi," which meant something in Chinese. I loved the easy words like "bah," which reminded me of the sound the little goats made.

Learning words was fun, but I soon found something I liked even better—my new teacher, Mr. Newman, helped me discover math. When I was eight, my sister Sophie taught me to multiply by nines on my fingers. That same year, my favorite shirt was covered with numbers and math symbols. I could add and subtract, divide and multiply as though this had been my language before I'd learned English. Even more important, I discovered the way it felt to be good at something. My brothers hated school, but my sisters liked it. And now I had a reason to like it too.

After I was done with multiplication work sheets, Mr. Newman fed me math questions, and I was happy to answer them for the whole class. As fast as he gave me problems, I could solve them. Part of it was comfort—numbers and formulas didn't change the way characters in history and paragraphs in English did—and part of it was the way it felt to get exactly the right answer, again and again. It was as though some of my classmates got lost in the woods and had to thrash their way out, but I instinctively knew where the path was and how to follow it. Math made sense. It didn't change, it wasn't subject to interpretation, it didn't jump back and surprise me; it seemed logical and linear, predictable and manageable, and I could *do* it.

As a payoff for my hard work, at the end of the year I won a school-wide math award. A few weeks before the awards ceremony, I broke my foot on some uneven asphalt at school. Nevertheless, with cast and crutches, I hobbled up to the stage in front of the entire school to accept my honor. I liked the attention, I liked the applause, and I especially loved the letter I brought home to show my family. It was signed by Ronald Reagan, the president of the United States. The signature was in blue ink, and even though I didn't care that it was clearly a stamp, I worried my family would think it less special. I prepared myself for what my brothers or Mom might say. "It's *mine*," I would yell back at them, "*and* even if the president doesn't know who I am, someone in his office does!" I wasn't going to give anybody permission to shatter my moment. I needn't have worried. They didn't notice the stamp. They barely even looked at the letter. "That's nice, honey," Mom said. "Now, you know it's your night for dishes, right?"

■ ■ ■

When my great-great-grandfather graduated from the University of California at Berkeley, the school presented him with an engraved silver mug because he was the first returning student to complete his degree while supporting a wife and children. The mug came with a note outlining specific instructions about how it should be passed down through his family. It is still our family's only heirloom.

In her twenties, Nana received the mug after she too graduated from the University of California at Berkeley, and for years it sat on a shelf in her living room. I used to go over to Nana's and polish it. "Graduate from Berkeley and it will be yours." She said it like it was a real possibility, and her position was firm. As long as she was alive, it would not move from her cabinet unless someone carried on the family legacy.

Given the family's track record, it sometimes seemed the mug might never leave the cabinet. My mother had dropped out of high school when she met my dad at fourteen. She took some community college classes in later years but never went further. My aunts and uncles didn't finish college, and neither Mom nor Steve ever had much to say to us about higher education other than to yell if we came home with bad grades. Good grades were greeted with indifference. Aside from joking that my brother would be a lawyer because he never gave up on an argument, there wasn't any discussion about our futures. My parents repeatedly warned us about "the real world," but they were never specific about what that meant or how we could make it on our own. In retrospect, I doubt they knew.

The spring my older sister Sky was about to turn eighteen, she called Sara and me and asked us to meet her at Fatte Albert's, a pizza place in Coalinga.

Turning eighteen means a lot of things to a lot of kids, but in our household it meant one big thing: time to move out. For as much coming and going as my brother and sisters had done (to my dad's, to an aunt's or a friend's, fighting with Steve and Mom and leaving, then coming back), eighteen meant no coming back. It was Steve's official "everybody out" age cutoff. Now it was Sky's turn.

Sara and I typically tried to see each other as little as possible. We shared a bedroom but had difficulty breathing the same air—we were so different. We might have both wished for a time machine so we could go back and stop her father and my mother from getting married. The only thing that bonded us was our baby brother, Ethan. We put aside our differences for him. Now Sky wanted both of us to see her, and she said it was important for us to meet outside the house. Sensing the weight of something momentous, we agreed to go.

Sky worked at Fatte's, and being there with her was always fun. But when I slid into the booth, I knew right away that this was different. Her face was tight—something in her eyes said this was not going to be the usual kind of talk about her rock-star career or wanting us to play decoy for her while she did some shoplifting. She asked me to slide over and let Sara sit on my side of the booth, so that she could look at us while we talked. "Your pizza and sodas are coming, don't worry."

Once Sara and I were settled, Sky leaned in toward us and instinctively we leaned toward her. "I have to tell you something," she said. "This is serious. You have to pay very close attention. And promise before you say anything that you'll listen to everything." Her voice was almost a whisper, drawing us in. I knew that whatever came next would be scary. She didn't wait for us to promise.

"Steve offered me money," she said. Then she took a breath. "He said . . . He said he knew somebody who would pay me money for my virginity." Sara and I looked at each other. *What?* "Sex," Sky said. "Virginity is when you haven't had sex yet. Do you understand? He's offering to pay me to have sex with somebody for the first time. But I don't think it's with somebody. I think he's talking about himself."

I slammed back against the booth. "That's gross!" I said.

"Shhh, we need to be quiet about this," Sky said. Steve's auto repair shop was diagonally across the street from where we were sitting at that very moment. What if he knew we were here? What if he or one of our brothers came in and saw us together? Sara shook her head in disbelief. I wondered if this meant Mom would leave Steve, as she had threatened to do on other occasions.

Sky shrugged. "I didn't want to be the one to tell you," she said. "But I thought you both needed to know because of your age. Sara is probably fine because she's his real daughter, but Carissa, he might try something with you. And I couldn't take it if you were hurt and I could've prevented it." Sky was a Jehovah's Witness; she took the beliefs seriously. I knew she stole from stores, little stuff, mostly— but she would never lie or make up a story, not one like this. And she wouldn't put up with being bullied by Steve, either. About a year earlier, he had tried to spank her and she had attacked him with her plastic hairbrush and made his chest bleed. He never tried that on her again.

The three of us sat in silence. No one knew what to say. We didn't know how to process this information. I knew that she was trying to protect us. But I felt more afraid, more alone than ever.

Finally Sky broke the silence. "Carissa, I think you should move with Dad. But you can't tell him any of this. If you do, you know he'll kill Steve. Then Ethan won't have a dad, and we won't either, because he'll go to jail forever."

I called my dad from Fatte's. Sky helped me ask him if I could come live there and bring my little brother Jacob with me. It was my idea to bring Jacob. I couldn't imagine leaving him behind. At nine, he was so small for his age; if I left, he'd be at the mercy of our stepbrothers. Dad agreed and said he'd have to make some plans but that it could happen soon. "Finish out this school year," he said, "and in the meantime I'll find us a bigger place to live."

Dad had never remarried, and he had never stopped loving my mother. He never told her that, just us. The two of them never spoke, and in their silence and hurt a lot more went unsaid. Regrets lingered, while memories of our family began to fade. By the time I called him from Fatte's, I couldn't even remember back to a day when we all shared a home together. Now we would be building something new.

As soon as I walked in the door, I saw Mom's face. She already knew. She was ready for me. "I'm going to move in with Dad," I said. "And Jacob is coming with me." It was final. I was leaving.

Sky walked in behind me. "Did you tell her?" she asked me.

Mom didn't wait for me to answer. "Yes, she told me. What's this all about?"

Sky took a deep breath and told Mom what Steve had done.

"You're lying," Mom said matter-of-factly, and before she could turn away, my sister's hand had flown toward her face.

Mom wasn't ready for the slap. She put her hand to her cheek, which was turning red, and looked at Sky in silence. No one said one word when Sky stormed out, and Mom didn't tell Steve about the slap. For that reason I knew that Mom believed that at least a small portion of what Sky had said was true.

"You can leave with Jacob," she said later, after a conversation with Steve where she explained why it would be a good idea for all of us to have a separation for a while. "But you'll see. You'll both be back."

■ ■ ■

I hadn't spent much time with my father before—a week here, an overnight there—so I really didn't know much about him except that he always said he loved us. I believed him; in fact, I was sure if he was mad enough, he might kill for us. So I kept my promise to Sky not to tell him why we were coming.

Almost from the time Jacob and I walked into Dad's house—a roomy duplex in Redding, California—we found ourselves in the middle of some kind of instant family theme park. Richie was already living with Dad, but now my father bought us new bicycles and installed an aboveground pool in the backyard. We were enrolled in tae kwon do lessons and gymnastics. Dad had a girlfriend, he told us—he was going to ask her to marry him and she would be our new stepmother. It was obvious Dad wanted to give us a real family, and for him this was what family looked like. He sat down with Richie, Jacob, and me to ask if that would be all right with us. "It's okay, you don't have to ask us, Dad," I said.

"You should be happy, Dad," said Richie. Jacob was silent. I'm not sure he understood any of it or even remembered that our mom and dad had ever been together.

Sadly, Dad's dream family didn't happen. His girlfriend turned down his proposal, and after that everything went downhill. Things with my older brother started to become uncomfortable, even weird. One afternoon, Richie pulled Jacob and me into the living room to watch what he said was the music video of "Parents Just Don't Understand" by Will Smith. Instead, we discovered it was a sex tape that belonged to my dad. At first, I wasn't sure what I was seeing. "Oh, yuck. Richie, shut it off." I covered Jacob's eyes but kept watching as he tried to peel my hands away from his face.

"Just wait, we just have to watch this one," Richie said. "Then the music video will come on."

The music video never came on. The movie, called *Taboo 3*, was about a father having sex with his high school–aged daughter. Richie gave me the hint, loud and clear, that if it wasn't going to happen with Steve, it might very well happen here at Dad's. My stomach rolled—wasn't I safe here? Was my brother threatening me or implying that my dad was going to do something to me?

A week after the video incident, Jacob and I were riding our bikes. Jacob wasn't very good at judging intersections yet, and I knew there was a freeway off-ramp we were going to have to pass just up ahead. "Okay, Jacob, when I say 'Go!' that means it's all clear," I told him. "Ride with me, and when I give you the signal, pedal just as fast as you can."

When it was clear, I said, "Go!" and took off, thinking he was right on my tail. I made it through, and when I turned around, Jacob was still at the top of the overpass. "What are you doing?" I yelled.

"I'm not a baby," he shouted. "I can do it by myself."

"Okay," I said, "but wait . . ." Before I could finish telling him to wait for my signal, he took off, pedaling clumsily through the intersection, but not nearly fast enough. We both saw the car at the same time. He was hit. Somehow, he kept riding. It was like a miracle. He came right to me. "Jacob, are you okay?" I couldn't decide whether to hug him or punch him.

"Yes," he said, shaking badly. I looked for blood on him and didn't see any. Then I looked at his rear wheel—just a few bent spokes. He might need a new rim, but that was all. He really was okay.

"Are you all right?" The woman driver was suddenly standing over us both. "Are you okay? I mean, I hit you. Are you okay?" She was shaking too.

"Yes, he's fine," I told the woman. "Just has a mind of his own and didn't want to listen to his big sister."

We rode off while the woman watched us. Jacob was a little wobbly, so we took it slow. When I told Dad what had happened, he didn't seem upset. "Your brother's fine, isn't he?" He shrugged. "Worse things happen."

A few nights later, Sky called to tell me that B.J., a boy from my class in Coalinga, had been killed in a car accident. He was a cute blond boy, the oldest of three blond brothers. He and another sixth-grade classmate had been on a trip to the beach. They were hit by a semi, and he was killed instantly.

I walked out of the kitchen and into the living room. Looking around at my brothers and my dad watching TV, I just wanted to leave and sit alone in the dark. I went outside, walked down the long driveway, and sat down on the curb. I could see B.J.'s smiling face.

I could hear his laugh. *Why did he die?* I wondered. Why did he leave his family? His brothers? Where was he now? Was he waiting to be in paradise? Was he automatically getting in because he was a kid? Did he feel anything? Did he hurt? I thought about Jacob's bike accident, how it ended up okay but just as easily could have been really bad, my little brother hurt or even dead. Could life really be this short? And if it was, did I want to be here, away from Mom and away from my friends?

I went back into the house and announced, "Dad, Jacob wants to go home. He's been crying for Mom every night. He needs her." Dad looked at me with disgust in his eyes.

"Is this true?" he asked Jacob.

"Yes," Jacob said meekly as tears began rolling down his cheeks. "I want to be with Mom."

Dad stormed to his room. I yelled at him for being so dramatic and told Jacob we could use the neighbor's phone to call Mom. "She'll come and get us."

I was leaving too. Although I hadn't told anyone, I'd figured out that my older brother had tricked Jacob and me into watching the porn tape. It was just too weird here, too uncertain. This wasn't the safe place Sky had hoped it would be, and I was beginning to wonder if any place was safe.

The next day, Dad left for work early and didn't come home until we were in bed. I felt bad—I'd asked him to take us in, and he'd done it without asking any questions. I knew he loved us, but he couldn't quite seem to figure out what to do with us.

Mom came to pick us up a few days later. As Jacob and I climbed into the car, Dad stayed inside the house watching TV. Mom had a smile on her face. She was happy to see us. We had done exactly what she'd expected we would do—rejected him and reached back to her. We'd always been a part of their game; every breakup they'd ever had was a fight over the kids. Dad got the boys; Mom got the girls. I knew she felt good about getting both of us back, but especially Jacob. He was one of my dad's treasures, one of the boys. The big question I had in my head was whether she would do enough to protect both of us back at home. Could she leave Steve? I decided to ask her flat out.

"Will you leave Steve?" I asked, pleading. "Leave him and choose us?"

Her face closed down again. "Aren't you the one who called me to come and get you and bring you home? Do you want me to turn the car around and take you back there?" She was speaking in her too-sweet-to-be-true voice, which meant her words were supposed to cut deep. They did.

Jacob was looking at me, fear on his face—he didn't want me to rock the boat. *Okay*, I thought. *No more challenges, no more questions. For Jacob's sake.*

We were not allowed to take our new things with us. We left our prized bikes behind, along with a backyard with a half-empty pool, a patio full of toys, and summer days full of fun things to do. Lying in my bed that first night home, I said my prayers the usual way, then added a prayer that Mom would leave Steve. I hoped that God would understand my reason for asking that she might get a place of her own where we could live together in peace—after all, it was only me, Jacob, and Ethan now; that wasn't too many. Steve could take Sara, Tanner, and Travis. *Maybe she could get a job*, I thought.

I knew Steve would never leave. He'd die before he left. Was that an okay thing to pray for?

I pulled the covers up to my chin and stared out the window, looking for the one star so bright that it actually sparkled. I concentrated on that star or planet, and whatever it was, I wished on it. I wished hard. The same way I prayed to wake up with a new life. I prayed night after night, but each morning, nothing had changed.

CHAPTER TWO

J unior high. As usual, the last week of August was hotter than hell in Coalinga, kids hollering and pushing, nobody telling us where to be or what to do. It felt like getting run over by a train.

The junior high was a beige, one-story stone building spread out into long hallways, one gray locker door after another. No art on the outside of the doors, like in elementary school. No teachers' names posted outside the classrooms, just numbers. Inside, every classroom was arranged the same way—desk facing forward, teacher barricaded behind it, rows of restless, fidgety students, and no windows. At least none you could see out of.

Fuck, I'm scared. I walked into my first homeroom class on day one and walked out of third period—and out of the building—just a few weeks later. "Fuck you!" I shouted at the substitute teacher, giving her the finger.

She furiously wrote out a referral and handed it to me, pointing to the classroom door. "Go to the principal's office." I tore up the triplicate pink/yellow/white referral slip in front of her and tossed the pieces into the trash on my way out. No principal would be seeing me. Not today.

When I left the school building, I felt free. I hated that place. It was so confusing. So many places to be, so many things to remember, different classrooms and teachers and substitute teachers. Homework. Binders. Required supplies. Lockers. And clueless people like this one, ordering me to be quiet when all I was doing was helping the kid at the desk next to mine figure out an assignment. Sometimes it seemed like the only thing grown-ups wanted was for kids to shut up.

The other students, the ones I knew, seemed to quickly find their place in school. My best friend, Mody, went to work on the yearbook. Lisa joined the softball team. The cheerleaders and football players lived and breathed school pride, all wearing their respective uniforms on game day.

Everyone else seemed dazed and confused. Most were children of migrant farmworkers, bused in from towns like Huron, which had an elementary school but no junior high of its own. Many kids came only part of the year and then disappeared. We were all in the same grade—seventh—and yet we were so different from one another. There was tension from the first day. The bused-in kids from Huron wanted to make this place their own. I wasn't stupid. I had a big mixed-up family. I knew what to expect. Fights. Lots of them.

In elementary school, fights on the playground had been rare, quickly broken up by watchful teachers and aides. Now the playground was gone. No more tetherball. No more monkey bars. No more recess. Just long walkways where most kids hung out during the six minutes between each bell, talking about whatever—a cute boy, a new pair of Reeboks or Ray-Bans. I wasn't in that bunch. I was alone, trying to figure out the maze of hallways and friendships, constantly lost and late. Anything could happen in those six minutes, and it did. Fights broke out almost daily, some between students but just as often between teachers and students, mostly the eighth graders. One long-haired stoner kid was thrown into his locker by a teacher for telling him to fuck off. The rumor was that high school would be worse than this, if you made it. This kid wasn't going to make it.

The new girls, the ones from Huron, didn't skulk down a hallway wanting to be invisible or stand at the edge of the school yard hoping nobody would call them out. They were tough and proud and did not look lost, ever. No girl in my class dared to make fun of them. Not to their faces, not behind their backs. If word got back to them, and it always did, you'd be dead. So instead of insulting their bright silk shirts, big hoop earrings, and multiple bracelets that jangled, the local girls looked away, as though these bused-in girls didn't exist. But they did. They were willing to fight to earn their place, but they'd settle for staring down or intimidating anyone who might've been thinking about calling them a wetback or a spic. Maybe it was something their parents had taught them: Fight before you have to and you'll fight less. Since fighting was likely to happen, I wanted to know how to do it, and I guessed that they could teach me.

I'd started wearing makeup when I started my period that summer. That was the deal with my mom. "Start your period, and you can wear makeup." I practiced my black-eyeliner-stare-down in the bathroom mirror. I found an old red lipstick in the bathroom too but saved it for when I got to school. Mody taught me how the Huron girls did their hair: Aqua Net, in the white can, and lots of it. To make the eyeliner even darker, I needed fire—matches, a lighter, a blow-dryer, anything hot would work. It went on very thick, like the coal along the railroad tracks. I loved my new look, but it always wore off by the middle of the day and disappeared entirely during gym class. So I skipped gym class—I needed more than five minutes for makeup alone and couldn't dream of starting over with my hair.

At home, my family noticed the new version of me. "What the hell?" said one of my stepbrothers. "We have a *chola* living here now?"

Those were fighting words, but instead of taking the bait, I decided to spend less time at home. I didn't care what they thought of me. I was sick of being picked on there, sick of the hassle—I'd always known I didn't fit in at home, and now everyone knew it. Unlike some kids at school, I wasn't a Latina wannabe; I *was* part Mexican. To complete the picture, I needed one more thing: pierced ears.

Mody's mom did it for me. She didn't speak English, but she didn't need to for this, since I knew the rules: Sit very still and don't be a whimpery baby. The ice was for numbing; the needle was for making the holes. The potato? Mody said it was to keep the needle and her mom's hand straight, so the holes would be even, front to back. And the white knotted string at the end of the thread? Those would be my earrings until I could get a pair of starters. I knew I needed to keep turning them in my ears until the holes healed enough that I could put in real earrings. I gripped Mody's hand hard and heard the skin pop twice. The needle went all the way through.

Those strings came out the next morning, replaced immediately with some hoops Mody let me borrow. I blinked against the pain of the little bloody holes that hadn't healed yet, but I didn't care. Big hoop earrings, melted black eyeliner, and red lipstick. I'll show you chola, I thought.

My birthday, September 12, always happened in the beginning of the new school year. For the first time ever, I was going to be able to have a party. A real party. Grandma Elaine provided the cash, forty dollars, for pizza and sodas at Fatte Albert's and maybe something sweet after.

I had three friends from Coalinga to invite; the rest lived in Huron. A couple of those people had said, "Well, maybe, if I can get a ride," but I knew they wouldn't. The only adult there would be my sister Sky, who had convinced Grandma Elaine that she'd be the best chaperone. Only I knew that she was also hoping to see a guy at the pizza place that night.

The plan was to go to the Oilers' football game at school. I had a crush on a boy named Fernando, a football player from Huron. I hoped to see him and maybe invite him to pizza after the game. We were going to the game on our own, then we'd walk over to Fatte's to meet Sky. She'd have the order in and I'd pay for the pizza with Grandma's forty bucks. But that's not what happened.

During Fernando's game, my friend Zizi, who loved that I'd mouthed off to the substitute, convinced me that we were bored. "I have some friends that live close by. Let's go there until this game is over."

"Cool." When we arrived at the apartment, things didn't look much better than at the game. If that was lame, this was scary. Five adults slouching around, looking like they were waiting for something to happen. They checked us up and down like we were meat. Instinctively I knew this was no place for me. I was thinking hard, trying to figure out a way to leave, when Zizi announced that it was my birthday and we were just stopping by on our way for pizza.

"Pizza!" One of the ladies on the couch laughed out loud and continued. "*Chica,* come back here when you know what a real party is about!" Two guys in white T-shirts, baggy jeans, and brown slippers approached me. They had massive, intricate tattoos running up and down their arms.

"Do you want us to show you how to party?" they said, all smooth and slick. "We will get some beer for you, show you a real party." I slowly pulled out my two birthday twenties from my front pocket. I don't remember exactly how the money went from my hands to theirs, but it was clear that I wasn't calling the shots. "We'll be right back." As I watched my grandma's money leave the apartment, I wished that I was going with it.

Fifteen minutes later, the two guys were back. They'd hit the Jiffy market and a dealer's house, scoring a bag of weed and enough red and white cans of Budweiser to fill a refrigerator. This was not my birthday party. What was I doing here? I'd never tasted beer, and I didn't want to smoke weed. I wanted to go back to the football game and find Fernando. It was past dark; the game would be ending soon. What if he left? What if I didn't get to spend any time with him? "I think we should go now," I whispered to Zizi, hoping she would come with me.

"Okay, are you sure? Because this is all your party."

"Yeah, I'm sure. We can come back after we go find Fernando."

We said good-bye to no one in particular, and as we left, someone handed each of us a beer "for the road." Once we were safely outside, about a block from the apartment, we cracked open our cans at the same time. We each took a swig. Disgusting. I spit it out on the grass and looked for a trash can to get rid of the evidence.

When we got back to the football field, I found Lisa first—she was with her cousin, who gave me a piece of gum; I wanted that beer taste out of my mouth. Next, I found Fernando. The apartment adventure with Zizi had left me kind of breathless. When Fernando walked toward me, I thought my head was going to explode. *Okay, girlfriends, see you later!*

"Hey, what about the pizza party?" Lisa asked. "My mom is picking us up at Fatte's." I felt bad, but what could I do? My pockets were empty.

"Zizi and I went to her friends' apartment," I explained, "and my money's gone. I don't want to go back there. The people were messed up and getting drunk. Is it cool if we do pizza another time?"

"Of course." She was a good friend.

Before I knew it, Fernando and I were lying together on an empty field behind school, the space was wide open, deserted. There were no lights. Just stars and grass. We held each other and rolled around. He'd changed out of his uniform, and his body felt so good against mine. We held on to each other, not wanting it to end. We were so wrapped up in what we were doing that we realized too late that he'd missed his bus back to Huron.

My heart raced. I knew this was all my fault. My fault for planning a birthday party where no one would show up, including me. My fault for going with Zizi to meet her friends. My fault for giving up that forty bucks. My fault for not calling to explain things to Sky. My fault for making out too long with Fernando, my fault he'd missed his bus. It was my responsibility to solve this.

I tracked down Lisa, and once again she understood. "You can stay overnight at my house," she said. We'd ask her older brother to give Fernando a ride home. But we'd have to give him gas money. Fernando had six bucks, so we headed to her house, hoping her brother would be there.

When we rounded the corner to Lisa's house, we both noticed the same thing at the same time. "Uh-oh, my brother's not home yet," she said.

I was okay, I could sleep over—but where would Fernando go? Lisa and I came up with a plan. He'd stay in the garage just until day-break, then we'd go in and wake up her brother. It would all work out, and it did: Fernando was home safely before the sun came up.

At eight in the morning, we heard the telephone ring. "Lisa, Carissa, can you come to the kitchen, please?" It was Lisa's mother, calling in through the bedroom door. "Carissa, why would your mother phone here and not know where you were?" she asked. "She said you didn't come home last night, and you didn't tell her where you were."

I thought fast. "She must not have got the message from one of my brothers."

I knew by the look on her face that Lisa's mother was not buying it. "She said she's on her way over, coming to get you." She made us pancakes while we waited, and I ate like it was my last meal ever.

In the car driving home, Mom had a few things to get off her chest. "I was up all night. Steve was too. We drove around looking for you, worried sick. Just so you know, you won't be going any-where or having any parties for a long time. You're grounded until you're eighteen."

Nothing about her response surprised me, except that Steve had been looking for me. But wait—grounded until eighteen? That was a joke, right? *Oh, no, no way,* I thought. That was not going to happen. I understood that almost every decision I'd made the night before had been bad, but grounding until I was eighteen? I'd be a prisoner, and then what would happen? It felt like an entire life sentence. Sleepy and pancake stuffed, I was on the defensive but too tired to fight with her. I was ashamed and sorry for the whole night. I wished there was someone else to blame, but it was all on me. Nothing I could tell Mom would make it better. At least no part of the truth. Beer, weed, overnight with a boy. I was silent and somewhat relieved that she also didn't seem interested in facing any of the facts.

"You'll learn your lesson," she said, echoing what I'd heard Steve say for years. "You'll never leave the house again." So this was not a joke; she was not kidding. I couldn't get my brain into gear to protest, and just then, we pulled up to the house. It looked like an audience had gathered. Neighbors from across the street. What were they doing? Drinking soda, eating candy, standing around waiting for the show.

■ ■ ■

The terms of the grounding were simple: I was expected to go to school, come home, and go to my room until Mom or Steve said I could come out. Day after day after day. Go, come back, keep your mouth shut. No after-school stuff, no hanging with friends, no plans on weekends, and no end in sight. All for one curfew busting and a blown forty bucks. This was overkill, and I wasn't having it.

Zizi showed up at noon to check in on me. She told me she was going off to have some fun, and I decided I couldn't stay put for another minute. I bolted. Out the bathroom window, onto the roof, and over the back fence. I ran away. I left without any plans of coming back. A surge of adrenaline rushed through me. I was everything I wanted to be—out of the house, out from under Steve's roof, away from the voices and the mess, out on my own. I was free.

At first, Zizi was a good running partner. She spent time between her mom's and her dad's places, and they both worked, so we could usually stay inside during the day. At night, she'd have to sneak me in, but that wasn't much of a problem. When Zizi's mom started asking questions, I went to her dad's. When her dad started asking questions, we decided it was time to go to Huron. Our new school friends there let us crash in their rooms, plus that's where the boys we liked lived. Huron wasn't like Coalinga; at night there was a lot to do. Kids were out, people were having parties, and when it got late, all I had to do was knock on someone's bedroom window to get let in. I slipped out before their parents woke up. *This*, I thought, *is a great adventure.*

Zizi went home after a few days, freaked out because she'd heard through the rumor mill that her older sister was looking for us, threatening to kick both of our asses. I didn't mind that she left—it was probably a good idea. Her sister was scary.

Mom and Steve, together and separately, searched for me in Coalinga, but since I wasn't hanging with any of the usual friends, they came up empty. They didn't know anyone in Huron, and they had no idea I was there until one of my aunts who lived there called and told them. I was staying at my friend Becky's—my aunt knew her mother. It was one thing to be ratted out, but it was another to learn that Mom had told my aunt to warn Becky's mom about me.

"Tell her that Carissa is trouble for her daughter," Mom had instructed. "She'll get her to run away." My own mother was trash-talking me.

After my aunt delivered the message, Becky's mom had a talk with me. "Carissa, you seem like a good girl, but your aunt says you're not going to school. I don't want you to be a bad influence on Becky." She said I could stay just that night, but the next day I had to find someplace else to go.

I didn't know what to do. I was borrowing Becky's clothes, but I couldn't take any of them with me. I couldn't take her daybed mattress that I was sleeping on, either. So that was it. I was out on the streets.

The more time I spent on the run, especially at night, the more I learned, strategizing about where to sleep and how (not even what) I was going to eat. I learned whose doors were locked and whose weren't. I learned whose parents weren't home during the day, so I could sneak in and take a shower. I learned to pocket homemade tortillas, I bought tacos for less than a dollar in the meat market, and I knew who would have space for me on the floor if I didn't find a bed for the night.

When I was tired of seeking out places, I would give up and go home. Nothing was worse than facing Mom and Steve. The first time I went back, their anger just about tore the roof off. The second time wasn't quite so bad, and the third time their yelling didn't even faze me. They tried other methods to try to get me to stay at home—Steve nailed the bathroom window shut, and later he nailed the one in my room too. So I just started walking out the front door. He once tried to physically block me, but I ran around him. It felt a little like a game to me, getting out despite their attempts to stop me. I was winning.

Eventually, Mom and Steve stopped playing. Instead, they called the police to tell them what was going on—if I did something stupid, they didn't want to be liable. Sometimes the cops brought me home, scolding me all the way. I was grounded again, over and over, forever and ever, until the next time. No one ever said, "We love you, and it matters to us that you're safe. Please stay home."

School ended for me in the seventh grade. Every time I ran, that was a day or a week of ditching. The truancies stacked up until finally I was put on informal probation. Eventually the county probation officer (his name was Tom Greene, I remember it well) had me labeled a "601"—the California legal code for kids who refuse to obey their parents' or guardians' "reasonable and proper orders" and are thus described as "beyond control." Being an official 601 also meant the state was keeping an eye on me, because statistically there was a good chance I was going to become a "602"—a minor who actually broke real laws. I didn't care what they called me; I wasn't scared and I wasn't going to change my ways. Finally Mom called Tom Greene and told him she needed to have me locked up.

"We can't lock her up," he said. "Technically she is not a criminal." He explained that there was one choice Mom could make if she was desperate.

She laid out her plan as though we were going over a shopping list. "This is what your probation officer says I can do: take you to juvenile hall and leave you there. And then they are going to have to find a place for you. A group home or something."

My heart sank, but I wasn't going to give her the satisfaction of seeing my hurt. I didn't blink an eye. "Okay," I said. I did not argue, didn't try to run or stop her from giving me up. I was fine.

"Can I grab some things?" I asked. "I don't have much, so it won't take long." I ran upstairs, choking on the tears I was determined not to shed in front of her.

The only bag I could find was an old, red fake-leather suitcase in the hall closet. I didn't know where it had come from; it belonged to no one in particular, like so many other things in that house. I crammed in a few tops, some underwear, shorts, and a tin of cookies. I didn't think anyone would miss the suitcase or the cookies. From the way things had been going, I didn't think anyone would miss me, either.

Mom and I had made the seventy-minute trip to Fresno a dozen times before, but this time everything was different. She was not happy with me, I was not happy with her. We did not exchange a single word. I stared out the window and focused on the crops that fanned out across the Central Valley flatland. One time, for a single moment when the car slowed, I thought, *I'll open the door and jump. She won't care.* But I couldn't do it.

When we finally arrived in front of the Fresno County juvenile hall, Mom circled around the parking lot. *Maybe she's changing her mind,* I thought—but she was looking for a parking space. She shut off the car, looked at me, and spoke for the first time since she'd told me to pack my bag. "This is what happened to me when I didn't want to go home to Nana," she said. "It was worse for me because they locked me up and I had to sit in an actual jail cell."

I was silent.

"But you're not going to be locked in a cell," she said.

Well, what, then? I wondered. *What are we doing here?* I followed her into the lobby. As she approached the counter, I sat down and put the suitcase at my feet. Pretending not to listen, I heard her explain to the guy behind the counter that she was leaving me on orders of my probation officer. He glanced at me, then back at her. "You can't do that," he said. "You're her mother."

"Yeah, I am," she replied. "But I can't control her." Without saying another word, she turned away from him, walked past me, and left. I recognized the look on her face—it was the same one she'd had when Steve threw me out the door in second grade. It was my fault. I had it coming. I should not have caused problems. The lobby door was propped open, and I watched my mother disappear. She was gone and she wasn't coming back.

■ ■ ■

I sat in that chair as though I'd been glued to it, waiting for some direction from somebody. Anybody. Was I just going to sit there all day? All night? The man at the counter obviously had no idea what to do with me. Alone in this lobby in a city I'd never been in by myself, I had no idea what to do. Running from here didn't seem like an option. Guards were walking in and out. Everyone had two-way radios, serious keys, real guns. I'd also noticed while driving into town that the streets outside were different from the ones at home. Scary looking. No houses, just buildings and stores. If I ran, it would be a long way back to Coalinga or Huron, back to friends' houses where I could sleep over or sneak food. I wouldn't know which direction to turn once I hit the sidewalk. So I just stayed still. Glued to the chair.

I spent the next three days in some kind of fog, sitting in the juvenile hall lobby while the staff called every group home in the city, looking for a space for me and finding none. I slept (not very well) on a plastic-covered mattress and used the visitors' bathroom in the lobby to brush my teeth and splash water on my face. I was told I could shower in the part of the facility where kids were booked and admitted, but I didn't want to go behind doors that were locked. I said I was fine with a small towel in the lobby bathroom. After I washed up, I changed into clean underwear from the little red suitcase; on the third day I was out of clean underwear. That morning, a sizable black woman with short, curly hair marched into the lobby, signed some papers, and impatiently waved her arm toward the door. "C'mon," she said to me. That was all it took to release me to a stranger. I left the building with her. Was she going to take me home?

She didn't tell me her name, she didn't ask me why I was there, and she didn't say where we were going or what I would do once we got there. Between long, labored breaths, she told me how I needed to live. "You need to learn to obey your parents," she said. "You have to do what you're told, go to school, straighten out. Bad things can happen to a girl like you, you know."

I snuck looks at her out of the corner of my eye. Who was she, and why was she telling me what to do? I wondered if she had kids. I wondered how many girls she gave speeches to and how many of them listened. Maybe she was a decent person in her other life. Maybe she thought this sermon was helpful, but it only made me angry. Why would I follow her directions to listen to parents who obviously didn't want me?

We finally stopped in front of a big Victorian house. "Come on," the woman said, getting out of the car. "This is where you're staying for a few weeks." I knew she was wrong. I'd be gone as soon as I had the chance.

She opened the big front door and we went through it, her in front, me behind. I watched her walk toward a small office, holding my little red suitcase. She put it on a table and started to open it. "That's mine!" I snapped from the office door, afraid to go too far into her space.

"Don't worry," she said. "You'll get it back. I'm just going through it to make sure you don't have any contraband."

"Any what? I don't have anything in there. Just some old tin with cookies in it and some clothes. What do you want with it? It's private!" I watched helplessly as this stranger touched all my stuff. My already worn underwear. My shorts. My socks. My stuff. I wanted her to stop, but she didn't. Those were the rules.

"Okay. Looks good. You can have it back." She said it as if she were giving me a gift or something, but in my eyes she had fucked up my shit, and I didn't want it back anymore. "I'm not the one who's going to process you," she said. "That will be Gary. He's in the office upstairs. Come with me."

The old house was huge. It seemed clean enough, but the walls were cold and bare. No pictures. No games or books. No pets being fed or jumping up to greet you. Just a big, empty place. "Here she is," the woman said, introducing me to Gary. "Our newest resident, a bad girl who doesn't listen to her parents."

What a bitch! I thought. I wanted to say it to her face, but I didn't. At least she was leaving. So now Gary. *Who's this guy?* He was middle-aged, which to me at that time meant older than dirt and nothing like me. He smoked. In fact, he chain-smoked, lighting one cigarette from the butt of the other, two or three in the first few minutes I was at the group home.

"I thought cigarettes were against the rules," I said. "Isn't that what she was checking for in my bag? Contraband?"

He didn't like my question. He didn't even answer it. "What's your name?" he asked. I watched his hand as he tried to write. It trembled. I spelled my name for him instead of saying it. I knew he'd never get it right.

"Do you know your date of birth?" Of course I knew it—did he get kids here who didn't? "Do you know your social security number?" Not by heart yet, but I'd soon learn it.

Within hours of my arrival, I was doing what I knew how to do best—running. I planned the escape with the girl who was sharing a room with me. Jennifer knew Fresno. She had grown up there and had been out on her own before. That's why she was here. Her dad was mad at her for running away with her boyfriend. I convinced her we could get out easily.

"How?" she asked. "We're on the second floor. What will we do, jump?"

Jenny was right. We couldn't use the window in our room. "We'll leave from the back stairway," I said. "That guy said it was the fire escape. It's there because of the law or something and can't be locked from the outside. It leads into the backyard. We'll go over the fence and no one will know we're gone."

The only thing was, we'd have to leave our stuff. Any bags would slow us down. I didn't care about my suitcase anymore, and somewhere out there I knew we'd find what we needed. The fire escape was right outside the bedroom door. We tiptoed to it and turned the knob slowly. The place was old and creaky, and we knew a staff person sat just down the hall, supposedly awake, supposedly listening for us.

Once the door was shut behind us, we were free, down the fire escape and running across the backyard. We had no trouble scaling the wooden fence. I was happy Jenny had been assigned as my roommate, rather than some wimpy kid who wouldn't run with me. She was smart too. "We can go to the hospital near here," she said. "We can call my boyfriend from the waiting room." If anyone asked why we were there, she instructed, we'd just say we're waiting for word about our sister, who was upstairs having a baby.

Less than thirty minutes after she'd made the phone call, her boyfriend showed up outside the hospital on his bike. He brought a friend, and the four of us took off toward an empty field near the railroad tracks. We stood around, we told some stories, and she did some making out.

■ ■ ■

Shortly before midnight, Jennifer's boyfriend said he had to get home or his parents would be looking for him. We said we'd be fine, but the only place we had to go was back to the hospital.

As we'd hoped, we were able to stay the night. One nurse asked why we were there, and we said it was because of our sister. She seemed to buy it. *This is too easy,* I thought. The hospital waiting room was so quiet at night, with fewer sick people and fewer people waiting for them. But the next night, as hard as we tried, we couldn't make our-selves invisible. "Weren't you here last night?" the same nurse asked.

"Yes, for our big sister," we said. "She's upstairs having a baby." This time the nurse didn't look convinced. Jennifer and I got scared. What if the police came? What if we got sent back to that home? That's when she called her dad and asked if he would come and get her. "Maybe he'll drop you back off at the group home," she said.

I didn't want to go back but didn't think I had many options. I wished I could've gone with Jenny, but she didn't offer and I didn't ask. We told the nurse that we had the hospitals wrong, we were sorry. I could feel her eyes on us as we went to the exit as fast as we could, then waited outside. It was cold. It was dark. I didn't have a boyfriend to call, or a dad, or my mom, who was the reason I'd landed at the group home in the first place. So I went back to the group home. My run for freedom was temporarily suspended, but maybe I could retrieve some of the things I'd left behind.

When they told me at the home that none of my belongings were still there—but wasn't I lucky that they had some space for me?—I almost lost it. What had happened to that little red suitcase? Who had eaten my tin of cookies? I was put into a different room, closer to the staff office and far away from the fire-escape door. My new roommate was Monica, a serial foster kid. She told me she had rela-tives around Fresno who sometimes took her in.

"This place sucks," I said. "They won't even give me my stuff back! I think they threw it away."

"Yeah, they do that," she said. "They don't care." We had a shared enemy, the staff who made things so hard. "Most are the same," she told me, "but some are better than others." She'd been in a lot of homes. She'd teach me a few things, and in exchange I'd never ask her why she was there.

There was a "common area" downstairs, a living-room kind of space that was more worn and crowded than my mother's couch. Ten or twelve other girls were there. Nobody acknowledged us; in fact, they weren't even talking to one another. They just sat and stared, as though a spell had been cast on them. One glassy-eyed girl rhythmically rocked her body back and forth, staring into nothing. *I can't stay here,* I thought, *or I will start to rock too.*

Monica and I ran a few nights later, making our way to her aunt's house. Her aunt didn't seem surprised to see Monica or too concerned about my tagging along with her niece. She had two teen daughters, did cocaine, smoked dope, and liked having company. I thought it was a nice deal.

■ ■ ■

One night Monica introduced me to three brothers who lived with their dad. They were older boys—maybe sixteen, eighteen, and nineteen. They had beer, they had music on the radio, and they had a house with nobody in it but us. One of them teased me a little about my hair. "Your bangs," he said. "They're wavy—is that because of that earthquake in Coalinga?" He grinned. "And you have a crooked tooth too, on the top." He didn't tell me I was pretty; he didn't say he liked me. He just teased me. He noticed that I was there. My little heart and mind fell to pieces.

Somebody suggested dancing. I forced myself to drink a beer, then another one. Dancing seemed like a good idea. Tone Loc's "Wild Thing" came on the radio, the beat felt like it was pulsing right through me. The teasing boy pulled me closer to him, my hips moving into his. "How about we dance the rest of this dance in my room?" he asked as he picked me up into his arms.

He took off my pants first, then his. I suddenly felt sober, and at the same time so grateful for his touch, for his kisses. He was being very gentle, nice, holding me and stroking me. I let him keep going because he wasn't being rough. And then I felt a sharp, stinging pain between my legs. I stifled the scream—I didn't want to be uncool, some scaredy girl who didn't know what she was doing. But was this how it was supposed to feel? I was in so much pain.

When he was done, he rolled off me, and it was then he noticed all the blood. He didn't say anything. I covered myself and went down the hall to the bathroom. I didn't understand. I wasn't having my period when I walked into the house, so what was this about? Where did all this blood come from? I cleaned myself up as best I could, went back to the bedroom, where the boy was already asleep, and fell asleep myself. Did this mean that I had a boyfriend?

The next morning, the three brothers kicked Monica and me out. Their real girlfriends were coming over, they said. I felt sick to my stomach and wanted to sleep some more, but no, we had to get out fast. I heard it in their voices: Out the door now, or they'll want to fight.

After that first time, sex was hard to turn down. I didn't go looking for it, but when you're an unanchored runaway whose hobbies include getting wasted, hanging out in parks at night, and crashing at strangers' houses, sex finds you. Sometimes, when Monica's aunt wasn't home, a guy named Raymond came over. He was twenty-one and brought Olde English malt liquor with him every time. Soon we were having sex regularly.

Raymond said he was my boyfriend, but he didn't do cute boy-friend things—we didn't joke or hold hands or go on dates or listen to our favorite songs. He made me promise I wouldn't tell anyone what we were doing together. One night, to get away from the crowd that routinely gathered at Monica's aunt's house, Raymond took me out for a ride. Abruptly, he pulled the car into a grocery store parking lot and turned off the engine. "Climb in the backseat," he said.

"What? I'm not even drinking yet."

"Come on, it'll be fun," he said.

I didn't want to have sex in a parking lot, especially without being drunk. The truth was I didn't want to have sex with Raymond at all. But I did want him to like me, so I choked back the fear of getting caught and crawled headfirst from the passenger seat into the back. I started to shake, and the heat rose to my face. Hives, I thought. I'd had them before. *Please God, don't make me have hives. If he sees me like that, he definitely won't like me.* My plea to God didn't work. In minutes, I was covered with bumps and my skin was on fire. If Raymond noticed, he didn't say anything. Afterward, he just pulled up his pants and went into the store to buy beer for the party. He knew I wouldn't leave the car—where would I go? Besides, as far as he knew, I liked sex. I wanted it. I'd never said no; I'd never pushed him off me.

Having little to keep me occupied—no school, no job—I did some chores around Monica's aunt's house but still had empty hours to fill. The first item on my "to do" list was "get better at shoplifting." I'd learned about stealing makeup and small things like gum and candy back in Coalinga, but now I needed other things—shampoo, condi-tioner, underwear, tampons. Lucky for me, one of Monica's cousins was an expert at going into stores empty-handed and walking out loaded with stuff.

I saw a Scrabble box one day in the store and immediately thought of my nana. Nobody I was hanging with played Scrabble. They hadn't even heard of it. Scrabble, solitaire, and crossword puzzles, Nana's favorites. "What's a six-letter word for a freshwater fish? It has to have a *u* in it." Or "Is 'axis' spelled with an *i* or an *e*?" I could picture her poker face, the one she wore when she was about to use a *Q* on a triple word score. She had a piano in her living room. *Frère Jacques, Frère Jacques, Dormez-vous? Dormez-vous?* Are you sleeping? Was I sleeping? Not much. I missed Nana; I missed the questions and the games. I called Emily, who had just moved to Vallejo for a new job.

"Please come see me, Carissa," she said, with real concern in her voice. "I'll send you a bus ticket." I gave her the address of Monica's aunt's house, and three or four days later the ticket came. I held it in my hand—it felt magical. The only problem was, I didn't have anything to wear. No actual shoes, just ratty old sneakers and T-shirts and the cutoff jeans I'd been wearing for weeks. I needed to make a big-item shoplifting run before my trip.

Everyone was there with me that day—Monica, her aunt, her two cousins. We circled the store a few times and figured out where all the security was. That's why I couldn't understand what I did, how I messed up so bad. I saw him look at me. He looked straight at me when I put that shirt in my bag. At that point I had a choice—put the bag down and walk out with nothing, or keep shopping. I took my chances and kept picking up items. We acted as if they weren't following us, as if there weren't more security guys posted at the front doors waiting for us to complete the crime. None of that mattered—we had a plan, to make the getaway through the garden department. No one ever watched that part of the store; it was where all the normal people shopped for houseplants and hoses. All we had to do was lose them in the main part of the store and get to the garden exit before they realized where we were. We'd be two blocks away before they knew we were gone.

I gave everyone the plan and asked Monica's aunt and her daughter to create a diversion. "Hold on to a bag just until the front-door exit," I said. "Then drop it near the register and walk out." The security guys would be watching them—meanwhile, we'd be in another section of the store, on the way out with the real goods.

We made it! We took about five seconds in the sunshine to congratulate ourselves, and then all we had to do was clear the parking lot. We walked very casually toward the edge of the lot, trying not to attract attention, just ordinary shoppers heading home after an ordinary shopping trip, when suddenly we heard the shout behind us. "There they go!" We started to run, but the bags were too heavy. They swung against our legs, tripping us up. Monica's cousin lost her sandal, and the black gravel was too hot for her to walk on. We turned around. And for the first time, we were caught.

The next stop was juvenile hall, behind locked doors, in my own cell, with no trace of that initial rush I'd had from running away. *This* was the reality of being on my own. Locked up. No one coming to get me. No one to be released to. No group home that would take a runner like me. And even if one did, I knew I'd be out of there as fast as my legs would carry me.

Someone who hasn't been through it might think that a group home would be better than sleeping on a stranger's floor or having to steal to survive. But a comfortable bed and a hot meal usually came with a high price tag: conformity, rules and regulations, and sometimes scary adults who were mean or borderline crazy. During those months on the run, I'd slept under bridges and in parks and scrounged food out of Dumpsters, eating other people's discarded pizza slices instead of going back home and behaving myself or submitting to the rules of a group home. Every day held the possibility of being beaten or raped by someone bigger and meaner. It was a high price to pay for freedom, and now, after going through all of that, I wasn't free at all. Inside the cold walls, I longed for some comfort. For some love. But all I felt was loneliness, dirtiness, aimlessness. This wasn't what I'd had planned.

■ ■ ■

I never caught that bus to Emily's in Vallejo, and after thirty days in juvy, I landed in another group home. I took off the first night, this time with a new friend, Mia. She had an aunt and uncle in Fresno who would let us stay with them. They liked to party, she said, and we could babysit their three boys while they were out or busy.

Mia only stuck around a couple of days, until she and her aunt got into a fight. I stayed. I decided it was a good setup, taking care of the kids in exchange for a cot in their room and a share of whatever fast food was left over. The boys quickly attached themselves to me, and after three weeks I was just another member of the family. I began to allow myself to feel safe. And then things went very badly wrong.

I was startled awake one night by someone playing with my leg. My bare leg. Scared, I sat up in the dark at the exact moment the bedroom light flicked on. Mia's aunt was standing in the doorway, and her husband was at the end of my cot. I sat up even straighter, bracing myself as she came running toward us.

She was a big woman, taller than her husband, who was now standing in a panic. She stopped when she reached him, looked down at him and shoved her hand between his legs. She grabbed hard and literally dragged him out of the room by his balls. He hit the front porch and let out a terrible scream. "You fucking bitch! Both of you fucking bitches!"

She turned to me. "Go back to bed," she said.

Her husband refused to leave the porch, and they yelled and screamed through the door for hours. Finally, he either fell asleep or went away, I didn't know which. When I got up enough courage to leave the boys' room in the morning and walk into the living room, their mother was pacing back and forth. She shook her head when she saw me. The phone was ringing and ringing—her husband, pleading to come home. I tried to busy myself with the kids, to look useful, to look necessary, but it was hard to concentrate. With each phone conversation, what little I heard told me she was caving. She was going to let him come home.

Later that afternoon, Mia's aunt sat me down at her kitchen table. I braced myself. She sighed. "He's a piece of shit," she said. "But I need a husband more than I need a twelve-year-old girl. I feel bad about doing this, but . . . you can't stay here. You have to leave before he gets home." With those words, my temporary home disappeared.

It was dusk when I left. I had nowhere to go. As it grew dark, lights were going on in houses. People were sitting around tables having family dinners. I walked along a four-lane commercial road with nothing other than the thin clothes I was wearing. The temperature was dropping, and I'd begun to shiver when an old brown lowrider U-turned around the highway's median strip and pulled up beside me. I knew the car. It belonged to Mia's other uncle, who'd been to the house before—she'd told me that he was a drug dealer and hard-core gangbanger who'd done time in prison. He stopped and reached across the seat to roll down the passenger-side window. "Where you going?" he asked.

I shrugged. "I dunno," I said.

"Do you wanna ride?" he asked.

I knew it was dangerous to get into his car. But I wasn't traveling in the usual pack of street kids and runaways on this night. I was alone, and without a ride I'd be wandering around all night with no place to go. It was dark, I was cold, and I was still young enough to worry about monsters jumping out of bushes. I put my hand on the car door handle and hesitated for a moment, waiting for the miracle of someone else, someone safer, to drive up and save me. Ten seconds. Twenty seconds. No one came. So I opened the door and climbed in.

Flaco—Spanish for "skinny"—didn't look skinny to me, but like the rest of the gangsters I knew, he'd gotten his name when he was much younger, probably before he even had hair on his chest. He had "Flaco" tattooed on the inside of his wrist, and he had other tattoos, more than I could count. The dark gang teardrops on his face made his deep acne scars appear even deeper. An oxygen tank took up the entire space in the back of his car. I'd heard Mia's aunt talk about Flaco's son before, and I knew the tank was for him because he was disabled. The large metal tank was somewhat reassuring, its presence a sign that Flaco would return to his family, that there was no way he would get me into the backseat—there wasn't enough room.

We drove around awhile, not speaking, then he pulled into the parking lot of a Johnny Quick gas station mini-mart and offered to get me something to eat. I realized I was very hungry, having been too nervous to eat much during the long, tense day. I waited while he bought me a hot dog and a fountain soda in a paper cup. He didn't wait for me to finish or even start eating before he said, "Come over here next to me." I scooted closer to him, the hot dog in one hand, the cold soda in the other. He put his arm around my shoulder and pulled me close as he spoke words he thought I should understand: "I'm going to take care of you and you're going to take care of me. All right?" I didn't want the hot dog anymore, but I also didn't want to be hungry. I ate and drank, wondering where we would go for the sex, since the backseat was out of the question.

"You need a place to stay," he said. "I'll get you a place for tonight. Does that sound good?" I nodded. He drove to Parkway Drive, a frontage road just off Highway 99 lined with dozens of cheap, one- and two-story motels. When he pulled into the parking lot of the Villa Motel, he told me to duck down—we were driving past the clerk's window. "They'll charge more if they see you," he said. I ducked—I didn't want to be seen. If I could've made myself invisible, a puddle on the passenger-side floor, I would've done it.

When we got to the room, he held the door while I walked in first. "Take your clothes off," he said before the door closed behind him. It was an ugly room, and it smelled. I couldn't look at the bed. I couldn't look at him. And I couldn't undress in front of him, either, so I headed for the bathroom. It had a small window, too small for me to crawl through. Nowhere to run, nowhere to hide. This was really going to happen. I knew I had to be strong. *I'll do what I have to do. Take care of him because he's taking care of me.*

When I opened the bathroom door, I was frightened. More tattoos. His naked body. Not skinny at all. His skin was wrinkled and old, not smooth like the boys and younger men I knew.

Robotically, my physical body moved toward the bed, while something inside me rose up and floated away. I was acting and watching myself act at the same time. I climbed on top of him and started moving the way I had with boys. He climaxed fast, and after he did, I had to physically control my urge to vomit all over him. I ran to the bathroom. "I need to clean up!" I yelled back as I turned on the faucet and the shower. I hoped he wouldn't want more.

He was up and dressed before I came out of the bathroom. "Stay here tonight," he ordered. "I'll be back tomorrow morning before I go to work at eight. I'll bring you a comb and a toothbrush. Anything else you need?"

I nodded obediently. Yes, I'd stay. No, there was nothing I needed. And he didn't need to waste any money on me. I would not be there when he returned in the morning.

I double-locked the door. I was alone. I wanted to stand in the shower and let the hot water pound me until all the hot water in the whole motel ran cold, but I knew that staying put was a bad idea. I might fall asleep and lose track of time. I wanted to get someplace else as soon as possible.

I peeked through the curtains to make sure Flaco was really gone. His car wasn't there. I grabbed the motel room key, closed the door, and walked fast across the parking lot toward the highway, taking care to stay in the shadows so no one would notice. When I hit the street, I stopped. I had a choice—walk left or walk right. I decided to walk right, and that's when I saw her.

The woman was several feet in front of me, walking toward me, every inch of her long brown legs fully exposed, her ass wrapped tightly in a tiny miniskirt. I realized immediately that she was pregnant, very pregnant, but only when I reached her, with a dim streetlight right above us, did I see her face—it was a mess. Her left eye socket was swollen, and her lip was split and puffy. We made brief eye contact as I walked by, then I looked away. I'd already learned the price of making eye contact at the wrong time. But when I was about five steps past her, something inside me told me to stop. In that moment, I had another choice—keep walking or turn around. She was hurt. I wondered if there was anything I could do for a pregnant, half-naked woman who'd obviously been beaten up, no doubt by somebody bigger than she was.

I had a key to a motel room. It was something. So I turned around. "Are you okay?" I asked in a little voice, afraid she might tell me to fuck off.

We were still about five feet apart. She turned to look at me a moment, then shrugged. "You got any drugs?" she asked.

She walked closer, and I felt pressure to answer her question with a resounding yes, wishing I could throw some drugs at her and run. "No," I said, "but maybe I can get you some. This guy who got me a room, he's a dealer. Cocaine, I think."

"My name's Natara," she said, and together we walked back to the motel room I'd just fled.

...

Once inside, Natara plopped her half-naked self on the floor, pulled up her knees, and hugged her bare legs close to her chest. She took off her sunglasses and I stepped back—her eyeball looked as if it had been popped out of her head and was holding on by a thin piece of bloody skin. I rinsed out a small towel from the bathroom and handed it to her. She dabbed at her face as I sat on the bed and told her about Mia's uncles, how I had been kicked out, how I had ended up here with this dealer. She nodded like it was an old story.

"Me and my boyfriend ran out of gas about a week ago," she said. "He was so pissed, he hauled off and smacked me in the face with the empty gas can. That's how my eye got fucked up." His name was Icey, she said. "He apologized. It was an accident. He didn't mean to hit me in the face." After the accident, he took her to the hospital and they left the car on the side of the road. When Icey went back later, it was gone—impounded. They needed $250 to get it out.

"It's hard for me to make money like this," she said, gesturing to her belly, "and now with my face . . ." She was about ten years older than me, and underneath the bruises and swelling she was kind of pretty. She was looking around the room. There wasn't anything in it except the furniture and her and me. Nothing for her to steal, nothing for me to give her. I worried that she would leave me alone. *I can help her,* I thought. *I can make her some money.*

"I should call my boyfriend," she said. "He's probably worried about me." She headed for the phone next to the bed. I listened to her explain to him that she was in a motel room with "some girl" who was trying to get away from "some guy." "You need to come over here," she told him.

He said he'd be right over. We continued talking, and in the middle of my story about not knowing I would bleed when I lost my virginity, there was a knock on the door. Natara jumped up and opened it as though the room were now hers, and Icey sauntered in, as casual as could be. Everything looked pretty average about him except his hair. It was braided. Long, in tight cornrows that made him look different from other black guys I'd hung out with. I wondered how he got the name Icey. He was tough looking, but when he looked at me, he wore a sweet smile. I knew instantly that he'd want to help me. Wasting no time, he started asking me questions.

"Who is this guy you're trying to get away from?" he asked. "A trick? A friend? Do you know if he has a gun? Is he in a gang? I can call my brothers if you think he's coming back tonight. We'll protect you." He was calm and polite, like he was asking about the weather or what I had for breakfast. But the words had some kind of tension to them, and I wasn't sure how to answer.

"He has a wife and a son," I said. "I'm sure he's with them. He won't be back tonight. But he'll come back in the morning for sure, and that's when I want to be gone. I was getting out of here when I ran into your girlfriend."

He nodded. "All right, then. We'll help you and get you out of here." He looked at Natara, and the expression on his face changed. "Bitch is all fucked up and pregnant," he said. "Worthless. She can show you what to do, since she can't make any money. Stupid ass did this to herself all on her own." Dropping her eyes, Natara hugged her legs again. I was afraid for her but at the same time relieved. At least his anger wasn't directed at me. I hadn't done anything wrong.

Icey looked at me again, a long, slow look, as though he were taking inventory. "You turn a few tricks, you make enough money to bail out my car, I'll help you out," he said. It was like a math problem, I thought. A favor. We'll do each other a favor. *I'll get the money, they'll keep me safe, and then I can decide what I do next.* "Go with her. She'll show you how to do it and will take the money, so them thieves won't try to get away without paying for what they get."

Natara looked up at me from the floor. "Come on, you've got to watch me first. I'll show you how to pick up a trick."

Picking up the trick was the last thing on my mind. What about the sex? Who were these guys? What did they want? Should I be scared?

Natara stood up and walked toward me. Icey took a seat on the bed. "I'll wait here. Bitch, you better come back with my money." I knew Icey was talking to Natara. He didn't have any reason to talk to me like that. Besides, I was coming back. I had no place else to go.

In minutes, Natara and I were out in the dark together, walking along Parkway Drive, where we had met less than two hours earlier. "Listen, honey. Out here, these tricks, they'll try everything with you. You have to tell them what they can and can't do. And for how much. All the money is negotiated up front. Get the money first. Always. And always cash. You don't count it, just hand it to me. Then I'll give you the sign when it's okay to get in the car."

"Okay," I said. My heart was racing, but I was glad she was out there with me. She was at least going to show me how to do this right. *Then, when it's over, I'll be able to get away from Flaco. Get away from this place.*

One of the first cars that drove past us was full of high school boys. "Fuckin' whores!" they yelled out the window. "Hookers! Bitches!" I was shocked. Natara seemed to me to be down on her luck—Mom and Steve were always taking care of people who were down on their luck—but she didn't seem to be a bad person, certainly not a whore or a bitch, and I knew I wasn't, either. *Stupid fucking high school boys don't know shit. Why should I care what they say? They're not part of my world.* I should've been starting eighth grade, but I hadn't been to school in a year. Now, instead of going on field trips to the Fresno Chaffee Zoo, which was practically across the street, I was walking along Parkway Drive with a pregnant, beat-up prostitute.

Natara showed me how to stand on the side of the road to let the cars going by know that they could stop and ask for a date. For now, she said, I should be quiet. I was glad, because I didn't think I'd ever be able to talk like she did. At least not out loud.

"Hey, honey, are you looking for a date? She'll make you happy." I didn't think the first two guys she hollered at were even American. And it turned out that they didn't speak much English. Natara knew a few words in Spanish and did the negotiating. She explained that she would give them a discount for both of us—forty dollars for me, only twenty for her, I guess because she was pregnant and messed up. One guy handed her eighty dollars. Only for her, he said pointing to me. They both wanted me.

In the hotel room, Natara directed the scene, telling me to bend over and hold myself up with my hands on the bed. Then she went outside, keeping the door open a little so she could "protect me" if "something went wrong." I worried about what could go wrong. What could be worse than this?

I'd never had sex this way. I don't remember if it hurt. I don't remember if I felt a thing. Both men had paid Natara money to have sex with me, and I couldn't do anything to make them mad or make her mad. My body did what it was supposed to do, as though it were separate from me. I had the strange sensation again, the one I'd had with Flaco. I was not in the room. I was someplace else. Someplace safe. Outside and above the room. What was happening was not happening to me—not to the spirit of me, the heart of me, the girl who knew how to do math problems, who knew how to bathe babies and ride a bike for miles. That girl wasn't there.

In less than ten minutes, it was over. Natara and I left the room, and on the way out I noticed the sign above the motel. "Children 12 and Under Stay for Free." I was twelve, and as far as I could tell, nothing was free.

CHAPTER THREE

R un. Everything in my body told me to run, to hide. But where? I didn't want to be out in the dark alone, not in this neighborhood, where it wasn't even safe to look into the faces of the men driving through, paying for what they wanted, then going back to their other lives. If I called Mom, if I went home or turned myself in, I'd be sent right back to juvenile hall. The only option I could see was to stay with Icey and Natara. Let them take care of me for a while. Natara was nice enough so far, and Icey seemed like he might really want to protect me.

And anyway, they were starting a family. I knew about babies; I could help. Even though they were asking me to do things I had never dreamed of doing before, it mattered to them that I was there.

Cops were cruising up and down the street, and one pulled over to the sidewalk where Natara and I were standing. "Stop right there," he said, jumping out of the car and walking toward us. "Yes, you two. We got a report of a black and a Mexican smoking crack in the bathroom here."

I didn't wait for Natara to talk. "That's not us," I snapped. I was kind of surprised when the words came out of my mouth, it was the first time I'd spoken up in days.

Natara chimed in. "We're getting something to eat," she said. "I was hungry."

He looked at her belly, then looked at me. "How old are you?"

"Sixteen," I said. "What does it matter to you, anyway?"

Natara smiled a little smile, watching me give this cop attitude. I knew if he ran my name, I'd be back in juvy within hours and in another group home right after that. I didn't know where she and Icey would take me, but I'd spent so much time in places where I wasn't wanted, how could hanging with them be any worse? "Can we go now?" I asked. I didn't want to give the cop any more time to think of something to arrest us for.

"You two be careful getting home. It's dangerous out here." He really sounded concerned. For a moment I felt bad for lying to him. But he was a cop. I had no reason to like cops.

After the first two tricks, the next ones weren't so scary. The actual physical act never got any easier—it wasn't sexy or exciting, and it was nothing like being held in Fernando's arms or fantasizing about boyfriends after I said my prayers at night. But everything leading up to making the deal felt like a game. I wanted to be as brave as Natara was, walking up to strangers, asking them straight for money. She was like a machine, no emotion, just saying and doing whatever she needed to get guys to say yes. She didn't care what anybody thought of her, or what she might feel like the next day, the next hour, or the next week. I wanted to be like that.

"Do you want me to get you out of here?" asked one trick. He'd given Natara the money and was driving away with me in his car.

Go with him where? For what? "I mean, you're a kid, right? A kid shouldn't be out here doing this."

"No. Just take me back when we're through."

He drove for a few more minutes and then parked. We were on a dark street. He never spoke after that, he just pulled his pants down, and when he was done, he drove me back to Natara.

We left the Villa Motel early the next morning, before Mia's uncle came back, if he ever did. I never saw him again. The sun was up and we were walking from the Villa to the next motel along Parkway Drive. I hadn't had much sleep, and I felt hungry and grungy and confused about all my feelings from the long night I'd just come through. Icey must have seen it on my face.

"You're going places, girl," he said in a reassuring voice. "You done good, and I'm going to repay the favor. I'm gonna take care of you. Would you like that?"

I nodded. Yes, I would like very much to be taken care of.

As we walked, he got closer and closer to me. And Natara was getting mad. I could tell because she had her arms folded in front of her, and she was stomping her heels on the sidewalk as she walked in front of us. She didn't want her boyfriend talking to me. Too bad. She got me into this in the first place.

I knew Icey was crossing a line when he put his arm over my shoulder, but Natara was so far ahead of us, I hoped she didn't notice. His arm was heavy around my neck, and the weight automatically tilted my head down toward the ground, where I noticed something I hadn't seen before. Icey was wearing yellow construction boots. The type I'd seen my stepdad lace up every morning before he went to the shop. "Those are work boots," I said.

"I drive a forklift," he explained. "Twenty dollars an hour to move heavy things around." He seemed happy to explain the details of his job. "But now I can't do that, not with her out here. Who would take care of her?" He convinced me. Natara needed his help, and now so did I. He pulled me closer under his arm and I stiffly moved toward him. My stomach curdled as I thought, *This is it. Maybe this is my life.*

Icey explained that we would not get a room right away because it was too early. "We're going to Twig's room," he yelled up to Natara.

She stopped in her tracks and turned around to yell back at him. "I hate that mean motherfucker!"

"Shut the fuck up and keep walking."

His voice changed when he talked to her, different from when he talked to me. I wanted him to take his arm off me, but I didn't know how to get him to move it. When we finally checked into the second motel room, Icey stretched out on the bed, picked up the TV remote control, and flipped Natara a twenty-dollar bill. "Go get her some makeup and anything else she wants at Kmart," he said. "She has to look older."

While Natara and I walked to Kmart, I tried to ask her a few personal questions, but she wasn't having it. "I'm not in the mood to talk," she said.

As soon as we walked into the store, I remembered the last time I'd been there, to shoplift a phone for Monica's aunt's house. High on coke, her aunt had washed the old phone in the soapy sink water and it had died. That seemed so long ago, even though it was just a couple of months. Going back in with Natara, with money, felt different—less fun, less free. I told her the shoplifting story. She laughed. "Girl, don't do any of that today." I started to tell her about my Kmart shopping spree with my mom and Sara. "At Christmas," I said, and something in her face shut down. There would be no girlfriends-sharing-holiday-stories between us.

When we returned from Kmart, I was carrying twenty dollars' worth of makeup that had actually been paid for. We hadn't been gone long, but we knew immediately that Icey's mood had changed. He stopped us before we got all the way through the door.

"Get out of here and make us some fucking money," he said to Natara. Glaring, she turned around and went outside. The door closed. I was alone with him. "Take your clothes off," he said to me. "All of them."

I froze. "Take your fuckin' clothes off!" he said again.

I started to take off my pants. He watched me. I felt uncomfortable. Everything was off except my underwear. "That too!" he ordered. He'd drawn the curtains closed tight, but he walked over to them, opened them a little. It was still early, no cops around at this time and no way to make the room dark, to hide my nakedness.

Icey walked toward me, his eyes so wildly alive in his head that I had to look away. But he yanked my face up, put his fingers inside my mouth and then put them between my legs and into my vagina. It was not sexual—it was a cavity search, and it was rough. He was looking for money. "It's all right, I'm just checking you," he said, "seeing if you bitches are trying to get away with turning tricks when I'm not watching you and then not giving me the money. Anything happen while you were out there? Got anything to give me?"

"No," was all I could say. I wanted to tell him that all we did was get what he told us, the makeup at Kmart. But I couldn't get any words out.

He let me go after the search. "Put your clothes back on." I did it and tried to make sense of the last few minutes. *This is the way it works. You go out, you come back, you get checked.*

As one day ran into the next, I lost any sense of time. I never got to hold or use any of the money I was making for them, but I knew not to ask. I was conscious of Icey's changing moods and Natara's pregnant belly. I remembered putting my hands and then my head on my mother's eight-months-pregnant belly. I wondered what my baby brother was doing right this minute.

From one motel to another, they smoked crack, using a little glass pipe. One night Icey put the glass pipe up to my mouth. "Smoke it," he said softly. I pulled my head back.

"I don't know how." I wasn't lying. I had never smoked crack.

"I'll show you." He put the pipe in front of my face again and showed me where to put my lips. He lit the yellow rock and I watched it melt.

"Breathe in," he said. "Inhale it."

The smoke hit my lungs like shards of glass, and numbness immediately followed. It took only seconds for my heart to start racing and my body to tremble. I exhaled. My chest felt like someone was standing on it. I gasped for air. Icey watched me. "Feels good, don't it?"

But it didn't. I was scared, I couldn't breathe, and I was sure I was going to die. Icey's face grew more concerned. "I think I'm dying," I said.

"Oh, fuck, are you having a seizure or something?" he asked.

Yes, that's what it was, a *seizure*—I knew the word because of a *Punky Brewster* episode. Punky's friend had a seizure. She was epileptic. "Yeah, I'm epileptic," I blurted. "I have seizures." I didn't have to fake the shaking.

In his crack-induced paranoia, Icey believed me. His panic turned to anger. "Bitch, you better not die." He waved his hand at the bathroom door and gave me a shove. "Get your ass in there. Take a cold shower," he said.

I was so relieved to go into the bathroom alone. I stood under the shower for a few minutes, and the cold water helped me breathe better, but it could not stop the fear. Was I really having a seizure? Was I going to die?

"My mom," I yelled to Icey from the shower, "she'll know what to do."

"Get out, then. Get out of the shower and call her." He was really scared. I wrapped around me a thin, cheap motel towel that barely covered me up. It felt like my blood was freezing inside me.

Natara watched from the bed as Icey dialed the number I gave him, and then he handed me the receiver.

When Mom answered the phone, I was so happy to hear her voice that I almost forgot why I'd called. I knew I couldn't use the words "seizure" or "epilepsy," or she'd know I was lying. "Um, hi, Mom. It's me," I said. "I'm in Fresno, and I'm really sick. Can you come and get me?"

There was a silence on the other end of the phone. Icey looked like he was going to take the phone away, but I put my hand up to my heart and patted it. I was desperate. Mom would know what to do. I waited for a response.

"Honey, you ran away," she said. Her voice was calm and soft. "You got yourself there. You can get yourself home, can't you?"

She didn't hear me right. "Mom . . ."

"You don't sound sick to me." She was right; I didn't sound sick. I sounded like myself. Which wasn't good enough for her.

I'm not sure who hung up first, but the conversation was over. She wouldn't come. Nobody would.

I knew for sure that I was on my own, and now Icey knew it too. Maybe I wasn't going to do any more crack with him, but now he knew there was no chance of anyone coming to my rescue. I had no one, so I belonged to him.

■ ■ ■

Every day, often more than once a day, Icey and Natara needed more crack. "Don't talk to none of these fools," Icey said about the dealers who came around. Then one day, he announced I was going with him to pick up the drugs. I didn't know why until we arrived at the two-story, faded yellow apartment building. "Get out of the car. If any of these motherfuckers ask, you're sixteen." I nodded, knowing better than to talk back to him when he was like this.

"Do you understand that you are sixteen?" he said. "They find out that you're twelve and they'll kill you, and me."

The tall wooden fence was behind me. Icey left me alone there while he went upstairs and into an apartment. I stayed where I was and rehearsed "sixteen, sixteen" in my head. Nothing could've pre-pared me for what would happen next. When Icey came back to the car with two other guys, I assumed they were the dealers. "How old are you?" one asked, getting up too close to my face.

"Sixteen." I said it just like I'd been told.

They looked at me suspiciously, then nodded to Icey. "Get up there, bitch," Icey barked. I didn't dare ask why. I followed the three of them up the stairs and into an apartment. It didn't contain much furniture—an old couch, a small wooden table. When Icey walked toward the kitchen, I started to follow him but was told to turn left down the hall and wait in the bathroom. There was a sink on the right side with a mirror above it. A toilet, a tub, and a shower stall with a fake-glass shower door. It wasn't dirty or cluttered like my house. It was just empty, as though no one really lived there. I was alone for a moment. One moment.

The first guy walked in, holding a large chrome handgun. He put it down on the back of the toilet. The heavy clunk told me that it was real. The next thing I heard was an order. His pants were down. "Do it." He glanced at his gun and back at me. I moved in closer to him and bent down. My mouth was too small. I was too small. He finished on his own, picked up the gun, and left. He wouldn't shoot me. I had done everything he asked.

Alone again. Another moment, sitting on the floor, making myself as small as I could in the corner between a bare wall and the bathtub, my legs curled underneath me. The next guy walked in and shut the door. He looked at me, shook his head, and left the bathroom. He didn't want anything from me.

The third guy came in, holding a different gun. This one wasn't as big. Not as heavy. "Take your clothes off," he said with his gun still in hand. "He didn't fuck you, did he? Cuz I don't want to catch no shit!" He put the gun down on the sink.

I took everything off. The last thing was my underwear. They were on the floor behind me when he was inside of me. I looked at them. They were dirty. They were white panties with red ruffles. Garfield was on the front of them. Garfield looked back at me.

The man pushed himself into me. This time, I wasn't numb enough to keep from registering the pain. I could barely stand it, it hurt so much. I bit my tongue. I didn't make a sound. I didn't want to do anything wrong.

Icey came in and told me it was time to get dressed, then he walked me back through the apartment. "Keep your head down," he said. He shoved me into the car. "We're not going back to the motel tonight." Natara was meeting us at his sister-in-law's townhouse, he said, in a neighborhood I did not know. I didn't care. I only thought one thing when we left that apartment building. *Never go back there with him ever again.*

■ ■ ■

The sister-in-law's house had wall-to-wall carpet, a couch along one wall, and mismatched chairs surrounding an old table that was more in the living room than the dining room, which was empty. Upstairs were two bedrooms, but Icey, Natara, and I slept downstairs, Icey on the couch, Natara and me on the floor. Icey's sister-in-law slept upstairs with her two little girls, who were eight and ten. The girls were not supposed to talk to Natara, but I was okay.

Icey's sister-in-law never said anything to me directly; she only talked to Icey and to her children. Even so, she was the most normal-seeming person I'd seen in weeks. I think she had some kind of normal job. I sensed that she wanted us gone, but for some reason she could not tell us to leave. I didn't know why. It wasn't a place I could run from. There was a deadbolt that locked with a key from the inside. I didn't know where the apartment was with the men with the guns, but if I was caught trying to run, there was a chance I could end up there again.

After the drug-house bathroom, Icey left me alone for a few days. One day the eight-year-old came home excited. "Carissa, I'm counting in Spanish." She jumped up on my lap. *"Uno, dos, tres, cuatro, cinco, seis . . ."* She went all the way to ten and said she was going to learn up to twenty soon. She smiled wide at me and I remembered the afternoon my sister Sophie had taught me to multiply by nine on my fingers. I'd been this girl's age. "Want to learn a trick to do math fast?" I asked.

"Sure," she said.

"Okay, first put your hands up like this. Then count the number you want to multiply." It was all coming back to me.

The peaceful interlude ended one afternoon. "It's time for you to get back out there," Icey said. "There are fewer cops, and Natara can introduce you around the neighborhood."

Natara came in a few minutes later with a black garbage bag full of used clothes that she said a church had given to her. She dumped the clothes on the floor and scavenged through the pile, tossing items around like it was Christmas morning. "That's cute," I said, reaching for a shirt, and Natara snatched it away. "It's mine," she said. She handed me what she wanted me to have from the bag and kept the rest for herself.

The next morning she was still asleep on the living room floor when Icey woke me up. "Come with me," he whispered as he led me into the kitchen. No one else was home. I didn't know where the little girls and the sister-in-law were. I wasn't even fully awake when he ordered me to drop the jean shorts that Natara had given me from the bag of used clothes.

He took off his belt. I had never noticed it before. He wrapped it around his hand once and made a loop with it. "Come here, put your head down."

I did what he said. I was awake. And there was a belt around my neck. How had I gotten to this place? Why was this happening? Icey yanked his pants down to his knees, then lifted me up onto the kitchen counter. It was cold. All I could think was, *This won't work for long.* There was no physical way for him to keep a tight grip, to choke me at the same time he was pushing himself inside me. I had to hold on to him or I would fall into the sink. I closed my eyes. *This won't last long.*

I was right. He couldn't keep it up. He told me to jump down, then dragged me with the belt around my neck into the empty dining room. "Get down," he ordered. As he pushed harder, my shirt came up and my back was on fire. He lifted my legs. I wanted to scream. Natara was only a few feet away on the living room floor. She couldn't be sleeping. I saw the pile of blankets move. She pulled the covers over her head. I didn't blame her. She was afraid.

I started to pray. *This hurts. Please finish.* The belt was still around my neck. I tried my best to wait for the relief that I knew would come once he was done. Finally, he finished on my stomach. I stayed still. Relieved but terrified. I wished that Natara would throw me her blanket. Icey stood up and got dressed in the kitchen.

"Get up!" he yelled at me. "Clean yourself up."

He pulled me to the table, where he sat down on a chair and pulled me closer with the belt. "Get on your knees, lower than me." He pushed my shoulders to put me on my knees facing him. He pulled the belt tighter around my neck and started to explain the rules. "You're a fucking bitch," he said. "Do you understand that? You belong to me. You came from my rib, the Bible says that. I own you, just like all men own women, and I can do whatever I want with you."

My heart ached.

He was lying to me, just like everyone else. He was full of shit, but there was nothing I could do. No way to run, no place to go. I knew for a fact that his version of the Bible was wrong. No Bible, no God, ever gave him permission to do these things. All those hours studying, all that time in the Kingdom Hall answering questions, I knew God didn't want this for me.

Salty tears began to roll down my face, and the belt got tighter around my throat. "If you're going to cry, you fucking cry! I want to hear you cry out loud, like you mean it." But I could not. I could not cry out loud. Only silent tears. Tears for him and for me and for Natara and for the little girls and the sister-in-law and everyone else I could think of. *He is wrong. He is wrong. He is wrong.*

"I'll get you to cry," he said, and stood up, pulling the belt as though it were a dog leash. "You're going to make me a lot of fucking money taking it in the ass, so I'm going to teach you how to do it, and one of these days you'll even like it. You'll beg for it like that bitch does." Natara was still faking sleep.

When we got to the upstairs bathroom, he bent me over the sink. In the mirror, I looked directly into my own eyes for the first time in weeks. And finally I found my voice. "Mom, Mom, I want my mom!" I was crying out loud. I wanted her. I was crying for her.

"Get in the shower," Icey said when he was done, and he finally loosened the noose around my neck. "You need to push that shit out of you in the shower, so you don't end up like Natara. Get it all out."

He hadn't done what he'd said he'd do. He hadn't raped me the way he'd threatened. Maybe he stopped because I cried for my mom.

His false compassion did its job. I never wanted to leave the shower, but I knew there wasn't enough hot water in the entire world to wash him off me, to wash him out of me, to erase the image in the mirror, me crying for my mother, she not being able to get to me.

That night, some friends of Icey and Natara's came to the townhouse, and Icey got drunk. I had seen him high on crack but never blind drunk. He started yelling at Natara, who yelled back about wanting crack, about needing to get high. He called her a lot of names, and this time she gave it right back to him.

I shrank back against the living room wall, praying that no one would notice me. I couldn't make myself small enough; eventually Icey turned his rising anger on me. "Come here!" he yelled. When I got to my feet and stood in front of him, he grabbed me with one hand and held a glass bottle up to my neck with the other. "I'm going to break this fucking bottle and cut your throat and cut you up. Would you like that? Huh?" He had a smile on his face, as though the idea of slicing me up made him happy.

"Knock that shit off," his friend said, looking nervously over at Icey. I was grateful. Icey let me go.

■ ■ ■

Less than twenty-four hours later, I sat in the backseat of a white Pinto next to another girl—Natara was out on Parkway, and we were going to pick her up to get more drugs. The other girl looked about sixteen and was with Twig, who sat shotgun while Icey drove.

Something in their silence led me to believe they were going to kill me. I felt so heavy, like a bag of dirt, useless and taking up too much space. In some ways I felt like I was already dead. We stopped at a gas station at Parkway Drive and Belmont, and there was Natara. I can still see her strutting across the street from Triangle Burger, hugely pregnant and chomping on French fries. Suddenly and finally, I hated her. She probably wanted me to die.

Natara got into the car on Icey's side and climbed into the back-seat, pushing me into the middle. We didn't get far. Icey had only driven about twenty feet when a cop car lit up behind us and pulled him over—for picking up a prostitute.

"License and registration," the cop said to Icey, who reached into the glove compartment like he was searching for papers. Of course, he didn't find anything, because there was nothing there. "My name's Reginald Jackson," Icey said. He was lying about his name, which was actually Jimmy Jackson—he was giving the cops his brother's name. The policeman walked back to his car and called for backup; in minutes, another flashing cop car parked sideways in front of the Pinto, blocking our path. Two more cops ordered Icey out of the car.

"What's the problem, Officer?" Icey asked, innocent as a choirboy.

"There's a warrant for your arrest."

I looked at the back of Icey's head and thought about how dumb he was. He gave the cops a fake name and it turned out to be some-body with an outstanding warrant. *Idiot.*

Then the cop slowly looked at the rest of us. "I need all of you to get out of the vehicle, and keep your hands where I can see them. You, come over here." He was talking to me.

Icey and I had rehearsed this a hundred times, and I tried to stick to the script. I got out. When the cop told me to get into the squad car, I did as I was told. Icey had warned me that the cops would want to trap me. To take me in. To lock me up. "How old are you?" the cop asked.

"I'm eighteen." I said it with a smart-ass attitude, the one I'd learned to put on in front of pushy cops just like this one.

"You are not eighteen," he said.

I shrugged. "I am. I'm eighteen." Icey and I were now in the backs of two separate cop cars; Natara and the two others stood outside the car while their names were run through the computer by another cop.

Being inside the back of a cop car was familiar to me. You can't get out. I was trapped. I was being arrested, locked up, just like Icey had warned me would happen. I was the criminal again. I was the bad one. All of them were looking at me in the back of the car. I was waiting for whatever would happen next. I knew what was next: After the cops there was juvy, then court, and then a probation officer who would recommend I be placed in a group home. I had been through it enough times before that I wasn't afraid and I didn't feel like any of it was punishment. It would almost be a relief after Icey and Natara. In a strange way I was looking forward to starting down a road I knew, one where no one would rape me or torture me or buy me or sell me.

The cop's car smelled like he did—stale and smoky, like a bag of old clothes. He smoked cigars; he had one in his mouth while he questioned me. I was probably safer there than I'd been in months, but I felt like I was sitting with the enemy. The one I was running from in the first place. "How old are you?" he asked again.

"Eighteen," I repeated. He didn't want to help me; he just was trying to catch me in a lie, to lock me up. At least that's what my broken senses were screaming.

"I don't think so," he said.

The cop didn't buy my lie, but he never really bothered to ask me about my truth. He never looked into my eyes or said, "Who are you? How are you doing? How did you end up here? Where would you like to go?" I might have told him something if he'd asked me those questions, but he didn't. The questions he asked were standard. Name. Age. Date of birth. I had easy lies for all of them. I didn't want him to know anything—not my real age, not my real name, not that I had violated probation and run away from more than one group home. I didn't want him or anyone to know all the ugly things I'd done. It was too big, like an earthquake or a tidal wave, too big for me to even think about, let alone put into words in front of this smelly, grumpy man. I didn't want to go home. I didn't want to live in a group home. And I didn't want to be locked up again. I just wanted someone, anyone, to take care of me.

Right before the cop drove away with me in the backseat, I turned my head and saw Icey in the back of the other squad car. He turned and winked at me through the window, then blew me a kiss. For a split second, I thought, *Wait, don't go.* I thought he was nice, even after he raped me. I believed in that moment that he might want me to be all right. I was relieved—he wasn't mad at me. Where were they taking him? I learned later that he had been found guilty of other crimes and ended up in prison for 144 years. I never saw him again.

Except, of course, I did see him. Over and over, in my dreams. Every night. Every day. Even in the sunshine, years later, it would come back, the haunting feeling that somehow he'd find me. I'd have nowhere to go and he'd find me alone. Only this time, I'd be the one with the gun.

All my fantasies about killing Icey were the same. My weapon was a light handgun, like the second one I'd seen in the bathroom. It fit my hand perfectly and it wasn't too heavy. Icey never moved in my dream. He didn't run. He didn't ask for forgiveness. He just sat there, waiting for me to decide to kill him. And I sat there too, feeling the gun in my hand, the coolness of it, the perfect weight of it, thinking about what it would be like to pull the trigger. But I never did it, not once. *I can't,* I thought, even in my nightmares. *I'm not him.*

CHAPTER FOUR

That kiss through the window from Icey lingered on for years, unmet, unreturned. The little girl in the back of the police car silenced by a small sign of affection, a kiss that carried a message: *I know I hurt you. I know you can tell the cops everything. But I also know that you won't.* Icey was right. As tough as I wanted the cop to think I was, as defiant as I wanted to be, I didn't blame Icey or anyone else for what had happened to me. I'd been warned repeatedly that bad choices would lead to bad consequences, and sure enough, here I was. At twelve, my life might have been out of control, but I still knew how things added up—my bad decisions were my fault. The selling of my body, the belt around my neck, being forced to do crack and raped at gunpoint, it was all on me. Why bother telling on Icey, sending him to jail? I was used to taking the blame.

The cop just kept asking the usual questions, knowing every word out of my mouth was a lie. He took me to juvenile hall, and as soon as we walked into booking, somebody behind the desk recognized me. "Back again, Carissa?" That was it for the cop—just as he'd guessed, I was a bad girl with a record. He turned me over without so much as a "Good luck, kid," and walked away.

The booking officer processed me for violation of probation. Since I'd repeatedly demonstrated I'd go back on the streets if they released me, it was an automatic lockup for thirty days. I turned thirteen in juvy.

I spent the next few months ricocheting around like a pinball—in and out of group homes, in Fresno County juvenile hall for probation violations, running away to stay with friends, babysitting in exchange for food and a couch. I knew which doughnut places threw out day-old doughnuts in the morning, so I wouldn't starve. I could've gone home anytime—and I tried, a few times. But I wasn't that girl anymore, asking for lunch money and doing homework. There was nothing Mom and Steve could threaten me with that was worse than what I'd gone through.

I had no idea Mom sat up at night worrying about where I was. I was on my own, with no one to trust. My family became other girls, always changing but always finding something in common. When I was running with another girl, we had our stories— the risks, the near misses, the wrong place at the wrong time with the wrong person. One of my stories was about my time with Icey. The next time I saw Mia (in a group home, of course), we took off together. I told her what had happened when her aunt kicked me out, about her perv uncle really being a perv, and about Natara and Icey. I was a little surprised at her reaction, which was basically none at all.

"But it's cool now, right?" she asked. *I guess it has to be,* I thought.

Mia was that girl—the one who didn't care who caught her, because all she wanted was attention, even more than I did, and she didn't care what she had to do to get it. She was easy to run with because she didn't care about where we ended up, as long as she got a guy out of the deal.

The first night, we left the home and hit Kings Canyon Boulevard. It was a little early, but we thought we'd get lucky and catch a few guys who were cruising. If we were lucky, we'd get picked up fast, and by someone cute—maybe even two someones. When Alex pulled up in his burgundy Grand Am, I was pretty sure he'd be mine and whoever his passenger was would be for Mia. I jumped in the front seat, and Mia climbed in back. Even though she was behind me, I knew she was pissed, and before any of us even exchanged names, she blurted, "You know, Carissa is a prostitute."

"Fuck you, bitch—at least I'm not an ugly whore!" I wanted to jump over the seat and beat the shit out of her but changed my mind when Alex reached over and touched my leg.

"It's cool," he said. "We're all just having a good time tonight, all right?" I exhaled and refocused my attention on him. He was nice looking—obviously not a street thug or a pimp—and it was a nice car. I settled in.

Alex turned down the music. "We cruise here all the time and haven't ever seen girls as cute as you," he said. Was he kidding? I had a crooked front tooth and hair with a mind of its own, but Mia was the flat-out opposite of cute—massive buckteeth and an Olive Oyl body. *Whatever*, I thought. We weren't walking, and we had less chance of being caught. Maybe we'd even have someplace to sleep.

Mikey, the guy in the back with Mia, didn't have much to say. He and Mia were getting along okay. "Mikey, how about we go to your house for some beer?" Alex suggested.

"Yeah, let's do it," Mikey said. "Maybe my mom will fix us something to eat." Mikey's place was a converted garage behind his mother's house. I was glad when Mia and Mikey left to look for food in the kitchen. I sat down on the couch, Alex sat down next to me, and we began to talk like any couple on a date, or at least what I imagined that might be like.

"How old are you?" I asked.

"Eighteen," he said. "You?"

I thought about it for a second. The truth? Or the Icey truth? "Thirteen," I said.

"You look older," he said. "I'd have guessed fifteen or sixteen." I was flattered. When he leaned in and kissed me, it was nice, a make-out session with a nice-looking boy on a couch. When he wrapped his arms around me, I leaned into his body. His tongue felt warm. Another long kiss. A third. And then something changed. He pushed his pelvis into mine, and I pulled back to let him know I wasn't quite ready for that. He pushed in harder and frantically began yanking at my jeans. "No, no," I said, trying to wiggle away. "Please, Alex, don't. No, stop it, please."

He was tall, well over six feet, and broad in the shoulders and back—he probably lifted weights. I tried to sit up, pushing against him with my hands, but he didn't budge. I hoped Mia and Mikey would walk back in. But they didn't. No one did. Shoving me back down, he pinned me to the couch, one hand over my mouth, the other one working my jeans down around my kicking legs. He pushed my knees up and plunged himself inside me, tearing my skin. From first kiss to the rip of pain, it took less than ten minutes.

When he was done, he pulled up his pants and told me to pull up mine, paying little attention to the look of disgust and even sadness on my face. "C'mon, you wanted it as soon as you got in my car," he said with a half laugh, and walked out of the garage.

I waited for Mia to come back. When she did, she was carrying a plate of food and giggling—and high. Maybe Mikey had this all planned. I wasn't sure, but I needed to get her alone.

"Mia, we have to leave," I said. "I'm not messing around, let's go!"

She rolled her eyes and laughed again. "I'm staying here," she said, shrugging. "You can do whatever, but they have food and beer and weed. I'm not going anywhere."

I finally convinced her to go outside with me, and I told her what had happened while she'd been in the house with Mikey. She just shook her head, echoing Alex: "You know you wanted it."

If I'd ever liked her, even a little bit, I didn't anymore. But I had nowhere to go, so I sat on the couch for a half hour, an hour. Alex was gone for a while, then came back into the room, a beer in one hand, a joint in the other. "Hey, let's go out and have you make us some money," he said. I was the only sober one there. I glared at Mia, the one who'd used the word: "prostitute."

Alex drove us to a nearby apartment, where he instructed two Norteña girls to "make her look older. So she can hit the streets and make me some money." It was a big joke to him. Dumbly, I followed the girls into the bathroom. I had no fight left.

One of them handed me a stub of eyeliner and a pink and green tube of Maybelline mascara. "Where'd you meet Alex?" she asked.

"On Kings Canyon."

"You know that Cynthia is his girlfriend, right?"

I just looked at her blankly.

"She'll kick your ass if you mess with him."

"I'm not messing with him," I said. "I'm just doing what he says."

"Okay, *heina*, because little girls like you shouldn't fuck around with someone's boyfriend." I wished I could tell her what Alex had done, but she would have blamed me. I was the slut.

When she left the bathroom, I shut the door and watched myself in the mirror like I was watching TV, putting on the mascara as slowly as I could, caking my eyes in black. How could I tell them I wasn't who they thought I was, that I didn't want to be here and I didn't want to go back out on the street? I painted my lips red and teased my hair high. *What the hell,* I thought. *Maybe this is me.*

I went back into the living room. Nobody said a word. Mia, Mikey, and I followed Alex back to the car and drove to Blackstone Avenue, a four-lane commercial boulevard lined with restaurants and cheap motels. After cruising up and down the street a couple of times, Alex pulled the Grand Am into a dirt lot. "Get out," he said. "Go over to the curb." I did as I was told, standing on the side of the street while the three of them sat in the car getting high and laughing.

Alex was not a pimp any more than I was a prostitute, and neither of us knew what we were doing. Standing alone in the dark on Blackstone, I felt the anxiety burn in my empty stomach. For ten or fifteen minutes, I just stood there, waiting for a car to slow down, to stop, but none did. I couldn't call out to them like Natara had. I knew there was a signal I was supposed to send with my body, but I didn't know what it was, so I just stood there as the cars drove past. It was pathetic. Not even the johns wanted me. I didn't mind the rejection—I knew I was better off being invisible.

Eventually, tired of waiting for me to get a date, Alex called me back to the car. "It's a bad spot," he said. In a few minutes, we all admitted defeat and headed back to Mikey's garage.

The next morning, I woke up with an ache in my shoulders and mascara smeared all over my face. I wanted out of there, fast. Mia woke up a few minutes later but seemed in no hurry to leave. We barely had time to use the bathroom before the boys kicked us out. I split from her as soon as I could and never saw her again.

■ ■ ■

"Cough and squat." I heard it every time I was booked into juvy. In front of a hard-eyed female guard, I took off all my clothes in the cold, tiled shower area and bent down and coughed. If the cough wasn't hard enough, we'd have to cough again, so I always tried to cough hard the first time. They were looking for drugs or weapons smuggled in our private parts.

I didn't tell the guard that I was used to this by now and that I didn't care anymore. I was a stranger to my body; it belonged to others as much as it had ever belonged to me. The only part I didn't let anyone touch was my backside. That's why cough and squat seemed so silly to me—what kid was ever going to intentionally stick something up there? It scared me to even think about Icey raping me there like he'd threatened to do. It was a place no one had the right to touch, ever.

Three days before this most recent lockup, I'd passed out in a group home because of the worst pain I'd ever felt, a sharp cramp that stabbed me in my side. I hit the floor and realized I was bleeding. Group-home staff called an ambulance after taking my temperature—104 degrees. I couldn't fake that.

The ambulance rushed me to the ER for an exam. I'd never had this kind of exam before. I recognized the examining table but had never been told to remove all my clothes. I'd never been given a paper gown. I didn't know which way to put it on. When the doctor came in, he asked me to lie down on the table. I did as he asked, nervously watching as he pulled metal rods from the side of the table and told me to scoot my butt down toward him and put my feet in the straps. All I really wanted to do was roll over on my side and curl up inside the pain, but he promised he could only help with the pain if I did as he said. The doctor looked up at me from his seat between the stirrups. "This won't hurt," he said. "I have to put a cotton swab in here, so we can run tests and see what's going on." I cringed but tried my best to relax. The metal was cold on my bare feet and the thing he put inside me was cold as well. It clamped, and I jumped.

When I felt the cold thing come out, I let out a sigh of relief, only to jump again when I felt his fingers at my backside.

"No!" I screamed, and pushed him back with my raised feet.

"It's okay, it's okay," he said, shushing me. "We have to check everything, or we may not be able to figure out what's hurting you."

"No!" I said. "No, you can't. Nothing has ever been in there, so nothing is wrong there."

"Okay, okay." The doctor stopped the exam. For the first time, I had said no and someone had listened.

Before I left the hospital, a nurse told me I had something called PID—pelvic inflammatory disease. And probably from chlamydia. "It's the most common STD," she said. My cure was a prescription for antibiotics and a brochure that talked about symptoms and treatment. The nurse mentioned condoms, but that was contraband, not allowed at the group home. There were other diseases they were checking me for, and she told me I could have my results in less than a week, but I'd be back in juvy, locked up, before that.

■ ■ ■

Most of the windows in juvenile hall were made up of dozens of small glass squares so thick that I could barely see anything on the other side, especially at night. During the day, weak sunlight seeped in through the panes, providing a constant reminder of the world on the other side—what we called the "outs."

Inside, the hall's low ceilings and concrete walls were the color of pale white skin. The institutional air was familiar, a combination of cheap paint, the cleaning products used to wipe and mop all the gritty surfaces, and cold, stale air. It was a desperation smell, a lonely smell, and it surrounded me every time I entered the booking room. The more time I spent in juvy, though, the more comforting the air became. The routine was familiar, and although nobody would've said they liked it, in a way, the regulars did.

For most of my shorter stints—two weeks or thirty days—I slept in a narrow little cell with a stainless-steel sink and toilet and a bunk bed sealed to the adjacent wall and nailed to the floor. The plastic-covered cot and pillow were now softer, as were the scratchy and stiff gray blankets. Nothing about the cell was enjoyable, but at least I was inside.

As inmates, we were given wall-to-wall rules that left no room for improvisation. Staff told us when to go out and when to come in, when to wake up and when to go to the bathroom. When to return our trays after meals and even when to brush our teeth. Food and shelter and keep your mouth shut. When we were allowed outside for fresh air, tall fences topped with razor wire surrounded the blacktopped yard and vacant field, reminding us that we were not good enough, not trustworthy enough, to be anyplace on the outs.

In juvy I was never quite sure what I looked like. The closest thing we had to a mirror was a flat, shiny piece of metal affixed to the wall. Over the years, girls had scratched away at that mirror to the point where it barely reflected at all; it was just a plate of graffiti. I was lucky if I could find a corner big enough to see my eye. But that was enough for us as we applied Vaseline to our lips and eyelashes—after all, juvy was coed, and there were reasons to want to look half decent in public.

Alex showed up during one of my short stays in juvy. When I first saw him, I thought, *What the hell? He's eighteen. What's he doing here with us?* He must've guessed what I was thinking, since the look on his face grew dark, almost angry. He'd never expected to see me again, either.

After a moment of mutual shock, he shifted his shoulders and cheerfully called out to me, "What's up, girl?"

I turned away and ignored him. I didn't want him to be there. But instead of leaving me alone, Alex darted out of his line and followed me into my classroom. "Hey, you don't say hello?" he asked. It was only the two of us and the over-sixty female teacher in the room. His tone of voice wasn't exactly long-lost best friends, but it wasn't obviously aggressive, either. Nevertheless, I didn't want to talk to him or act like we were cool. The teacher watched us closely but was not about to intervene. Sensing I was on my own, I grabbed a plastic chair, lifted it off the ground, and braced myself to throw it at Alex if he came any closer. Everything unfolded in slow motion, even as my pulse raced.

Moments later, Dot Jones, the rare counselor I actually respected, rushed in. She must've noticed Alex's detour. As soon as she came in, I knew I was safe. I put down the chair. She led me back to the girls' unit, and even though no one had laid a hand on me, she could sense I was afraid.

As Dot steered me into my cell, my breathing slowed a little. I was back in the girls' unit. Alex couldn't come in here. Dot stayed with me, sitting next to me on my bunk, our backs against the wall. She waited patiently until I was ready to talk. "What happened with that boy?" she asked, lowering her voice.

I told her almost everything. How I met Alex and how he raped me on a couch in a garage. How my friend didn't believe me. Then I stopped. That was enough to justify why I felt threatened by him, why I'd picked up the chair. I didn't tell her that I'd put on heavy makeup and stood on a curb for him. I didn't want her to think like I did—that it was all my fault.

Dot was still sitting with me when the other girls returned to the unit and two of Alex's homegirls walked past my cell. Information moves fast in juvy—too fast to be right. People get it wrong, they want to make drama, and some of them, the ones with nothing better to do, are invested in feuds and claiming sides even when there's no reason for it. "We're gonna get you, *puta*," one of the girls yelled out.

The second one, the one who was about to go up to Youth Authority for another year, made it clear. "Alex is my homeboy. You give him any time, and I'll kick your ass before I leave here."

I curled up on my bunk, trying to get small. "This is so stupid," I told Dot. "Those girls were my friends this morning. Now they want to fight me."

"Don't worry," she said calmly. "I'll take care of it."

Dot Jones was a fifteen-time championship arm wrestler who'd been a shot-put winner in college. She'd gone to South Korea in 1988 to compete in the Olympics. She was buff and dignified and deserved all the respect she was given, because she never once used her size or strength against us. Nobody, from the guards to the toughest kids, ever tested her.

I never found out what Dot said to those girls—it could've been a look, a sentence, a word. All I knew was, by dinnertime that night, they didn't even look my way. I had nothing to worry about.

I'm not sure how long Alex was locked up or if Dot ever went over to his unit to talk to him. But I had a hunch that she did and that she also had something to do with what happened later that same afternoon.

At first it wasn't difficult to get out of juvy with a placement in a group home. But after I ran a few times, the various group-home staffs caught on. So I was rarely interviewed, was usually the last one to get placed, and felt lucky every time a group home finally agreed to take custody of me. I wasn't always planning to run, but after a day or two, I'd feel anxious and restless and know I'd have to get out. Sometimes it was for obvious reasons, like not getting along with other girls. Small rules frustrated me, like having to wake up early in the morning on weekends just to do chores, including making our beds with "hospital corners." In the end, it was always something and I always ran.

A few hours after my talk with Dot, I had an unexpected interview with a familiar group-home staffer.

"Carissa." Dot called my name from the control center. She walked me toward the dining area where we did our group-home interviews. "You have someone here who knows you," she said. "She may have some space for you in the next week."

"Who is it?" I looked into the dining area and knew exactly. This was a staffer I loved, a warm, grandmother type. She looked back at me, smiled, and waved me over. I sat down across from her and listened as she reminded me—firmly—about the rules at the home. "Will you stay this time?" she asked. "Will you please not run?"

I asked if certain girls who'd given me trouble were still there.

"Yes," she said. "But they've all come a long way. And everyone's worried about you. You're not safe out there, and you're not making any progress."

"Okay," I said finally. "I'll stay."

My release from juvy was unceremonious. I didn't graduate from any program; I was just another girl rotating out, making room for someone new to come in. I went back through booking to return the clothes and shoes I'd been issued and pick up my bag of personal belongings. I put on the dirty clothes that had been sitting in a clear plastic bag for a few weeks. I wished I could have kept the clean underwear they'd issued me.

As I was leaving, two new girls came in. It was always easy to tell when someone had just been booked. Their skin was fresh and their hair still wet from the mandatory shower. Even though my skin was pale and my clothes were dirty, I was happy to be going in the other direction.

I didn't know the woman who picked me up, so I stayed quiet on the drive to the house. When we arrived, the grandmotherly staffer emerged from the sliding glass door. "Carissa, welcome home," she said. That felt nice. I knew I'd try to stay this time, just for her.

The first time I had been at this group home, I had run away the day school started. This time, if I wanted to stay, I would have to go to school. It was close by, only a two-block walk from the house, a continuation school for junior high kids. Technically, I should have been in the eighth grade, but I'd fallen far behind.

All of us girls from the home went to school together, some to junior high, some to the high school next door. The high school girls looked tough, and I didn't want to mess with them. The weather was cold, so each morning we started the day with a hot Cup Noodles for breakfast. Our classrooms were two trailers, two rooms in each, one teacher to a room.

My teacher, Mr. Clark, was a fifty-year-old black man with a funny disposition. After the first few minutes in his class, I sensed he was probably more uncomfortable than I was. The classroom had no security guards; it was just him and us. He took time each day to remind us of the basic rules. Instead of pushing us, he made suggestions. Our assignments were less about grades or failure than they were about his wanting to give us an opportunity to learn more about ourselves, more about the world we would live in, far beyond the mean streets or juvy or a group home. "Think about an essay on the United States of America," he said one day, "and what it means to be a citizen." I thought about his question for a few minutes and then started to write. Other kids were drawing and passing notes to one another, but I kept writing. At the end of three hours, I handed in five pages.

The following day, I was in the yard when Mr. Clark walked over to me. "I'd like to talk to you for a moment." He looked happy, so I smiled and waited. "I read your essay about being American," he said. "I wanted to know if you'd read it to the class today."

I wasn't quite sure what I was hearing. "Yeah, sure," I said, "but . . . do you think they want to listen to me?"

He laughed. "Probably more than they want to listen to me!"

The first two hours of class went by too slowly for my comfort. When was he going to call me up to speak? Would it be at the end of the day? Would the other kids be in a hurry to leave? Was he setting me up to be a dork in front of everyone? Why couldn't he read to them instead? Then it happened: "Students." This was how Mr. Clark got our attention. "I've asked Carissa to read her essay to us. Please pay attention. She has something important to say."

I went blank. I couldn't even remember what I'd written. Was it good? Why would they care? Slowly, I stood up to read, as Crystal and Devonne looked at me. Then Johnny and Demitrius looked up from their desks. I began:

Our books say that being American is about being free. Freedom is important. Americans died for it, we are willing to fight wars for it, but this essay is not about what our books say about being American. This essay is about what I can say about being American.

The papers were shaking a little in my hand. I took a deep breath and continued:

As I look around this trailer, I begin to understand where I am. I see different faces. Different shapes. Different colors. And I know instantly what being American means to me. No racism. No prejudice. No judgment. We are all starting in the same place, and we are free to become something more. Free to grow. Free to write and free to learn.

I was surprised when I got to the last page and everyone was still listening. I looked at Mr. Clark. With only one sentence left to read, I suddenly knew that it was the most important one to him.

For me, being American is about being here today in this classroom and learning about being me.

Some of the class applauded. I remembered my fifth-grade math award and the parents and teachers clapping for me. But those were grown-ups. These were kids like me. Did they clap just because that's what they were expected to do?

The next day I had a request of Mr. Clark—or, as he'd put it, a suggestion. "I think we should all read in class," I said. "Take turns sharing what we're learning."

He agreed. That day, Juan shared a poem he'd written in juvy, and Rachel shared a letter she had written to her grandmother who'd died.

On the way back to the group home that afternoon, I felt like everything was different. I belonged in that classroom. This class was not going to be a problem for me.

■ ■ ■

Mom started visiting me at the group home after I'd been there for three weeks. I thought that seeing her would make me angry all over again; instead, I was relieved. I didn't want to fight. She didn't want to fight, either; she was always ready to forget about bad stuff for the sake of a peaceful moment. By the fifth week, I was allowed to go out with her for the day. We usually went to lunch, my choice—Taco Bell or maybe KFC for strawberry shortcake. The most memorable outing was when Mom brought Nana with her. Because I was doing so well in school, Nana said she wanted to buy me something special. "What would you like?" she asked. It was all I could do not to throw my arms around her and hug her to pieces.

"Black boots," I said.

"Fine, let's go to the mall."

It took about an hour to find the ones I wanted, the soft suede ones I'd seen other girls wearing. We were in a small retail store, not a big department store, and I was thrilled to find them in my size. I was just about to try them on when Mom and I both noticed something at the same time: Nana's face had gone deathly pale.

"What's wrong?" Mom asked.

Nana, who'd worn a colostomy bag ever since her cancer surgery, whispered that she needed the bathroom, quickly.

"I'm sorry, ma'am," said the salesman who'd overheard, "but we do not have a restroom for the public. There's one at Penney's." But that was on the other side of the mall.

At that point, my quiet mother became someone I hardly recognized. She even seemed to get taller. "Do you understand that my mother needs a restroom now!" she said, her voice strong and clear. Other customers were looking at us. "She can't leave here without going to the restroom. She won't make it!"

Quickly, the manager stepped out from behind the counter and guided Nana to the store restroom in the back. I was proud of everyone in that moment—my mother, who'd stood up for her mom, my grandmother, who had such dignity, and the store manager for being decent to a stranger in trouble.

When we went back to the group home, Mom walked in with me while Nana waited in the car. All the girls wanted to know what I had in the bag. I hugged Mom good-bye and ran over to show off my brand-new boots. I think when Mom drove home that day, she left feeling that everything would finally be okay between us. She always wanted things to be okay but never wanted to talk about all the facts that made them *not* okay. Those subjects were off limits, closed, not available for discussion. Just behave. Don't be dramatic. Neither of us had any idea that this was the last afternoon we'd have together for a very long time.

■ ■ ■

The day after we went shopping, one of the girls asked me to run away with her. I liked her and felt bad for her because she missed her boyfriend on the outs. I didn't want to leave, though. I liked school. I liked having a bed. And I liked the staff, all of whom had grown on me in some way. But I also knew what it was like to be in need of a friend, of someone to borrow strength from, and I didn't want to disappoint her. "I know what—let's just sneak out for a few hours tonight." I explained that I knew how to get our window open without the alarm going off. I'd need her help to do it.

"You think we can?" She sounded doubtful.

"Of course we can." I was confident it would work, and I needed her to be confident too.

Most group homes had alarm systems, as much for keeping us in as for keeping strangers out. Every window and door had a buzzer that would sound when it was opened, but at this home I had noticed, if just one of the buzzers was disarmed, none of the others would go off. A glitch. An opportunity.

The plan was all about timing. I would take the garbage out after dinner and leave the back sliding glass door open just a little. At that same time, she would prop our window open, which essentially canceled out the alarm. We'd be able to get out, and we'd be able to get back in. But it was risky—if we were discovered, we'd probably be kicked out, be taken back to juvy on probation violation, and say good-bye to school and friends.

The grandmotherly staff member who'd given me another chance smiled at me as I walked past her carrying the trash in one hand. I felt a familiar twinge of guilt, knowing I shouldn't run, but now my friend was counting on me. I smiled back and walked out the door. As she looked back at the TV, I had my chance. I left the glass door open just enough. When I walked back in, I shut the door all the way and locked it. The timing was perfect. My friend had gotten our bedroom window open. I felt smart.

That first night we snuck out, I wasn't afraid—we weren't running away; we were just taking a break. It wasn't until we were safely back in our beds that I realized what we'd done. We were fooling people who were trying their best to help us.

The next night she wanted to go out again. "It's too cold outside,"

I said. "And anyway, we couldn't find your boyfriend last night. What makes you think we'll find him tonight?" In fact, the night before had been boring. Only one person had stopped to ask us to party, and it had been a creepy drunk. "Besides," I said, "I have a funny feeling, like this time we'll get caught."

My friend wasn't worried. The following morning she was gone. And so were my new black suede boots. I hoped that she was just borrowing them, that she'd come back, but of course she never did. I felt like the fool—I'd lost my boots, my friend had turned out not to be my friend, and I was the one who had made the plan so she could get away!

It took everything in me to get through the school day. Mr. Clark noticed something was up and asked me if I was all right. I just shrugged it off, too embarrassed to tell him. I ignored his questions and didn't turn in any new work. All I could think of was my "friend," the one I'd taken a risk for, the one who had paid me back by taking something I couldn't replace. I asked everyone if they'd heard from her. "If you do," I growled, "tell her I'm going to find her, and I'm going to kick her ass."

Within a few days, I had a tip. She'd been caught and locked up and was heading back to the home. I got to her within five minutes of her arrival. "Where the hell are my boots, bitch?" I didn't care if staff heard me; they knew I was pissed.

"I didn't take them," she said. "It was somebody else. It wasn't me."

I thought of my mom and my nana and the day we bought my boots. I wanted those boots back—I wanted that day back. Without the boots, it felt like the day had never really happened.

Instead of ripping the girl's hair out, I reported her theft to the group-home staff and everyone else I knew. Maybe this would stop her from stealing from anyone else, but she just shrugged her shoulders; she didn't seem to care.

At school the next day, I decided not to go back to the home. It had turned out like all the others—nothing there for me. No one who mattered and no one I mattered *to*. After school, two older girls caught me wandering and asked if I wanted to go to a party with them. I knew I'd be kicked out if I went. I left with them and didn't look back.

■ ■ ■

I missed my old friends in Coalinga. I decided to hitch a ride back, but needed someone to stay with. Someone who'd never stolen from me, someone I could trust. In no time, I was back hanging with Zizi and our newest friend, Shorty. Zizi and I were one year older now, on probation, and convinced we were at least one year smarter. The only problem was, outside of school, nothing was happening in our small town. The streets were empty. It felt like you could die waiting for something to happen. We could shoplift, but we'd be spotted too easily; we could camp out in the creek and smoke, but last we'd heard, the cops knew about our spot. We decided to hole up at Zizi's dad's house, where there was a fan and cold beer to relieve the heat. We'd both grown a taste for beer, but only when we chugged it.

As we were strolling down the streets, Shorty kept doing something I couldn't figure out—walking close to all the cars, peering inside. I figured he was looking to steal something, a wallet or a stereo, which I'd seen him do before. I was surprised he went anywhere near the big two-door Lincoln. I didn't know what he could want from that car, a rusted-out old junker; even the plates were rusty, hanging on by a single screw.

"Hey," Shorty yelled. "We can steal that car! Ride it to Huron. It'd be easy—look, there's a wrench in the ignition-key slot."

Suddenly, Zizi and I were both into something we didn't know anything about. Grand theft auto—GTA. We didn't know how to drive, either, and Shorty, well, he was short—from outside the car he'd look like what he was, a little kid. No doubt the cops would pull us over if they saw him behind the wheel. Earlier that day we'd run into Leah, older than us and taller too. We guessed she knew how to drive. We went back to her house and told her the plan. A joyride to Huron! She was in. Shorty ordered all three of us to wait in the alley. He'd go back and bring the car to us.

As we stood behind a fence in the alley, we joked and laughed. It wasn't until we saw the car turning toward us that we realized we were actually stealing it. Shorty's little head barely came up over the steering wheel. He was driving so slowly, the cautious new driver, foot on the pedal a little, then off. When he stopped, we jumped in the passenger-side door. "I was afraid it wouldn't start," he said, "so I rolled it a few feet from the house before I tried it. Nobody heard a thing."

Leah was supposed to drive, but when she saw the car she balked. "I don't think I can. This car is damn big." Shorty didn't care; he'd drive and take his chances on being pegged. As soon as we got out of town, the car started to smoke. We knew we'd have to dump it once we were in Huron, but we were terrified of its breaking down before we even got there. With ten miles to go, smoke was pouring out from under the hood.

"Pull off the road when you see the smallest dirt road, right up here," I said. "I know someplace where we can find water for the car." This may have been the only piece of workable knowledge I'd ever gotten from Steve, my stepfather, the mechanic on the scene when Mom was broken down and helpless. I guessed that the radiator had a leak, and when we finally popped the hood, I was proved right. Once filled with cool water, the car started back up with no smoke. "We can make it to Huron," I said.

Shorty jumped back in the driver's seat, and we were on our way. Almost.

As we pulled into Huron, an unmarked police car flashed its lights behind us and hit the siren. Instead of stopping, Shorty laid on the gas. In seconds, we had three cop cars behind us and no way to outrun them in the clunker. Shorty threw the car into park and I watched as he, Zizi, and then Leah all scrambled to get out. Leah threw back the front seat and shut the door behind her, stranding me in the back. I didn't have time to think—I flew through the open passenger-side window, landed on all fours, then ran like crazy, following the three of them into an abandoned building.

When we thought it was all clear, we came out. Shorty took off on his own, while Zizi, Leah, and I ran into a backyard and hid under the trailer of a big rig. Hyped up from the chase and fully in survival mode, I told the others to stay put while I checked around. I crept through the yard, spotted a little kid on his bike, and asked what was happening.

"The cops are all out of their cars and walking around," he said, his eyes big with excitement.

I went back to the other girls and quickly laid out the plan. We could avoid the cops if we raced through backyards and hopped the fences. We took off running toward our next stop, the back of a duplex, but suddenly found ourselves trapped by two cops, one on each side of the duplex's back patios. When Leah saw one cop in front of us, she turned to run in the other direction and promptly ran right into another one. She was caught. Zizi and I ran around and past the second cop, who was bigger and slower than his partner. I knew we could lose him if we ran fast enough.

Running down the street, I caught sight of the little boy we'd seen earlier. "He's right behind you!" he yelled. Just then, I heard something I had never heard before.

"Stop or I'll shoot!"

We froze. Up until that moment, it had all been a game with the cops—stealing clothes, shoplifting makeup, sneaking out of group homes. All the chases before had been a pure adrenaline rush—I ran because I could. Now it was something else. No cop had ever threatened to shoot me. Zizi and I slowly turned around, and sure enough, the undercover was standing there, pointing a gun at us . . . but his pants were falling down! He was trying to hold them up with one hand and aim the gun with the other, but could not do both. I knew right then that even if he pulled the trigger, there was no way we were going to get shot.

"Keep running!" I screamed at Zizi. She hesitated. "Go! Go! Go!" I yelled, and she took off like lightning behind me.

The cop turned and headed for his car, probably to call for backup. Zizi and I knew we had only a few seconds to find a hiding place. We saw a group of four guys hanging outside a house and figured they were selling drugs and wouldn't rat us out. I led Zizi to the side of the house, where I pushed in a broken door of what appeared to be a shed—the perfect spot. Zizi followed me into the cramped, dark space, which was dusty and covered in cobwebs. We held the door shut, waited, and listened, panting as quietly as we could, trying to catch our breath. The sound of police radios got closer, and then we heard the voices of the guys in front of the house.

"No, Officer," said one, "we didn't see anything."

"Don't know what you're talking about, Officer," said another.

About ten minutes later, when everything was quiet, one of the guys spoke to us through the shed door. "Is there someone we can call to get you out of here?" he asked. "They'll be back soon, and they'll have dogs and more cops."

Zizi gave him the phone number of her brother, Junior—and it turned out they actually knew him! A lucky break. Our new friend went inside the house, called Junior, and told him where to pick us up. Twenty minutes later, we hopped the back fence and met Junior in the alley. The police were still circling the neighborhood, so we sank low in the backseat. We had gotten away.

But not for long. To avoid doing any jail time, Leah gave the police all our names. Plus, the cops found my bag in the back of the car—along with Leah's testimony, this was enough to charge me.

They picked up Shorty first, then Zizi, and because I was already out on probation, I bit the bullet and turned myself in. My probation officer told me I'd get less time if I admitted Shorty and Zizi were in on stealing the car, but I refused. I wanted Shorty and Zizi to know I wasn't the rat.

We had different attorneys and weren't allowed to talk about our cases. I met my public defender just before the first court date—like all the others, she wanted me to cut a deal. Her bleached blond hair and long red fingernails told me that she didn't have time to hear the whole story. She was nice enough as she interviewed me in a tiny room at the juvenile hall courthouse, but the two-inch-high stack of files that sat between us on the table told her only one thing. I was guilty. "It's your history," she said, tapping the files with one of her long red fingernails. Shoplifting, possession of stolen property, running away from group homes, probation violations, and, of course, this latest and most serious offense. She said because I wasn't the driver she thought she could get the district attorney to reduce the GTA, get it down to something like joyriding.

"You're going to do time," she said. "If you are willing to plead guilty to joyriding, you'll get less time. There's really no alternative." I knew she was right. What I didn't know was that my real stories— the stuff that was not in those files, like Icey and Alex and the realities of life on the street—might have helped me get counseling and possibly a reduced sentence.

In the court's eyes, I was uncooperative because I wouldn't snitch on my friends in exchange for a lighter punishment. I was given the full sentence that my probation officer recommended: 221 days in the California Youth Authority. Nearly eight months, with credit for time served.

I cried when I heard the recommendation. I knew how to deal with juvy, but Youth Authority was a different story. YA was not a "detention facility"; it was a prison with a reputation for turning kids into gangsters. It housed hard-core criminals and turned you into one. With no gang affiliations on the inside and very few gang connections out on the street, I'd be jumped immediately and have to claim to survive. Every girl I'd ever known who'd gone into YA had the same story: They went in alone and came out a true gang member, with missing teeth and chunks of hair missing to prove it. I knew if I was going up, I'd be forced to be something I wasn't. I wouldn't have a choice. I'd get my ass kicked every day if I refused. If I went along, I'd get my ass kicked only once, just to prove I was worthy of being accepted.

Within days of my being sentenced, three other girls (between thirteen and fifteen, with crimes unrelated to mine) also received six-month sentences in YA. Now the chief probation officer was faced with a question: Send these girls up? Or create something new for them, similar to what the local county authorities were doing for boys?

The C.K. Wakefield School for Boys in Fresno was a six-month rehabilitation program for teenage boys who were on the brink of being shipped to the California Youth Authority. The boys had this one last chance before the county handed them over to the state prison system, where the odds were against them. Unlike the regular juvenile-detention units, Wakefield was a structured program with social workers and teachers, with real classes in math and English. Wakefield also taught basic life skills, like budgeting, filling out job applications, and paying bills.

Wakefield had never taken girls—and the number of girls committing these types of crimes was low. That's why the girls' program had been shut down a few years earlier—the number of girls who needed it didn't warrant the extra cost of the staff. Now that was all changing. With no extra money in the budget and a clear need to do something different, we four girls were about to be launched as a trial balloon for coed rehab at Wakefield.

It was another chance, and I knew it. Of the four of us, a girl named Vanessa and I were the two chronic offenders, with a long list of crimes and probation violations. The other two, Jessica and Amanda, were both looking at six-month sentences on their first offenses, which had been pretty bad, but both were considered ideal candidates for a rehab program. They'd make it in Wakefield, but they wouldn't stand a chance in YA. They knew it too, and fearing the alternative, they both walked the line from day one.

Vanessa and I were defiant and harder to deal with. The first day at Wakefield, I watched as Vanessa began to test the boundaries. She mouthed off to staff and was immediately kicked out. At the end of the week, we were told, she was going up.

It was a quick lesson for the rest of us: This is what happens if you don't follow the rules. I was terrified to start a program with sixty guys. The first week of the program, I didn't get smart with staff, but the only way I could hold back my anger—at the system, at the rules—was to put my head down in my arms and cry. This wasn't freedom; this was a lockup, no matter what kind of nice name they wanted to put on it. I was in jail. I cried for the entire first day and was demoted to a lower level.

The next day I was told that if I didn't participate by the end of the week, I'd be going to YA with Vanessa, on the same bus. That night, I went back to the girls' unit where we slept and showered. Vanessa was there, in her bunk, burrowed under her scratchy gray blanket. Even though I was on the other side of the dorm, I could hear her weeping. This wasn't a tough girl; this was a young girl, crying for her mom. I knew what I had to do the next day. I made a choice. I'd be good, seriously good. Otherwise, I'd lose what was left of me forever.

For two years, my life had resembled a car spinning out of control.

Now the spinning had stopped, and I was intact. It didn't occur to me to thank anyone at the time. I didn't know about the people responsible for making the alternative to YA available; I didn't know it was a gift. All I knew was that someone thought I was worth saving. Because I had never stopped praying, I figured God had something to do with it. And even though I felt lost, I trusted that someone somewhere knew who I was and what I needed.

CHAPTER FIVE

■

For you did not receive a spirit that makes
you a slave again to fear, but you received the Spirit
of adoption. And by him we cry, "Abba, Father."

Before Wakefield—in juvy, waiting for my final hearing with
the judge—good behavior got me promoted from "blue" status
to "gold," which came with privileges: I was allowed to use a juvy-
issued razor to shave my legs, I could wear mascara, I could use a real
zit medicine on my face, and I could put real curlers in my hair. Gold
status also meant I was one of the first girls allowed to choose my
clothes each day. This was a big deal because it gave me access to
the nicest, cleanest underwear. Girls in the back of the line (the ones
who got in catfights or swore at the staff) ended up with the shabby,
worn-out stuff no one wanted.

On weekends we were visited by volunteers from various
churches. As part of their ministry, they spent time talking to us,
showing their care and concern in ways that most staff either weren't
allowed to do or didn't have time for. Hearing their words, seeing
the strength of their belief, reminded me that God existed, that
He loved me, even when I kept testing boundaries. The volunteers
echoed my nana's words: *God loves you, Carissa. Trust God, do what*

you know is right, and everything will be as it should be. I wasn't so sure. I still believed in God. I did believe in Nana, so I tried to hang on to the thread of my faith.

In juvy, unlike on the streets, we could make the choice to not fight—or fight back. If somebody gave me shit—a jealous girl or a new girl who came in with street attitude—vigilant staff members stepped in and stopped it. Even so, the mood in the hall could quickly change from upbeat to brutal. On family visit days, there were lots of happy girls. On days probation officers came to give updates on when you might be able to leave or what infractions were going to keep you there longer or get you sent up, there were always tears. If anyone had asked me at that point where I expected to be in five years, I would've said, "Dead or in prison." I couldn't imagine graduation or a job. Every occupation from parking attendant to cleaning lady seemed far out of reach.

So far, there'd been little about being a girl—or becoming a young woman—that hadn't been painful or shameful, but at least the small privileges I'd earned in juvy were a kind of armor between my worth and the world that judged me. When I started the program at Wakefield, that armor was taken away. It was back to square one: no privileges, not without earning them. The long dorm room most of us shared didn't offer any privacy or peace. Each morning, seven days a week, a crackling voice came over the intercom and announced it was time to get up. Still half asleep, we shuffled to the bathroom with our flimsy combs and cheap toothbrushes that were the same pale beige as the walls. We had to be quick, because the faucet turned off as soon as we let go of the stainless-steel button. Worse, we lost points for taking too long.

We girls never saw where the boys showered, and they never saw where we showered. We used the staff bathroom, while the Wakefield boys used the common stalls. But all meals were co-ed and so were our daily group sessions in the activity room.

Ron Jenkins was the chief counselor for the boys, and now he became our counselor too. A recent college graduate with only a few years of experience in the facility, Ron had been a star football player at Fresno State with dreams of playing for the pros—when I learned that, I couldn't understand why he wasn't bitter that the dream hadn't been realized. Instead of appearing to be stuck and unhappy, Ron arrived for his shifts smiling and full of energy. His shirts were spotless and his nails were always clean. He took a kind of pride in his job, and in himself, that I hadn't seen before. At times he even broke out in song. He'd sing whatever he knew or had heard on the radio last. His off-key rendition of a Luther Vandross love song would make even the toughest kids smile. He would walk around snapping his fingers to the rhythm and joking with the kids he passed. I would roll my eyes, and we'd all laugh. "You're terrible. Please stop."

Ron was cool, which gave us one more reason not to push him away. If anything, the awful singing drew us in. I think now he wanted us to know that if we could laugh at him—with him—then maybe we'd learn how not to take our missteps so seriously, learn how to laugh at ourselves and be laughed at by others.

Because this was the first year with girls at Wakefield, and there were so few of us, staff members kept a close eye on how we adjusted to the routine and how the boys adjusted to us. At every meeting, every class, and every meal, staff watched us. In the dining hall, from the time we stood in line until we were done with our plates and cleared our trays, we could feel eyes on us. Ron was usually right there too. He didn't eat with us, but he didn't guard us, either. Instead he just interacted, making his presence feel natural.

For a big man, he wasn't intimidating. He seemed to be where he wanted to be, and I didn't know many people who felt that way. His office was in the cement-and-Plexiglas watch-command area, where we could see him and he could see us, but he was hardly ever there. Instead, he was out on the floor with us, looking into our eyes, checking our posture, our hair. Who was bent over in sadness or frustration or loneliness? Who was paying attention to things like showers and appearance? Whose grades were getting better or worse? He didn't miss much. The extra attention didn't feel overbearing or Big Brother–ish. He just was who he was and available whether we asked him to be or not.

Two weeks into the program, I had fallen into a comfortable groove. I was participating. The new routine was now my only routine. New faces became familiar, staff members called me by name, and rarely, if ever, did anyone bark an order or a criticism. Compassion poured out from the staff in small ways—extra time in the yard for recreational activities, more time to read or write or draw after our kitchen duty.

Ron made a point to smile at everyone in the hall and greet us when he walked past us in the cafeteria. I had spent so much time with men his age on the streets, men who wanted more from me, wanted me to be grown up, sexy, available, docile. Without understanding why, I knew this man was different. He wasn't gritty or ugly or mean. As far as I could see, he was good and he meant no harm.

One of our first real conversations happened when Ron noticed my eating habits. While I was locked up, I'd decided I was a vegetarian—mostly because I wasn't going to eat anything I couldn't identify. If it was bread, I knew it was bread. Butter was butter; milk was milk; vegetables were mostly recognizable. But all that other stuff—vaguely meatlike, vaguely sauce, some kind of soup—it went down less easily. Ron had been eyeing my dinner tray for a while when he started laughing. "You're gonna get constipated with all that corn." Without thinking about it, I laughed too, then remembered my big bucktooth. I couldn't cover my face with my hand the way I usually did, because I was holding the tray. For the first time, I didn't care.

"You don't need to cover your mouth when you laugh, you know," he teased. "You have a nice smile."

Later, this moment came back to me when I read and understood Romans. I was a child of God all along—not a slave to fear and not under law, but under grace. In Ron's eyes, I was under grace.

Soon Ron started asking me a question or two. Not like a cop with a notebook trying to build a case or catch me in a lie, more like someone who just wanted to know what I thought. Each attempt to connect was so unassuming, even goofy, that sometimes it seemed he was talking nonsense.

"What's your favorite color?" he asked one day.

What? It hadn't ever occurred to me that I had one. *Pink? Yellow? Green? Why does he want to know, anyway?* I didn't know how someone even picked a favorite color. Plus there were only so many colors. Sara, my stepsister, had chosen purple. She told everyone, all the time. Purple, purple, purple. My sister Sky loved black. I didn't know why or how purple or black had become their favorites, but they let the world know it. Was I worth a color? If so, how would I know for sure it was my favorite? I imagined Sara's world had been full of purple and pink before our families collided; she'd had all those little-girl things that I'd never had. Maybe Sky had chosen black because that was the color of our favorite family dog.

"Do you have a favorite color?" Ron repeated. Such an innocent question. Why was I so quick to be on the defensive? Was he writing a book? I kept these doubts to myself. Mom, so good at discarding her own feelings, always said, "If you don't have something nice to say, don't say anything at all." Her golden rule, meant to create manners and consideration, built a barricade between me and the world: *Don't ever tell people what you really think.* But now Ron wanted to know what was actually on my mind. "I don't know," I finally said. "I guess I don't have one. I like all colors."

"What's your favorite team?" he asked.

"What do you mean?"

"Some people choose favorite colors based on favorite teams," he explained.

"Oh. You mean like basketball, right? Or football? I don't have a favorite team."

"You're silly, girl," he said. "You're out there running around, stealing and making a mess, and you don't even know your own favorite color." He had a point.

"You don't belong out there," he said once. "You have potential. Do you know what that means?"

I shrugged my shoulders. I wasn't sure what "potential" meant, but I couldn't bring myself to admit it to him. I'd rather use a dictionary in one of our classrooms than tell him what I didn't know.

After group one day, Ron asked me why I didn't talk in front of other kids. "You don't say much in the circle. Would you rather talk one on one?" I nodded. "Let me get the dinner crew started," he said. "We'll talk later. I'll come find you."

Ron found me at the table writing letters after dinner. "So, you ready to talk?"

I sat, silent, and waited for Ron to say something. When he finally did, it was another question. "So, Carissa, how did you get here? What happened?"

It was the first time that anyone had asked that question.

What did happen? How did I get here?

Ron didn't push me to tell him everything right away. Instead he held out a college-ruled spiral notebook, bright yellow, and asked, "If I give you this will you write in it?"

"Write what?" I asked.

"Write what happened. Why you're here. Tell your story."

"My story, for what?"

"For me. I want to read it." Him, a juvenile hall counselor, reading something I wrote. The idea made me nervous. What if I misspelled words? What if I didn't know how to say what I so desperately wanted to say? I was full of doubt, but I liked Ron and I didn't want to give up on him. I was afraid if I did, he'd give up on me.

"Okay," I said. "I'll try."

I started with what I knew. "Dear Ron . . ." He read my letter to him the very next day.

"Great, that's a start," he told me. "You're a great writer, Carissa, better than some of the staff here." He laughed and handed the notebook back to me. "Fill it up."

Within a week, I did, each new entry starting "Dear Ron." The first journal became a second one, and then a third. Yellow, purple, green. The white ruled pages were sacred spaces. Sitting at one of the large circular tables in the cafeteria, I'd hunch over the page, my legs dangling from the chair and my shorts stretched down over my thighs so my skin wouldn't touch the cold metal seat. There was no order or chronology to what I wrote, and I started writing letters about my days when Ron wasn't on shift, explaining how something had set me off or reminded me of something from the past. After he read the letters, we talked about the entries, and before long we both had come to the same conclusion: How I had gotten to Wakefield was really about the last year and a half. *That's* how it had all happened. I started to talk to Ron about the hardest stuff, and he'd say to me, "Okay, we'll talk, and then you should write it down." I couldn't say everything that came into my mind, but when I wrote, I didn't hold anything back.

The entries surprised me, not the details as much as the feelings. *I'm still afraid that I'll see him again. I'm happy that part of my life is over.* Putting the pencil to paper in a place where I felt safe was like giving myself a small valve to release the pressure of holding the memories down. Little by little my story was being told, and someone important was bothering to read it.

As Ron had promised, he read every word, initialing the pages as he finished them. RQJ. RQJ. RQJ. "Is that your signature for when you're famous?" I asked. "An autograph you practiced for when you were going to be a professional football player?"

Ron looked at me. I worried that I'd said more than he wanted to hear, that I'd hurt his feelings. Then he broke the silence. "Yes, that's my autograph," he said proudly. "Hold on to it, because it will be worth something someday."

I was being honest with Ron about a lot of things, but the one thing I thought I'd never be able to tell him was how important it was to me that he was black.

I knew racism was bad. My father, Richard, whose own father was from Guadalajara, Mexico, had been adopted by white people. According to family accounts, he was the eldest of two babies created between a *bracero* in the lumberyard and a poor white woman working alongside him while her husband was away at war. Dad told us stories about being brown at a time when it was not okay to be brown. He had to sit in a separate part of the movie theater, he was jumped and beaten by guys calling him ugly names, and the white girls he dated were forbidden to go out with him once their parents saw his skin color. I didn't want to be like all the people in my father's life who had hurt him; I didn't want to think like that. And most of all, I didn't want the bitterness inside Icey to settle inside me. The worst days of my life had been because of a black man, and now here was Ron Jenkins. Ron patiently and selflessly gave me the best of himself and somehow brought out the good in me.

As I shared my story with Ron, he began sharing some of his with our group. I learned why he had chosen to work with kids and why we mattered so much to him.

Ron's mom died when he was only two, and he spent years in foster care in South Central Los Angeles, often abused and almost always lonely. When he was a young boy, a woman took both him and one of his brothers. Their basic needs—shelter, food, and clothing—were all met. "But even then," he said, "I knew it wasn't because she loved us. It was because she got money from the state." He also figured out pretty quickly that any extra money went toward drugs she bought to sell. Ron learned to keep his head down and stay out of his foster mom's way.

One day when he was thirteen, Ron, along with a few other kids, decided to throw a ball through someone's window. The owner, a man named Harrel Burnett, figured out easily who the culprit was. That night, Harrel walked over to Ron's house and knocked on the door.

Ron heard the knock and stood quietly in his room. Maybe this knock was not about the broken window. Maybe his foster mom would forget that he was even there. He listened from his bedroom as Mr. Burnett explained the broken window, along with the cost for the repairs.

"Okay. Harrel, just tell me again how much," his foster mom said impatiently. "I'll pay you for it. These damn boys, always breakin' somethin'."

"No, I don't want your money," Harrel said. "I want the boy to pay for it." Ron held his breath. "He'll come to work with me. He can work until he pays for it." Mr. Burnett told Ron when he needed to be at his house and what he should wear. He didn't yell, didn't swear, didn't threaten. Ron went to work that Saturday.

For reasons of his own, Harrel Burnett believed in kids and was especially partial to kids in his own neighborhood. He wouldn't listen to the complaints from his neighbors about this boy, or that gang, unless he knew for certain that they had tried to invite that boy or a single member of the gang over to their house for dinner. "Teach them," he'd always tell his neighbors. "Teach them, take them in, then you can start complaining about them."

When Ron's work had repaid the broken-window debt, he had one question. "Can I come back again next Saturday?" Harrel said yes. In time, Harrel's wife, Rosetta, and their daughter Dezetta became Ron's de facto family. He ate meals with them, did his homework under Rosetta's guidance, and was given permission to call Harrel "Dad"—the first time anyone in his life had responded to the word. He played his high school football games with the Burnetts cheering him on from the bleachers.

By the time he was twenty-one, two of Ron's biological brothers and two adopted brothers were dead, in a neighborhood collapsing under drugs, gangs, and violence. Ron knew exactly why he was still alive. A shield—the love of one man—had protected him. Guided and encouraged by the Burnetts, Ron graduated from high school (the first in his family to do so), earned a football scholarship to Fresno State, and showed up for every game ready to play. Scouts and recruiters asked for meetings with him, and his dream of a pro career began to look like reality.

In one of his final college games, Ron was running hard when he felt his feet suddenly give out under him. "What happened to your feet?" the ER doctor asked as he looked up at the X-rays. There, in shades of black and white, were the bones, broken and crowded, mended crookedly together and misshapen beyond fixing. Ron's mind started to race as the doctor explained how rare his condition was: bone and tendon damage, caused by years of his feet being cramped into too-small, too-cheap shoes while the rest of his body was growing tall and strong. And just like that, the pro football dreams were gone.

"I didn't want to spend my life mad. I could have been mad at the system, or at my foster mom, but I wasn't," Ron said. "I had broken feet, but I also had this man in my life who hadn't missed a single game."

When Harrel heard the news, he had one thing to say. "Ron, those feet look good to me. Got you to college, didn't they?"

Harrel was there when Ron earned his degree in social work. After graduation, his first position was at Fresno County juvenile hall. With the instinct and grace of a born athlete, Ron worked juvy as if it were a sport, getting to know each kid's attitudes, weaknesses, and strengths—he figured out each kid's game. I'd seen my share of angry, control-freak adults before, facing off with angry kids and creating only more anger. Ron didn't do that. He sensed when a kid had reached the boiling point, and time after time he stepped in ahead of the explosion and defused it. His thoughtfulness and good judgment, his care and devotion, made us all feel safe.

After hearing his story, I watched and wrote with more purpose. Through Ron I saw myself for the first time in a clear light. I did have potential.

At Wakefield I moved. I ran sprints, I did push-ups (boy style), and I always volunteered to lead my group in stretching, jumping jacks, and some gymnastics. I was faster and stronger than all the girls and even many of the boys. Remembering the long, sweet hours on my bike, the cartwheels on Kristie's green lawn, I learned to be at home in my body, with its broad shoulders, small breasts, and large bottom. Now, rather than wishing that none of those parts existed, I was learning to respect every part of me that made me faster, tougher, or more flexible than the others. Running wasn't just something I needed to get away; it was something I could do for fun, something that made me feel great. I loved how it felt to run to exhaustion and to win.

In the beginning, schoolwork came a little more slowly. I chose, like most of the kids, to stay quiet and sit in the back as much as possible. It was better that way, hiding, so no one would know how much I didn't know about history, job applications, and adverbs versus adjectives.

Wakefield classrooms were located across the hall from the unit, a little closer to "home." We had three classes—English, math, and life skills—each with its own teacher. This faculty was not the revolving roster of retirees and substitutes at juvy. The teachers didn't sit behind their desks—they were up, moving around, and they got close to us, approaching our desks if they thought we needed help. For students, there was no half-asleep staring into space or doodling gang tags on an empty piece of paper. Some teachers read to us, some had us read to one another, but every one of them always had something specific for us to do. A mock job application, a talk about responsibilities in life—how to get a job or open a checking or savings account.

I tuned out most of the life skills stuff; I wasn't even fourteen yet and didn't think any of it mattered. Still, I listened when my classmates read aloud or had questions. I was amazed at how many kids struggled with reading, even those older than I was, but unlike on the outs, nobody here laughed or made fun of a kid struggling with one word at a time to finish a sentence We didn't judge or laugh when someone wanted to leave the room. We knew the way it felt to be not good enough at something or not good enough, period.

In my first week at Wakefield, I decided that our math teacher was the person in the world most different from me, the one most like the grown-ups I'd learned to avoid. Her starched, flowered dress, tight curls, and glasses were just the start, but what put me over the top was the way she looked me directly in the eyes, spoke with a firm voice, and sent a clear message: I am not your babysitter or your probation officer; I am your teacher. "My name is Mrs. Wegermann," she said. "If you can't say that, then you can call me Mrs. W."

Even though Mrs. W had only been at Wakefield for one year, her reputation made it seem as though she'd come with the place. "Mrs. W doesn't cut you any slack," kids whispered when they'd get into trouble for not doing work in her class. None of us knew that this was her first teaching job, or that she and her husband were competitive ballroom dancers, or that she had a daughter and diabetes and had scrimped and saved so she could go back to college in her thirties. All we knew was that in Mrs. W's class, you didn't nap or draw roses. It didn't matter if you were thirteen or seventeen, a Norteño or Soreño, a drug dealer or an addict, you were there to do one thing: learn math.

For the first few days, I sat in the back of the room and never raised my hand or volunteered answers. I just did the work sheets that Mrs. W passed out, and when I finished, I tried to look busy or occasionally rested my head in the crook of my arm. I didn't notice at first that others were finishing long after I did. One boy sitting near me had a glass eye and arms covered with tattoos and knife scars, but as tough as he wanted to be, he could not multiply. After watching him struggle, mumbling under his breath, pencil digging holes in the paper, I scooted over and showed him how to multiply by nines using his fingers, the same way my sister Sophie had taught me in third grade. He got it immediately, and his face lit up with relief, even excitement. It was clear that he wanted to learn.

One day, minutes after Mrs. W had us tear pieces of paper into neat sections—first in half, then in quarters, then in eighths—as an exercise in fractions, Ron came into class and asked her how I was doing. He told her I was "a very special young lady."

The next day, I was doing a fraction work sheet when Mrs. W came up to my desk and knelt down beside me. "This is pretty easy for you, isn't it?" It wasn't a question. She knew the answer. I shrugged my shoulders, unsure of what she wanted me to say.

"Do you think you're ready for algebra?" Again, it wasn't a question. "I have six hundred students a year. Most are not ready for algebra. You are."

I felt dazed. Then she explained. "If you learn algebra here, when you leave Wakefield and go to high school you can start right up with geometry." *Leave Wakefield? Geometry?* She was talking about my future, about things I didn't understand, but then I heard Ron's words: *You have potential.*

"I won't be able to work with you in class," Mrs. W said. "If you want to learn algebra, it will be up to you to teach yourself. You'll have to learn the lessons on your own. If you have questions, write them down and bring them to me."

I squinted and gave her a nervous smile. Mrs. W wasn't the type to take no for an answer. Maybe she was more like me than I'd thought. "Okay," I said, "but can I work on it in my free time, outside of class?"

"Of course." She was pleased. Mrs. W stood up and walked back to the front of the room.

On a sticky afternoon a few days later, I sat on a plastic chair in the far corner of Wakefield's community room, writing in my journal, when I noticed Mrs. W walk in, searching for someone. My eyes widened. It was rare for teachers to enter the part of the hall where students lived. Then she spotted me. Was she breaking a rule? She was walking in my direction with a big stack of papers in her arms. She didn't smile or acknowledge anyone else on her way toward me. When she reached me, she put the papers down on the table in front of me.

"You wanted to learn algebra in your free time, right? These are photocopied chapters from one of my algebra books," she said. "The answers to the odd-numbered problems are on the back pages. I'll collect these next week and bring you more. I'll also have a test for you to take in class."

"Thank you." I meant it. I liked having this work. It was the kind of challenge I felt ready for.

"You're welcome. And if you get stuck on a problem, try to figure it out with the examples. If you can't get it, I'll try to help you in class." Then she left the room with the same deliberate walk with which she'd entered.

Staring at the pages on the table, I felt two sensations: First, worry. It looked difficult—what if I couldn't do it? I didn't want to make Mrs. W angry. I didn't want to disappoint her. But I also felt a weird kind of confidence. *I can do this*, I thought. *And she thinks I can too. This is my potential.*

How much potential did I have? I didn't know, but Mrs. W did. Before photocopying a single page, she'd asked the school principal if she could photocopy chapters of an algebra textbook for a student who wanted to learn in her free time. "No, sorry," he'd said. "There are copyright laws." Mrs. W had already been told by the staff that she couldn't bring in one of her own books for me to use, because it was a hardcover—a dangerous weapon.

Mrs. W had taken the job at Wakefield, the only one she had been offered, because she knew that God had a plan for her there. She had met me and decided that it was the right moment for her to teach, no matter what. Her boss had said no, but she figured God's answer was yes and went ahead and made the photocopies for me.

Free flowing through my journals. Focusing steadily on every math problem. No matter what else had gone wrong in my world, at least I had blank paper, and filling it up meant filling the time and filling up the places inside me that only weeks earlier had felt so empty.

■ ■ ■

When you're locked up, visiting day starts with possibility and often ends in disappointment. If your family doesn't visit, you feel left out. It never happened to me, but I saw it happen to other kids. A visitor meant everything. Mail brought a reassuring voice from the outside world, but an actual person making the trip, passing through security, and spending time . . . Well, I wouldn't have known enough then to call it a healing gesture, but I know now that it was. When my name was called for mail, I was happy, but when my name was called on visiting day, my heart leaped.

I had one regular visitor at Wakefield—my mother. Once a week, sometimes twice, she drove the dusty hour-plus from Coalinga to Fresno to see me on visiting days.

Mom and I sat across from each other on folding chairs set up in Wakefield's gymnasium, surrounded by basketball hoops and other kids talking to their family members. Because visiting day was one of the only times kids had access to candy and soda, Mom always brought a Snickers bar or M&M's for me and a cold grape soda. For the entire hour I nibbled at the chocolate and barely sipped the drink, trying to make the sweetness last while Mom talked in her slow, girlish whisper about what my family was up to back in Coalinga.

No one under eighteen was allowed to visit, so I never saw my younger siblings. I learned later that they did come, but they had to wait in the car in the hot sun or, if they were lucky, sit at Fosters Freeze with a cool treat. Afterward Mom took them to the mall and gave them a report on how I was doing.

We always kept our visits about normal day-to-day things, stuff happening at home, with Nana, with my siblings and aunts and uncles. We avoided the two toughest issues: my relationship with Steve and my past. During our time together we did not fight; we didn't raise our voices. I did not run. We hugged hello when she came in, and she kissed me good-bye when she left. "I love you, honey," she always said. I'd go to bed at night hearing those words, and they mattered. I would push away the bad feelings or confusion I'd had about her. There was no room for hard feelings when I was locked up. I missed her. I missed my family.

More than once, Mom brought Nana along on visiting day. My grandmother, with her heart in her eyes, pleaded with me. "Be good.

You need to be good," she repeated, as if it were that simple. "Your mother loves you. You need to say your prayers. Talk to Jesus, and ask for help to be good."

In my journals I had written about these visits, so Ron asked if he could meet my mother the next time she came. "Sure," I said, then immediately started worrying. When the day finally came, there was a knot in my stomach. How would I introduce them? What would she say to him about me? What if they didn't like each other?

And then Ron just walked over to us. "Hi, I'm Ron Jenkins," he said, and put out his hand to shake hers. I looked up at him gratefully as he stood over us.

Mom smiled. "Hello, I'm Sharol, Carissa's mother," Mom said in her quiet voice. She remained sitting; so did I. My heart thumped hard as their conversation continued.

"You have an amazing daughter," Ron said, as though I had just discovered a cure for cancer.

His enthusiasm about me seemed to be contagious. "I know, she is amazing!" Mom said. "If she could only realize it herself."

We all smiled at one another for a few seconds, and then Ron excused himself. "I hope I'll see you on your next visit," he said to Mom. "I can give you more updates on her progress." As he walked away, I took a deep breath, relieved that the encounter had ended.

"He's a nice man," Mom commented.

"Yeah, he's cool. I'm writing a journal about my life, and he's reading it."

"That's nice, sweetie. You know, I keep a journal every day too." Hearing the chipper tone she took, I knew she didn't realize what I was writing. There was no way to put it into words for her—the suffering, the ugliness. I wasn't sure she had the capacity to understand. If I let the truth come up in front of her, something would explode. The tenuous connection between us might rip and tear apart. Maybe she wouldn't come visit me. Maybe she'd leave me again and just walk away. She'd done it before. I needed to be good. In Wakefield, I was. I could feel it. Good was happening inside me.

Later that day, after visits were over, Ron sat in his office and read about Icey raping me. He had counseled boys about rape and molestation but had never heard about rape like this, not with all the details and not from a girl. He didn't let on how much my stories frightened him, but that evening at dinner, his face wore an expression I hadn't seen before. "What's wrong with you?" I asked. "Did you have a fight with your girlfriend?"

He paused a moment. "Let's talk one on one," he said. I'd talked alone with Ron many times and never worried about it, but now something was different. I didn't want to face him, but I didn't know how to refuse.

Ron stood up and asked me to follow him into the control deck. There was fear inside me. *Stop. Stop. Stop being afraid. Walk. Get up and walk.* Ron looked back at me and smiled. It was his usual smile. "You coming or what?"

"Yeah," I said as I packed up my stuff and stood up.

When we stepped up to the control deck, Ron pulled out two office chairs and motioned for me to take a seat. He sat in front of me and said, "Carissa, I don't want our relationship to change. I want to be able to keep helping you, but there's something you have to do."

I gulped and nodded my head up and down. *What?*

"Your mom and you need to talk more, about everything." I let out an involuntary laugh. "Why is that funny?" he asked.

I got a grip. "It's not funny. Sorry, you're right, we do." I was relieved, but I could never have told him why.

"I've talked to a female counselor on staff, Georgetta, and she contacted the psychologist who comes into the hall once a week," he said. His face was very somber. "Georgetta is willing to see you and your mom weekly, and the psychologist would also like to meet with both of you." By now Ron had earned enough of my trust for me to listen without protesting, but this felt contrary to me. Talking to people I didn't know? Telling my mother the truth? Weren't the notebooks enough? But after all he'd done, I couldn't say no to him.

"Sure," I said. "I think Mom will agree to it. But she drives far. Can it be on visiting days?"

Ron was excited to hear my answer. "That's what I thought you'd say. I'll let Georgetta know. I think she's already called your mom to arrange it."

Through Ron and family counseling sessions, Mom slowly learned the details about what had happened to me while I was on the streets, including Icey and the rapes. I could not read the expressions in her eyes, and she said almost nothing to me directly. She asked questions, but mostly to Georgetta or the psychologist. She never once cried. When I finally confronted her about her lack of emotion, she answered me in the same even tone she always used in the most tense situations. "I cried so much when I was a little girl," she said. "I cried all the time. And then one day, I just decided not to ever cry again, about anything, about anybody. And so I didn't." She had decided she would never let her sadness show ever again.

Over time it seemed like Mom had lost access to her sad feelings. She didn't mind, she said, because she had her faith. "I believe there is another life for us after this one," she said. "I can't be sad for you because I know that someday you will be happy. Here or somewhere else."

As reasonable as Mom made it all sound, it still made me feel like I wasn't worth it to her. I wasn't worth a single tear. Facing that made me want to die.

■ ■ ■

Mrs. W's algebra chapters flew past me like calendar pages flipping in old-timey black-and-white movies. At first I checked every problem in the back of the book, knowing that if I applied a rule incorrectly, everything in the section would be wrong. Something in my brain, which was so lost in so many other ways, just seemed to connect with algebra. Over and over again I got it. "I got it, I got it," I'd whisper, seeing the solutions appear on the page as if by magic. Soon I stopped checking every answer and only checked every five. Then I only checked after I'd completed entire sections. Eventually I stopped needing proof I was right—I was right, and I knew it. I loved the way it felt to work the problems and to be right. I loved the challenge on every page. I loved beating it every time. When I finished three or four chapters, I showed them to Mrs. W, who looked over my answers, quizzed me, and then gave me a test. I scored 90 percent or better on every exam and finished the entire book in less than three months.

Mrs. W recognized what I had inside my head. She didn't care about my stepfather or my crazy family or poverty or Icey. She cared about me and I knew it. I wanted to be worthy of her belief and worthy of Ron's as well. No one had ever given me what they gave me, and all I wanted was a chance to prove that I was worthy of that gift.

■ ■ ■

Toward the end of my time at Wakefield, Ron brought me some news: I was going to summer camp for a week.

Camp Esteem was a program for troubled girls, most of whom still lived with their families or in foster care. Even though I was locked up, my good behavior had earned me permission to attend. The camp was in the mountains somewhere near Oakhurst, California. There would be swimming and hiking and lots of outdoor stuff, a sanctioned break from Wakefield.

I didn't know what to make of the opportunity. The mental image I had of camp was from sixth grade, when I didn't know what pimps or juvy were. Camp kids came from loving families, lived in clean houses, and went to school. They were "normal." And I was pretty sure I wasn't that kind of normal.

To his credit, Ron didn't push me. "It's up to you," he said casually. "I think you'd have fun."

I thought about it. I missed the sky. I missed the air outside. I thought about trees and clouds and clear water, and mostly being someplace else, far away from any place I'd been before. I went to Ron and asked him a burning question: "Will I have to wear juvy clothes? I have no clothes." How could I have fun with nothing to wear? Sitting in Ron's office, I could feel the tears coming. "I guess I won't go," I said, shaking my head.

He got it immediately. "Hold on a minute," he said. "I've got an idea."

That night, before he was done with his shift, he made a call to Nina, a counselor in another boys' unit. I only knew Nina by reputation; she was cool and tough. She was also short for a grown-up. Ron mentioned me and camp and didn't even have to ask. Nina offered to lend me her own clothes. It was a small thing, but it was everything. Khaki shorts, long pants for hiking, sweatshirts, T-shirts, a visor, nice soap, even new underwear and socks. Everything fit! Even better, Nina did not stuff all the clothes in a big garbage bag—she packed everything in a real duffel. I was prepared! I had everything I would need for a week, even a sleeping bag. I felt like a real camper.

■ ■ ■

When the big day came, Ron gave me a ride to meet my most recent probation officer, who'd be driving me to camp. The ride would be a reminder that I was still locked up. The official transportation guidelines required that I be taken in a secure vehicle to and from my furlough location, so I would be sitting behind the black fence grille between me and the driver. He and Ron spoke for a few moments, then Ron grabbed the bag with Nina's clothes from the trunk of his car. "Okay, girl," he said. "See you when you get back."

"All right," I said, all smiles. I hopped into the back of the probation van.

"Don't be scared to try new things," Ron said. "And stay out of trouble," he added just as the sliding van door was closing.

"Of course!" I was excited. Something fun was about to happen.

As we drove, my PO's eyes flashed back at me in the rearview.

He was new, and I'd never met him before. "Mr. Jenkins went to great lengths to make sure you were ready for camp," he said.

"I'm ready," I told him. During the ride, we talked more. He wanted to know all about Mrs. W, about the algebra work I'd been doing. I flashed some of my work from my spiral notebook, which contained problems and dozens of letters to Ron. I wanted him to know I was good. I was worth their effort.

As soon as I arrived at Camp Esteem, I knew I was not at sixth-grade camp. A dozen counselors, with twice that many girls, had already arrived on a big yellow bus that picked them up at the Pinedale Boys and Girls Club. Some girls were already swimming in the lake. Others were sitting on the side, not wanting to ruin their hair. The clear air, the mountains, the blue water, everything I'd fantasized about was right there in front of me. But the landscape, as beautiful as it was, didn't lessen my nervousness. I made a mental note of who was who and where they were. Then I spotted a familiar face bobbing in the lake—it was the first girl I'd ever run away with! She looked a little confused—maybe I was a dimmer memory to her than she was to me. "It's Carissa," I said, thinking, *Please let me have one friend here. Please let her remember.*

She did. "Oh, hey, Carissa! Come on in, it's nice."

The counselors, most of them recent college grads, had planned different activities to begin every few hours to keep us busy. That afternoon after the swim in the lake, they gave us an overview of the rules and the expectations and included some information about wild plants and bears. *Bears?*

There were maybe twenty girls at Camp Esteem. Most were black or Mexican, and without exception each of us was from a poor family. The counselors were mostly white and seemed like they were from better backgrounds. They had things—new shoes, new clothes, earrings, watches. The most obvious difference was that they were polite and well mannered, which meant they probably wouldn't like us much by the time we all left.

At the end of the first meeting, we learned we'd be sleeping in cabins, four to a room in bunk beds, with one counselor and a shared bathroom. That night, we had camp songs and a few scary stories. I think I was asleep three minutes after my head hit my pillow.

The next morning we had early breakfast. (It was much better than Wakefield; I could identify everything on the plate, and I ate every last bite of it.) Then we went on a hike up a mountain to a big vertical rock. One of the counselors pointed out the route. "We're going all the way up there," she said. It was such a steep climb that some girls refused to go. One counselor escorted them back to camp for other activities, but most of us adjusted our packs and continued. *Don't be scared.* I heard Ron's voice.

Once we reached the top of the rock, sweaty and out of breath, we watched in nervous anticipation while our breakfast guests, climbing instructors we had met that morning—all women—unloaded their equipment and began to set up. They were going to show us how to rappel down this rock by ourselves. We would be in safety harnesses, and we would be tethered, but still . . . we would go alone.

I didn't want to do it. None of us wanted to. We were scared, so scared that some of us were in tears. Rappel or walk back down, those were our options. It looked dangerous, somehow more so than what I'd seen on the streets. The first instructor went down slowly. None of us took our eyes off her, making sure we watched her every move. I took note of each place she put her feet and every part of the rock she touched.

"Any volunteers?" she hollered when she was safely down below, in a position to spot us.

"Hell, no," one of the older girls said, and began walking back toward the hiking trail.

I gulped. In that moment, I thought about walking back down, about not volunteering, but I just couldn't do it. It would be like leaving a math page blank, undone. Something inside me knew I would survive. I looked around to see who the first volunteer would be, and then my hand went up in the air all by itself. *Oh no, it's going to be me.*

Pushing myself off that rock was a leap of faith. I had butterflies in my stomach, but the familiar adrenaline rush—from running, from escaping—fueled my first kickoff from the ledge. Even with the harness, I didn't feel like I was tethered to anything or anyone. I was falling backward in the air, no longer on steady ground. I thought of my favorite female action heroes—She-Ra and Wonder Woman. I bounced a little, swung back to the ledge, and kicked off again, and the thick nylon line both held me and spun me down. When I landed on the ground, everyone cheered. I looked back up to the top of the rock, amazed at where I'd been. *I did it,* I thought. "I made it down a rock face that was as high as a three-story building."

After me, down came the next girl, and another right behind her. I cheered them all on. Then one girl got really scared about halfway down. It was clear in her body language and in her eyes. She couldn't seem to propel herself forward, and she sure as hell couldn't go back. Street culture is hard on anybody who shows fear, and everyone watching had spent time on the streets, looking and acting tough even if they weren't feeling it. But that day on the rock, it was okay to be scared. "You can do it," somebody called out to her. "You're doing great up there," someone else said. And then a third voice joined, and a fourth. I screamed up at her, "You've got it! If I can do it, you can too!" In moments, we had talked her down. Once her feet hit the ground, her face lit up in a huge, incredible smile.

The days in the sun, and the nights in exhausted sleep, passed quickly. Before we left, the counselors wrote us notes describing impressive things we had done and presented the cards to us at a good-bye ceremony. Each camper had something special and individual on her card—something specific she'd done or said during the week that was worthy of praise and encouragement. Although I don't recall the exact words on my card, I do remember that I was praised for being brave and for helping someone—it wasn't stated specifically, but I knew it was the girl coming down from the rock ledge. The words said something about my spirit and my soul. The street in me didn't cry, but the girl in me did. Luckily, no one was looking—they were all reading their own cards, understanding that in this one camp experience, something special had happened that would stay with us for a long time—maybe forever.

■ ■ ■

When I returned to Wakefield, I had two weeks to go before my early release. Ron placed two plastic chairs in the center of the community room. "Wanna sit down?" he asked, but I knew it really wasn't a question.

"For what?"

"To talk," he explained. I searched my mind for something I had done wrong. Did I forget something at camp that belonged to Nina?

Did he think that I stole it? Did my PO find out and tell him that I sneaked out and ran around the camp in the middle of the night with a few of the girls?

"What's wrong?" I asked. His face looked so sad. He didn't answer, but the well-placed chairs and his serious expression signaled a serious conversation. He sat down and looked at me more deeply, more intensely, than anyone ever had. His eyes were like lasers—a father looking at a child heading off to war.

"Carissa," he said, and my teeth clenched tight. "You may be leaving, but I am not going anywhere. Everything that happened to you here is real, and it's not going away, either. No one can take this experience from you." I leaned into his voice, sensing that I needed to hear and hold on to every word. He wasn't sure I was ready to go, and I wasn't sure if I wanted to. But we both knew I couldn't stay. He knew the challenges I'd face on the outs; he'd sent other kids out before. Only a month earlier, a seventeen-year-old from the girls' unit had been murdered on the streets—police found her body bloody and carved up with knife gashes. She had a three-year-old son who would never know her. I did not want to die like that. I wanted to live; I just wasn't sure how.

"You still don't like your stepdad. I get that," Ron said. "You don't have to like him, but you're going to have to listen. Follow the rules. Do what it takes." *No fighting. No stealing. No running away from home. And school. Always school.* "Get your education," he said. "Don't let anything turn you around." As he spoke, I gripped the seat of my chair as if I could hold myself in that place. "Remember how far you've come," he said, his mouth rising to a grin. "And take all the good memories with you."

A train of snapshots swept through my mind as Ron listed my

accomplishments. Camp Esteem and flying off a mountaintop. Daily group sessions with other kids who had it as bad as or worse than I did. Algebra, the pages stacking up like evidence in my favor. After I'd successfully finished my course work and aced the tests, Mrs. W had written an official letter addressed "To Whom It May Concern," stating that I was ready to take geometry. Aside from this letter, there was no official record documenting what I'd done.

And then there were my journals. I had filled three spiral notebooks, and each entry began with "Dear Ron." He wanted to give the journals back to me, but I felt they belonged to him. "Will you keep them?" I asked. "They're safer here, with you. I don't want to take them into that house."

"Okay, I'll keep the first three," he said. "But you take this fourth one, and keep writing in it." I agreed, even though I wondered whether I'd write if no one was there to read it. What would I do when life started coming at me from all directions? As my time in Wakefield came to an end, I'd thought half seriously about doing something to extend it—get in a fight, mouth off to somebody, buy another day inside, another week, another month. But I knew it was better to go with dignity, with respect. I'd earned the *right* to go, and now I needed to take it.

"By the way, I think it would be nice if you wrote Mrs. W a thank-you note for all she did for you," Ron said. This hadn't occurred to me, but I liked the idea.

I carefully selected several pieces of the cleanest paper I could find, sharpened my pencil, and in my best cursive handwriting began to try to say a proper thank-you. I had a dictionary to check the spelling and an eraser for mistakes. I stopped and started several times, with each attempt using a fresh piece of paper, then crumpling it into a ball. I put my hands on the shiny metal table, where I'd spent hours writing, hours doing math. I knew I wouldn't be coming back.

Finally I finished the thank-you letter to my satisfaction. I folded it up three times, leaving a little flap at the top, which I folded once more so the paper would fit in the short envelope that I had. The last day I saw Mrs. W, I gave her the envelope addressed to "Mrs. W."

6-28-90

Mrs. Wegermann,

Above learning math in your class, I learned a few other things. I learned that I could do things. Today Algebra before you know it a doctor or maybe a scientist. Whatever I decide to be, I won't forget your class & especially you. Thank you for believing in me, I needed it. Well I'll be happy & thinking about you in Geometry next year. I pray that you'll find yourself in the best of care this summer & through out every year.

Sincerely,

Carissa

a student with the potential to go anywhere she wants

I didn't know it then, but she was leaving Wakefield too—she was planning that day to turn in her own letter. No one could blame her. The constant stream of students at various education levels staying for unpredictable periods of time had taken its toll, and she and her husband had decided it was time to move on. I would not see her again for sixteen years.

CHAPTER SIX

As I stand inside the walls of Wakefield, which have held me prisoner for six months, waiting for someone to let me out, I am flooded with every kind of feeling—anxiety, happiness, fear, pride. All I know for sure is that I want everything to be different. I have spent the last days cataloging memories to hold, focusing on Ron's words about doing whatever it takes to make life work outside. This morning he walks with me down the long hall, stopping briefly at the booking area to retrieve what I came in with—dirty clothes and nothing else. We say nothing because we've already said everything.

Ron unlocks the door and I go out, turning toward Mom. Nana is there too. They are both smiling at me. As I walk toward Mom, I can feel my eyes welling up. She wraps her arms around me and says, "Honey, I'm so proud of you."

"Thanks, Mom," I reply, soaking up the way it feels to be held. To be loved. To be someone who made her mother proud. If she were sitting down, I'd climb into her lap and curl up like a cat.

Putting her hands on my shoulders, Mom looks directly at me.

"I'm counting on you staying home." I step back. *Why is she setting me up for failure? Not now, not in this moment.*

Then Nana hugs me. She feels smaller than I remember from the last time I saw her. "I hope you do better from now on and make better choices," she says, giving me a little pinch on the arm.

"Are you hungry?" Mom asks. "Do you want to get something to eat?"

This part I've been thinking of for days. "Yes! A burrito supreme, no meat, and extra sour cream." We say a long good-bye to Ron, jump in the car, and head straight to Taco Bell.

The warmth of the burrito wrapper feels good in my hand, but I hesitate before the first bite when I see that Mom's about to say something. I hope to hear reassurance, love. *We're all in this together. It's going to be a new day. Honey, it's okay to be nervous. It will all be all right. I won't leave your side until you feel safe again.* But that isn't what comes out. "I tear off the ends of the tortilla," she explains. "It's just empty there. All those extra calories aren't worth it."

■ ■ ■

The seventy-mile trip went by too fast; sitting quietly in the car with Nana and Mom, it would've been okay with me if the trip had been seven hundred miles long. Mom recounted my last big homecoming, when I was three years old. I'd spent almost two weeks in the hospital after a serious reaction to a spider bite. "I was a nervous wreck," she said. "I never left you." I didn't remember any of the tests, the monitoring or IVs, and I had no picture in my head of her being there, but hearing her say it made me want to believe it. She never left me. Then, closer to home, we stopped for take-out chicken for the family, and suddenly I was brought back to the present—they were all waiting, the others. The stepsiblings who'd never missed me for a second. My stepfather.

My chest tightened a little as we pulled up to the house. It didn't look much different, except the door had been spray-painted dark brown, with uneven zigzag blotches from the top to the bottom. "What happened to the door?" I asked.

"Oh, Grandpa Mac did it," Mom said, referring to Steve's father. "He hasn't been the same since his surgery. We don't think they gave him enough oxygen."

"Mom?" I was scared. I felt like I was about to walk into a trap.

"Yes, dear?"

"Can I stay out here just a few more minutes?" I asked.

"Sure, honey, you can stay, but I'm going in. I don't want the chicken to get colder than it already is." She and Nana were already out of the car. I couldn't put it off. I had to go into the house.

I breathed a little easier when I saw my older sister Sophie in the living room. "I wanted to ride with Mom to pick you up," she said, "but I had to cover a shift." Sophie worked at Denny's and rented a small studio a few blocks away while she finished up at community college, hopeful that she'd be able to transfer to UCLA. She'd written to me while I was locked up, always positive and encouraging in her letters.

The pressure on my chest loosened when I realized Steve wasn't there. Sara, my stepsister, was waiting to say something to me; I could see it in her eyes. She had given evidence to the cops the last time I was arrested. I didn't doubt she'd do it again in a heartbeat. With her arms folded, she made her well-rehearsed proclamation:

"I've cleared out the bottom two drawers for you, plus you can have most of the closet, because I'm locking my things in a metal locker in the hall."

"Yeah, cuz everybody knows that Carissa's a thief!" cracked one of my stepbrothers. I clenched my fists, tensing to punch.

Sophie intervened. "Hey, want to go for a ride?" she asked. "There's a new *ampm* near I-5 out on Jane. They have great soft-serve ice cream."

"I'll go with you." As soon as we were settled in the car, I confessed, "I didn't really want ice cream."

"I know," she said. "Let's just drive out there so you can see it. Maybe you'll change your mind."

■ ■ ■

During my time away, rumors about my life on the streets had made their way around town. The fact that I'd been threatened and raped and scared for my life didn't make it into the stories. In most of them, I was a straight-out prostitute. My brothers, my parents, my aunts and uncles, they all seemed to be part of the gossip chain. "She's a strawberry," one of my older stepbrothers said, using street slang for a girl who slept around a lot. It took everything I had not to scream at him.

According to my probation officer, not only was I prohibited from seeing Zizi and Shorty, but I also wasn't supposed to hang out with anyone on probation, which was nearly everyone I'd been friends with just before Wakefield. Most of the girls I'd known in sixth grade had parents who didn't want me anywhere near their homes or their daughters.

The morning of my appointment with the high school guidance counselor, I reached for my spiral journal, which I'd kept hidden at the top of the bedroom closet. Inside was the small note from Mrs. W about my being ready to take geometry. I'd stashed it away instead of handing it over to my mother, who might've lost track of it just as she'd done with the second-grade emergency card. To me, Mrs. W's note meant more than any other piece of paper—it was the starting point of a treasure map. All I had to do was find out where it led.

Once in the high school counselor's office, I did all the talking while Mom sat close by to sign any necessary paperwork. I had not completed a single class in junior high. All that I had was this note. Would it be enough? I answered the doubt in the counselor's eyes by adding, "You can call Ron Jenkins at Wakefield. He'd tell you more about the work I did there." I put every ounce of confidence I could find into my voice, taking care to sit up straight in my chair when I spoke.

"I think this will be fine, Carissa. We'll just have to choose your other classes, besides geometry."

Other classes? I'd been thinking only about math. The counselor disappeared for a few minutes into a back office and returned moments later with my seven-period schedule. It was official: I was a freshman, taking geometry, ninth-grade English, history, science, computer lab, typing, and PE.

My first morning was a failure. Compared to the lineups, rules, and routines of Wakefield, high school was madness. A sea of kids shoving, yelling, slamming metal lockers. Textbooks and pencils (forbidden weapons in juvy) were tossed around as though they held no value. Boys I hadn't seen since sixth grade were taller and spoke with deep voices. I had street survival skills but was at a loss in this environment—everyone had a two-year head start on me in terms of how to behave, what to wear, how to speak to one another, how to simply get from one room to another. I wanted more than anything to fit in, but I didn't, and no outfit or cool hairstyle was going to get me to class on time or help me feel at ease once I got there.

Just as I'd done in my first days in Wakefield, I sat at the back of the room and made myself small. The first day, there weren't enough seats in the computer lab class, and there weren't enough computers. The room was packed; just in case I needed a quick exit, I chose to get as close as I could to the back window. The day went downhill from there: I didn't understand the English assignment and didn't know how to ask for help. I got a glare from my history teacher when I arrived in class late after spending five extra minutes alone staring at my reflection in the bathroom mirror, wishing it would change. I quickly fell behind; within a few days, my default eighth-period class was detention, the penalty for being chronically tardy. Not wanting detention, I quickly learned how to forge excuses for my tardiness and my absences.

I did only my geometry homework, using the textbook as my guide. I searched every page to find answers, decoding symbols I'd never seen before. Out of fear that I'd be sent back to algebra, I didn't reach out to the teacher for help. I felt caught halfway between a dream and reality. Had my time and achievements at Wakefield even been real? Was I supposed to be in high school?

I didn't like how I looked—in broad daylight and bad classroom lighting, my crooked teeth and bad complexion could not be hidden. I went back to keeping my mouth shut, never smiling; if I spoke at all, I put my hand over the lower half of my face. I couldn't relax, couldn't share a laugh. Ron's "You have a nice smile" rang hollow in my ears. Braces, clear skin, new clothes, I needed all of it to fit in—to feel normal—but how was I going to get it?

After I was finally caught with a fake note from home, I started skipping classes. I made some new friends, girls I had nothing in common with—except that they skipped classes too. They also knew where the parties were, even during the day. Anyplace we headed outside school was fine with me.

At home, Steve rarely acknowledged me. He'd agreed with Mom to back off, as long as it was understood that there were two rules I had to obey: The first was to stay out of his way, and the second was to not cause problems in his house. "I won't try to make rules for you here," said Mom. I was fourteen, the age she'd been when she first ran away with my father. Whatever "raising" of me still needed doing I was expected to do myself. I could wear what I wanted, date who I wanted, go where I pleased and not meet a curfew, just as long as I didn't run up phone bills or make any scenes. It was an interesting tactic, and a side benefit was that it made Sara furious. Mom was giving me what I wanted—freedom. No boundaries. No rules. No limits.

Then one morning I overheard Sara's loud complaints about the unequal rules and treatment. "Why does Carissa get to do what she wants?" she demanded. "I'm a year older than she is, but she has way more freedom than me!" Still groggy from a long night out, I jumped out of bed when I heard my name and eavesdropped from upstairs in the hall.

"Carissa doesn't have a curfew like you do because she's gotten around," Mom said. "Everyone knows it. That's what your dad doesn't want for . . ."

Before she could finish her sentence, I bolted down the stairs and got in her face. "So you let me do what I want because you think I'm a whore!" I was furious. I'd deceived myself that the freedom she'd given me was a privilege I'd earned—in Wakefield or on the streets or in the horrors of the days with Icey. But no, I was just trash, no longer worth making rules for.

My mother looked back at me in shock and tried to take back her words. "No, that's not what I meant," she started, but I waved her off.

"You were in counseling sessions with me!" I shouted. "You know what happened. How could you say that to her? How could you say that to anyone! I'm not a whore!"

Mom shook her head. "I didn't call you that name."

"No?" I said. "What does 'gotten around' mean, exactly? Go ahead, call me a slut and a whore. Next time, just do it to my face!" I turned and ran back upstairs, yanked my hair into a ponytail, changed my clothes, and stuffed some clean underwear into the front pocket of my jean shorts. I was heading out as though I were propelled by rocket fuel, but I knew enough to want clean underwear wherever I landed. When I went downstairs and out the door, my mother said nothing. She didn't call the cops or my probation officer. We both understood that it was way past that for us.

Just like that, home was the place I checked into and out of like a hotel. I ate there, washed my clothes there, and sometimes slept there, as long as I arrived before closing hours. If I didn't make it in before the lights were out, I was on my own.

I threw myself into a life of partying. As open as I'd been with

Ron and in my counseling sessions, I'd never thought that drugs or alcohol were an issue for me, and I never promised anyone not to party. It was an escape, a way to fit in instantly with a group that accepted me. The "real" addicts, I thought, smoked crack, slammed heroin, did the serious drugs that messed people up. But what I was doing, I reasoned, was "recreation." Everybody did it.

On the few nights I made it home, I'd lie awake replaying the days over and over in my head. My mind ran off to ugly places. Sometimes I went back to the dream where I faced Icey. In my fantasy, I put the gun right to his head but even awake I could not actually pull the trigger. I wanted the satisfaction of making him as scared as I had been. I wanted to see him frozen, begging for mercy. I thought about Ron, about Mrs. W and about God's grace, but something big was missing, a void I couldn't seem to fill no matter what I tried.

■ ■ ■

At Wakefield there had been boys I liked—and maybe would have liked to be with on the outs—but kids were always coming and going, so it was hard to know who would be around from one day to the next. Now here I was with all this freedom to do whatever I wanted, to party, to stay out late, to ignore home—and it wasn't fun at all. While I waited for drugs to wear off, I felt more miserable than I'd ever felt on the streets. Tired of spending nights alone and afraid I'd end up being labeled even more, I decided it was time I got a real boyfriend, somebody who wanted something more than sex from me. I prayed about it. *God, please let me find a guy that likes me like a normal girl.*

Danny, a first-generation Mexican American, had a sweet-faced immigrant mom who always had something good on the stove and a dad who worked long hours in the fields as a supervisor in exchange for a paycheck and housing on the farm. Danny was a big guy—overweight, actually, but I didn't care. Sixteen, with dreamy brown eyes, the kind a girl could swim in, he had the sweetest disposition of anyone I knew. He was everyone's friend, and at the perfect moment, for whatever reason, he liked me. Danny wanted to take me on actual dates—basketball games, movies, fast food—and he did. We sat across the table from each other at Denny's and laughed. Sometimes I would just look at him and be amazed that he was with me.

Danny was kind and gentle. And even though we didn't wait long, I knew he had fallen in love with me before we had sex. It was easy to love Danny. For the first time I felt like I was making love. When we were together he was patient and sweet, and I felt safe. It made him happy when I responded with pleasure. He held me close afterward for as long as I'd let him. We always did it in the car, but it was fine with his parents that I stayed overnight. Out of respect for them, I slept in his sister's room; in the morning, everyone sat around the table while his mother served homemade tortillas and eggs. When we were in public, Danny held my hand, proud to be with me. With him by my side, I felt accepted at school. I didn't just have a boyfriend. I had Danny, and he let everyone know it.

His house soon became my second home. His family did all they could to make me feel welcome there, but I had trouble organizing a routine. My clothes were always in the wrong house, I didn't have the right makeup, and I didn't always enjoy the smiles that reminded me I was a guest in the house, especially early in the morning. In the bathroom, in the shower, in moments when I needed privacy or quiet, there wasn't any. I began to feel restless, crowded in. I recognized the feeling and tried to push it away. *No, this is good. Don't wreck it.* And then I wrecked it.

I got sick with some kind of respiratory flu, and though Danny's mom stayed up all night doctoring me, I didn't feel right about being there. I felt so disgusting, hacking and snuffing, my head sweaty on their pillow. I didn't see how Danny or anyone could want to be with me. I couldn't stop coughing. I didn't have the ability to do this, to be with a nice guy, to be a nice girl, to be sick and needy and vulnerable. How could he stand me when I couldn't stand me?

One night, I just flat-out told him to take me home—we were through. Time to run. "Don't call me," I insisted. When he left me at the doorstep, I didn't turn around. I didn't want to watch him drive away, but I didn't want to go inside my house, either. But where else could I go, now that the gentle, loving boy, the sweet one with a car and a family I loved, was driving away?

Danny would've given me anything, and I knew it. We could've done the Coalinga thing—gotten pregnant, gotten married, and lived in the love and certainty of his family. Those were choices I knew I wasn't ready to make. He loved the girl he thought I was, but I was still a mystery to myself. All his certainty in us made me feel like a liar. I put the gifts and memories from Danny into a shoe box and then I put the box away.

■ ■ ■

I had always been good at letting people go. Some people I might know for a night, a week, a month, or even an hour. New friends replaced old ones, their habits becoming my own, as if I had never existed before I met them. More and more, I lost myself in who my friends were—or in what I wanted them to see when they looked at me. One of my stepbrothers said I was getting "more white," trading in the ink black eyeliner for a soft beige eye shadow, wearing penny loafers instead of flat black Mary Janes. I was a willing chameleon, desperate to do whatever it took to push back the old Carissa. But as much as I tried, I couldn't make her disappear.

One morning, after days of skipping school, I woke up in my own bed and decided to give disappearing another try. Dragging myself out of bed, I tried to find something to wear. Nothing looked right. Nothing fit. I couldn't remember the last time I'd felt clean, so I took a long shower. Afterward, I still felt dirty inside and out. I brushed my hair but couldn't make it do what I wanted. I wet it again—still I couldn't make it right. Everything inside me hurt, and no amount of makeup or hair spray could dull the pain. I had lived with it for too long and wanted nothing but for it to stop.

Quickly, before I could change my mind, I went down to the kitchen, opened a cabinet, and grabbed a bunch of medicine bottles—a combination of prescription and over-the-counter drugs—and lined them up on the counter. Popping the little caps, I swallowed fistfuls of pills, including aspirin, which I knew I was allergic to. Clutching a couple of the little bottles, I went back upstairs, crawled into bed, and began to cry. A few minutes later, my stomach began to cramp.

"Carissa?" My mother's voice. "Are you up there? We're going to be late." She had made an appointment with a doctor, trying to call my bluff about being sick and get me to go to school.

"Just cancel the appointment!" I screamed back at her. "I don't need to go. I'm gonna die anyway." I heard her feet. She was coming up the stairs, which was rare for her. She opened the bedroom door.

"Get out of bed. If you're not going to school, you're going to the doctor."

She sighed. "And stop being like your real father, always so dramatic. You're not going to die."

"I'm not dramatic, Mom! I am really going to die. I want to die." I threw the empty bottles onto the floor. She looked down at them.

"Well, if that's true, then we should probably leave for the appointment," she said. It was hard to argue with her point. *Why not die at the doctor's office?*

When we arrived, Mom checked in, said my name through the glass window, and sat down with me to wait. There was no sense of urgency or crisis. The cramps were worse, and I felt a wave of heat rise up from my gut into my face. A nurse opened the door to the waiting room. "Carissa Phelps?" Without a word, Mom and I followed her into the small white examining room. A minute later, another nurse came in and took my blood pressure. "This is very high," she said. My mother said nothing.

A few minutes later, the doctor strolled in and turned down the lights to peer into my ears and throat for signs of infection. After looking into one ear with his light, he moved around me to look into the other. Mom grew impatient. Her arms folded across her chest, she finally spoke. "Are you going to tell him, or am I?"

"I'll tell him," I said.

The doctor looked at me. "Tell me what?" he said, stepping back to look at me in my eyes.

"I took aspirin this morning," I said. "I'm allergic to it."

"How many?" he shot back.

"The entire bottle. And other pills too. Prescription stuff." He bolted to the door, hit the overhead lights, and hollered down the hall to a nurse. In minutes I was on a gurney and loaded into an ambulance, heading to an emergency room a few blocks away. In the ER, a nurse put a lubed-up tube in my nose and down my throat. I retched up whole pills and a lot of other disgusting stuff. "This hurts," I gasped. The pumping out was followed by a pumping in of water and a black charcoal substance to absorb everything that did not make it out the first time. "Don't fight back," the nurse warned, "and don't yank on that tube. It will only hurt worse if we have to do it again."

My hands restlessly patted the hospital sheets as I watched the black tar drain out of me. I wanted to get up. Get out. Time jumped around in the hospital bed. My sister Sky was there, and she called my best friend, Jennifer. "Everyone out, I've got to check her vitals. We don't know how much is still in there." My blood pressure was returning to normal. The nurse left and Jennifer came in. She looked scared. "It's nothing," I said. "Just a few pills. And they're all gone now anyway." She started to cry, and so did I. I was saved. Nothing had changed.

"It hurts," I said.

"What does?" she asked, maybe thinking I was talking about the tubes or the IV in my arm.

"To live," I said. "Will you stay with me until I feel better?"

"Of course I will." She grabbed my hand.

When Mom returned, we learned that I couldn't be released without a psychologist's evaluation. Lying on the bed in a thin blue hospital gown, my throat burning like I'd swallowed thumbtacks,

I realized that I stood a good chance of being locked up in another institution, worse than juvy—a place where they sent crazy kids.

There was no psychologist on staff in Coalinga, so I was sent to a hospital in Fresno for evaluation, the same place where I was born. Mom drove, Sky came along, and Jennifer was in the backseat with me. My head hurt, I was thirsty, and I was thinking fast. By the time we arrived, I'd come up with a plan: The only way to not get locked up was to not be crazy. *Concentrate, Carissa—what do they need to hear, what do you need to say, to convince them you didn't mean it?* "I did it for attention," I rehearsed to myself. "It wasn't that many pills. No big deal. I knew I was going to the doctor and that I wouldn't actually die. I won't try anything like that again. I know I could've been seriously hurt."

Once inside the hospital, we sat in the psych ward waiting room. Eventually, a disheveled man with wrinkled khaki pants and messy hair emerged from the large double doors that led down a long hallway. "Phelps?" I knew the moment I laid eyes on him that he didn't have time for me. My rehearsed answers were going to work.

"How are you?" I asked him nicely.

"Just fine. And you?"

"I'm feeling better now, thank you." My act was on.

We went into a room with a single table and two chairs, and I took my seat facing him. "Do you understand why you are here tonight?" he asked.

"Yes," I said. "To make sure that I'm okay to be on my own. It's required." When he smiled, I knew it was the right answer.

"Correct," he said, "so the questions I need to ask you are required too. I'd like you to answer everything honestly. Do you understand?"

"Uh-huh." I nodded. I did understand, and I was confident that I'd be going home in a half hour or less.

Robotically, he went through the questions and marked up the papers in front of him each time I answered. This was a quiz.

"Have you had a change in sleeping patterns?" he asked.

"What do you mean?" I knew exactly what he meant, but he already believed he was smarter than me. I wanted to keep him in that mind-set so he didn't catch on to my act.

"Have you been sleeping a lot less or a lot more than normal?" he rephrased the question.

"No, no changes with sleep." I was lying. He noted my answer and continued to the next question. In total, there would be over twenty questions. It was like a math problem—I could see the answers a mile away.

Change in appetite? Change in weight? Increased irritation or anger? Loss of energy? Decreased concentration? Feeling of hopelessness, worthlessness, self-hate, or inappropriate guilt?

My answers: No, no, no, no, no, no, and "definitely not anymore."

My least favorite question to answer: "If you leave here, will you try to harm yourself again?"

I answered, "No, I would never do that again." But honestly, I was afraid. I wasn't sure what I'd do when I left, and if I didn't think it would have been an automatic lockup I would have answered his question with one of my own: Do *you* think if I leave here I will try to harm myself again?

At the end of it all, I passed the test. He looked as relieved as I felt—probably less paperwork if I was able to go home.

When we came to the end, he seemed satisfied. "Is there anything else you'd like to say?" he asked. "That you'd like to tell me?"

"No, I'm fine. Can I go home now?"

I wondered if he thought my attempt at suicide was real. I wasn't even sure myself how much I actually wanted to die. Before taking the pills, I hadn't threatened to kill myself. I hadn't talked about dying or suicide, and I really hadn't thought out my plans. I was just desperate, without hope, and sadder than I ever remembered being. How could I tell him that what I really wanted was to trade in my life for someone else's? I shrugged my shoulders and took a deep breath in. "No. Nothing more to add."

He took some final notes and looked up. "I don't see any problem with sending you home tonight." Then he led me back into the waiting room. A few minutes later, the nurse appeared with a medical folder and some forms. When Mom signed the last form, the nurse looked over at me. "Carissa, you're free to go. Take care of yourself."

The next day, to my horror, my mother called Ron. Even though it was against regulations for Ron to have contact with me once I was back on the outs, he took the call.

I was mortified, but I accepted the phone when my mother handed it to me.

"Carissa." I had never been so glad to hear someone say my name. "Carissa," he said again. "How are you?" I started to cry. I couldn't lie to Ron or put on a fake voice for him. Hearing me so upset, Ron didn't wait for me to say anything; he just started to talk. "I have to tell you something and you can't ever forget it, okay? Are you listening to me?"

"Yes." Of course I was listening. This was Ron. I respected him more than anyone, and he was talking to me about something important, something that mattered enough for him to bend the rules—and he was a rules person. I braced myself for what was next. "I'm here. I'm listening." I choked out the words and shut my eyes tight, as if blocking out everything around me would help me focus on his words.

"No matter what happens in your life—good, bad, ugly—suicide is not an option," he said. "You are going to break hearts and you are going to have your heart broken. You are going to make promises and you are going to have promises broken. Drugs, alcohol, all of that—but suicide," he paused for a deep breath, "is not an option."

There was a silence. I could picture his face the day he'd pulled the two chairs close together and spoken to me like a father sending his child into the world. "Do I need to repeat it again? Because I will." Then he did, word by word, as though the quiet force of his words would engrave them on the inside of my brain. "Suicide. Is. Not. An. Option."

"Okay," I said, barely able to get the two syllables out of my mouth. "Okay. I understand." *Suicide is not an option.*

After hanging up, I knew one door was closed. Now I'd have to find another one to open. I was fourteen and I needed a fresh start.

CHAPTER SEVEN

■

"[Get] them to realize that life [is] still expecting something from them."
—VIKTOR FRANKL

Ten months later, I walked up the long ramp into the brown double-wide trailer that housed Cambridge Continuation High School. Cambridge was the alternative to regular high school for students who'd been kicked out, had fallen behind, or had dropped out for any number of reasons. I was finally back in school, but the path had not been easy. Cambridge was just a short distance from home, but I had managed to travel six thousand miles to get there.

■ ■ ■

After the suicide attempt and my phone conversation with Ron, I knew I couldn't drop out on life, but high school was another matter. Living at home was not going to work; Mom and I had reached our limit with each other. So I called my dad in Florida, hoping that he'd take me in. Florida, I thought, will be far enough away from my mistakes. A month later, after Dad had saved up the money to buy me a ticket, I found myself on a cross-country Greyhound bus with a used Walkman and two sets of batteries to last me all the way. I'd never even been outside California, and now I was on my way across America.

When I finally got to Sarasota, I'd been on the bus for four days and three nights. I felt scraggly and tired; my hair was dirty and my scalp itched. I was ready to get some fresh air, ready to take a shower. When I stepped off the bus, my father was waiting. He looked a little older, but I would have known him anyplace.

"Hi, honey." Dad put his arms around me and gave me a big hug. "I'm glad you're here." As the bus driver got my box out from the cargo hold, Dad explained our living situation. "This place is only temporary," he said. "I'm going to find a bigger place. But right now, it's just a little studio cottage. I've carved out a space for you to sleep. Just for now."

On the drive there I was quiet. Sitting next to me in the front seat, with only an arm's length between us for the first time in almost two years, my dad felt unfamiliar to me. I didn't feel like his daughter. I wondered if he felt like my father. The way he was talking, it was more like we were going to be roommates: *You stay in your space, I'll stay in my space, and we'll get along fine.*

The tiny cottage had enough room for Dad's queen-size mattress and my fraction of the room, which was separated from his by a tall metal bookcase at the foot of his bed. It was my tiny nest—Dad reminded me that it was the best he could do for now. "You'll have your own room when I get a new job," he promised. In the meantime, he'd be in and out of town, sleeping in his camper shell while he looked for work around the state. I wanted to ask him to stay for a while, to show me around the city, to help me figure out what was where in his place. But I didn't want to seem like a baby. One thing I'd promised him over the phone was that I could pretty much take care of myself.

■ ■ ■

The fresh start I'd hoped for never quite materialized. The seeds of my old life had trekked cross-country with me and began to take root in my new world. In downtown Sarasota, there was a public center where local bands played live and anyone—even a fourteen-year-old wearing bright red lipstick—could buy a thin plastic cup of beer from a cart vendor. Day after day during my first weeks at my dad's, I hung out downtown, dancing and getting drunk. Since Dad might find a new job in another city at any moment, I wasn't enrolled in school, and soon the months started slipping by.

But even in this new world of blacking out, I was surprised to find pieces of myself, ways of being healthy that would become part of my way forward. One morning, after a few days recovering from a particularly nasty hangover, my restlessness pushed me to pick up a pen and paper. It wasn't my journal, but it would have to do. I needed to get the guilt and loneliness out of my body, the same way I'd done when I wrote to Ron about Icey. I wrote and wrote until the fog in my head lifted. Then I looked through the window. I could see the sunshine again, and I desperately wanted to feel it.

Today, I'll start something new. I pieced together a running outfit— some cut-off sweatpants, an old tank top, and my regular sneakers. Running had always been something my body did naturally, to get away from people or places, and it had given me a kind of exhilarating freedom in Wakefield. But doing it like this was different. I'd seen other people jogging around town—they seemed happy, relaxed. I wondered if I'd look like them when I ran. I hoped so.

I started off fast and then slowed my pace, one foot in front of the other, controlling my breathing, pushing myself forward even when the sun beat down. I guessed I probably didn't have the best form, but I didn't care, as long as I was on my feet. I'd flash a smile or nod as I passed other runners doing the same thing. This was something that normal people did, and for now, I was one of them.

Maybe it was the adrenaline or the music on my Walkman or the fresh air of the marina on my face. Maybe it was the freedom to decide whether to turn left or turn right and knowing that neither was a bad choice. But suddenly I felt good about my life. About where I lived and about who I was. I felt the burning in my legs as Black Crowes' "She Talks to Angels" streamed through my headphones.

There was something going on I'd never experienced before. I felt the music with my body, while the words took on a whole new meaning in my mind. This was new. The music, my thoughts, my body, and the landscape I ran through were all in sync, harmonized. *No one could understand this moment,* I thought. How could I ever explain it? I could have been alone in that moment forever; I didn't want to share it. The solitude was peaceful, and the smiles I received along the path filled the void of not knowing anyone. I felt far away from anything hurtful, running and breathing in a beautiful place with the blue-green ocean by my side. I had been fourteen for three months, and for the first time I felt like my surroundings fit me. I stopped where the road stopped, caught my breath. I was alone, and I was safe, at least until the sun went down. When the day ended, I never knew what was going to happen next.

■ ■ ■

One night when I was hanging out with some new friends at a motel, two good-looking college boys pulled into the motel parking lot in a shiny red convertible. Their combed hair, tans, and collared shirts told me they were from someplace else, someplace I hadn't been. "Hey, cutie—want to go to the beach with us?" It was clear that they were talking to me, and only to me, and I didn't have to think long. A red convertible versus a warm forty on a cement sidewalk in front of a roach motel? I promised my friends I'd see them later and climbed into the backseat of the convertible.

As we sped down the freeway, my hair whipping in the wind, I leaned between the two front seats to chat. They were in town for a game, they said. "Where are you from?" The passenger was interested in me, I could tell.

"California," I said. The driver half turned toward me.

"And how old are you, Miss California?" I didn't even think to lie. I was fourteen. Wasn't that old enough? I caught the look on the driver's face—he didn't like what he heard. When we pulled up to a beachfront resort, he parked the car and the guys had a little talk. The driver was tired. "See you guys later," he said, and he walked away.

"Don't worry," said the other guy. "I'll get you back. Let's have some fun first." He was headed toward the beach, and I was happy to follow. On one side of us, rows of hotel balcony lights flickered, and on the other was a long beach, with a moonrise low on the horizon. The gentle waves made swimming in the ocean seem possible, even though I didn't know how. "I'm going in!" he said, pulling off his shirt and then his shorts. I did the same, and in our underwear we walked into the warm ocean with ease. I sank in it up to my waist and laughed out loud. He couldn't know how new this was to me. He liked my laugh, he said as he kissed me—and then kissed me hard. I kissed him back. The salt water, the breeze. A cute, clean-looking boy on spring break. *This is what normal girls do,* I thought.

He held my hand and invited me back to the shore. I wasn't ready to get out, but I went along with him. He towered over me, and then our bodies fell naturally into the sand. Suddenly I felt him, his weight, his hardness, his insistence. All I had on was my underwear. I remembered Alex, and the light inside of me went out. This wasn't a date, and it wasn't a romantic movie. He wasn't going to wait for me to catch up, or for me to say yes or no. The sand that had felt soft between my toes was now in every crevice, rubbing me raw. He pushed himself in and out of me. *What am I doing? Why does this hurt so much?* I wanted it to be over. I focused on the bottomless sky, the stars, on the sound of the ocean. When he rolled off me and stood up, I walked into the water to wash him away. My legs felt shaky.

"I'm going to find you a ride," he said. He had his clothes on and was walking down the beach before I could say a word. I knew he wasn't coming back.

I walked away from the moon and water, stopping at the curb. The street was the street. I put my thumb out like I did in California whenever I needed a ride. More than a few cars passed before a black Corvette drove by me slowly, then made a U-turn to pull up beside me. A pretty brunette poked her head out of the passenger-side window. "Where are you going, sweetie?" I hesitated, and she said, "Meet us over there, at the hotel lobby. We have to check in, then we'll take you wherever you want to go."

I followed the Corvette as it pulled into the guest driveway, then walked into the lobby with the woman and the driver—both of them over forty, maybe married to each other, maybe just going out. I was the odd one, soaking wet in old shorts and flip-flops, suddenly aware of how young I was compared to everyone in the hotel lobby. It was a beautiful, massive room. I'd never seen anything like it; the lighting was bright but soft, and the furniture and decorations were clean and new. Music was coming from someplace, people were murmuring, and the elevator doors opened and closed with barely a trace of sound.

"Where are you going?" The woman spoke in a low, warm voice, very matter-of-fact, as though there were nothing out of the ordinary about the three of us walking into the hotel lobby together. I told her where I'd like to go, the motel where my friends were staying. She gave the information to her companion, who approached the young man behind the counter for directions. The woman stayed near the door and talked to me. I wasn't so sure of her guy, but something in her eyes said I was safe with her; she'd make sure I got to where I wanted to be.

The Corvette was a two-seater, no backseat, and for a minute I thought I was going to have to ride alone with him. But then she got in the car as well. "You can sit on my lap, if that's okay with you," she said.

I lowered my shivering, sandy body onto her lap. "Thank you." I meant it a hundred times over.

When we found the motel, I was both relieved and embarrassed. I couldn't let my friends know what had happened. But no matter how much I wanted to take back the entire night, I knew I had to get out of the tiny car. The woman was so nice. When she opened the door, I sprang from her lap. She didn't get out but looked at me from her rolled-down window with the same intensity that Ron had had when he looked at me in Wakefield. "Are you sure this is where you want to be?" she asked. "Is there someplace else we can take you?"

I wanted her to tell me where. I didn't belong here and I knew it. There *was* someplace else that was better; I just didn't know the direction or how I'd ever get there.

"I'm fine," I said, holding back tears. "Thank you so much for the ride." I needed her to leave fast or I was going to lose it.

■ ■ ■

A few days later, Dad got a job in Orlando, and we were on the move. Everything we owned fit into the camper on the back of his truck, and I was going to need to unpack most of it. He said he'd buy me a bed as soon as we got settled into our one-bedroom apartment. We were moving up in the world.

Dad had promised that I could get a dog to start jogging with me. We went to the animal shelter the first time he had an early night off from work. I immediately fell in love with the largest, most awkward-looking puppy I saw. "That's the one!" I said, pointing to the two-month-old red-haired German shepherd mix.

"I think she might be too big for our place," Dad said, but I insisted she was perfect. I named her SoBe after my favorite line in the 1980s movie *Pump Up the Volume.* "We're all in pain," says Christian Slater, playing an underground DJ talking to his flock of high school listeners. "But just remember one thing—it can't get any worse, it can only get better. . . . Being a teenager sucks, but that's the point, surviving is the whole point." He ended every broadcast with "So be it."

Naming my dog SoBe was brilliant, I thought. Dad didn't care what I named the dog as long as I understood that feeding and cleaning up after her was my job.

Instead of beaches and marinas to run around, Orlando had hidden lakes in the upscale neighborhoods that surrounded ours. They were small but had enough grass and trees to become a destination for me and SoBe. People, who smiled at me when I was jogging, smiled even longer and commented on how cute my puppy was. I started taking books on our jogs so I could stay gone longer. I sat down near the water and read, SoBe nearby.

Those days were invigorating, but evenings were still a struggle. Dad never seemed to really be there; he hardly ever listened to me. How could he know what I was feeling? Each night he turned on the TV and I headed to my room. Before long, I would grab SoBe and head out of the house for some air. It was a short walk to the nearest pay phone, where I'd quickly made a habit of calling both Ron and my mom.

Alone in Orlando, I needed people to talk to face-to-face, people who saw the world the way I did. I didn't know how I'd find other kids, but like answered prayers they started to suddenly and without reason begin to appear. Sadness connected us, our loneliness, our general sense of "lostness," our boredom—sealed our bonds. We weren't in school, and we all had problems. When we were together, those problems didn't seem as hard to carry. Without a sense of direction, we didn't judge one another about what was ahead or behind. Only the present moment was important, and we wanted it to be as much fun as possible. We searched out ways to fill the void—boys, drinking, smoking, staying up late, partying all night.

Quickly, my jogging, reading, and solitary days at the lake with SoBe became a memory. Once again I traded my sense of self for the company of others. And I lost my dog too. Or rather, I left her—for hours at a time, alone in the apartment, unexercised, unloved, but never hungry or thirsty. She made the inevitable messes and changed from an energetic, happy dog to a sad and lonely one.

Being a bad dog owner, a bad puppy raiser, was more than I could handle. I cared about her, but I didn't have it in me to be what she needed, and I knew it. I called the shelter and made some excuse about my life changing, and they said I could bring her back in. "I'm sorry, I'm sorry," I told her on our last trip to the lake. "You'll be better off without me." I thought of the last time I'd seen Danny standing at the front door of my house, so sad and hurt. I'd left him for the same reason. I didn't know how to love.

■ ■ ■

The only thing I didn't stop doing when I was hanging out with my new friends was writing letters. Ron's first letter back to me, written in pencil on the hand-sized spiral notepads that staff used at Wakefield, said he hoped I was in school and asked how I was getting along with my dad. A month later, he wrote on purple notepaper that he was proud of me for going to Florida because I'd realized that I needed to change. At the end of that letter, his "P.S." urged me to get in school by fall. "I'll be looking forward to getting those report cards with A's and B's." And in another letter: "I'll be glad when you get into school so you can blow your teachers' minds away with your street smarts and ability to learn in the classroom."

Each letter also included a sentence or two about my dad. "You're lucky you know who your dad is" wrote Ron, who had not known his until he met Harrel. When I called him one night from a pay phone, upset at my dad, he asked me to remember that my father was doing something many fathers did not—he was trying. "Tell him thanks sometime," Ron advised.

I wanted to do what Ron had told me. I said thanks, to Dad as much as possible. One afternoon when I realized that the big batch of bananas I had insisted on getting at the grocery store was going bad, I found a recipe for banana bread, which I'd never made before. I thought the fresh banana bread would make Dad happy, and for a little while it did. I walked back and forth to the store to fill our grocery list so he wouldn't have to worry about it, and I did my best to keep the apartment as clean as it had been when we moved in. I wanted to help, and when my father came home from work tired and ready for a drink, I gave him his space, either staying in my room or going out with my friends.

I knew the days were going by, that I was falling behind again. I knew I had to do something about school. Dad and I seemed to spend our days living around each other, as if we were still strangers. I came and went as I pleased, and sometimes I caught Dad sighing or harrumphing, signaling that my attitude was wearing thin. But as long as he said nothing, I kept pushing my limits. Finally I stretched his patience to its end when I invited a man whom I'd found on our landlord's porch to sleep over. That was it. Ten months after my arrival in Florida, the father/daughter experiment was over. I went to a pay phone and called my mom collect. "I want to come back," I said.

"You'll have to go to school," Mom countered.

"I promise to go to school, if you'll get me braces."

We made a deal. Dad was furious when he found out, but my mind was made up. I was headed back to California and back to school. Part of me wished he'd said, "I will love you no matter where you live, and I'll always be here for you, or at the other end of the phone. You can count on me." But I knew that wasn't going to happen. It's not who he was, and it's not how it was ever going to be between us.

■ ■ ■

Since I hadn't technically been kicked out of ninth grade, I entered Cambridge Continuation High School without a bad record; in fact, as far as I knew, I had no record at all. My classmates had all come in with labels—troublemakers who disrupted class, fought with other students or with teachers, got pregnant, or were otherwise struggling to fit in. All of us had one thing in common: We were dealing with life in ways that made sense only to us.

Every day, Mr. Doty, our one teacher, stood at the front door to greet each student. "How are you today?" he'd say.

"Doing good, Mr. Doty. How are you?" was the usual response.

This tiny daily connection was enough to get most of us in the door on time. Mr. Doty's routinely cheerful nature and neatly pressed outfits made us feel respected, encouraged to stay and take our student roles seriously. He had a football player's build and a calm air of authority that filled the room enough for us to know we were safe in his presence.

Barbara, Mr. Doty's teaching assistant, was the second greeter, available to us from the minute she walked into the trailer. "Barb," we'd call out across the room, and she'd be right there to help, to give direction, to answer questions.

The first week at Cambridge was easy, mostly spent learning the rules and the routine. The second week we began to work. "There are exactly two ways out of Cambridge," Mr. Doty said. "The first is the door you came in, leaving the same way you came in. The second way out is to work." I liked the idea of working. I was determined not to leave Cambridge the way my older brothers had. I was going to graduate from high school.

Once we were settled, as Mr. Doty moved to the front of the class, Barbara rose from her desk in the back of the room and quietly took a seat with us, facing him. She listened as he spoke, modeling what we should do. Mr. Doty wrote some numbers on the board. "This is how much a high school graduate can make, on average," he said. "And this is how much a college graduate makes, on average." The second number was three times higher than the first, and the raw facts of the difference made an impression.

That day, Mr. Doty gave us one common assignment: Complete an application to West Hills, the local community college. Once we'd filled out the forms correctly, we could stop there—or we could choose to earn more high school credits by walking five minutes from Cambridge to West Hills and actually turning in the paperwork to take classes. I was interested in the extra credits.

Students at Cambridge were at different levels, and worked independently in different booklets. I quickly fell into a pattern, finding my way into and out of math problems, completing sentences, and answering reading-comprehension questions. Most assignments took me ten minutes or less to complete, and when I was done I watched

Barbara move quietly around the room. She was ever sensitive to which students were struggling and moved in to help them before their frustration defeated them. When she saw me watching her, she walked toward me. "I'm done," I blurted before she got to me.

"Wow," she said with a big smile. "That's impressive!"

The next day, just as I finished my work sheet, Barbara asked me to come to her desk. I instinctively worried—had I done something wrong? But her question wasn't about something I'd done. "One of your sisters went to college, didn't she?"

"Yes, Emily did—she went to UC Davis." I said it proudly, because I was proud. I'd visited her at school and sat in the audience when she delivered the commencement speech at her graduation.

"Have you thought about taking your forms in and signing up for a college class at West Hills?" Barbara asked.

"Yes, I've thought about it." But I wasn't sure it was for me. That afternoon, Barbara asked if I wanted to call Emily to talk it over with her. "I guess I could do that."

My fears of not fitting in evaporated when I heard Emily's excitement. "This is going to be a really good thing for you!" she said with excitement. Per her advice I started with one class, and choosing it was easy: conversational Spanish. I needed the foreign-language credit, and Spanish was something I'd wished I'd known when I was on the streets. Not knowing it separated me from so many of the kids I'd hung around with, and it was one of the reasons I'd sometimes been a target—I was the white girl, the vulnerable girl with no family protection. The fact that my dad's father was from Guadalajara didn't seem to make a difference, but I thought that speaking Spanish would.

The sixteen-week class was free as long as I stayed enrolled in Cambridge, and if I completed it with a C or better, it would count as a full year's worth of high school foreign-language credit. The textbook cost more than fifty dollars, but somehow between my sister and my mom, the money was there. I fell into a comfortable routine, going to Cambridge for three hours each day, then crossing the football field to get to West Hills. The college classroom felt as normal as Cambridge. *"¡Hola!"* the teacher welcomed us. *"¿Cómo estás?"*

No matter how I felt, I replied, *"Bien"* or *"¡Muy bien!"*

School was by and large a positive force in my life, but bad days still happened, and there were times when I wasn't "very well" at all. One day I took a standardized writing test at Cambridge—we were instructed to respond to the prompt "Describe a challenging situation you have overcome." Without hesitation, I hunched over the table and wrote freely about juvy and Icey, just as I'd done in my journals to Ron. I put it all down just as it happened.

Time was called. *No, no, wait, I need to write more.* "Time. Stop writing now," Mr. Doty announced as Barbara began to walk around the tables collecting our essay booklets. Frantically I scribbled one more sentence: "And this isn't where it ends, but what he did burned me up inside, I want to stop . . ." And then I put down my pen.

A few weeks later Barbara passed back our sky-blue test booklets. I could hardly wait for her to get to mine, to hand it over. I watched her walk the entire room. She was getting to me last. I wondered why, but then I saw the red ink. One of the lowest grades in the class.

My heart sank. "What the fuck is this!" I couldn't believe I had said it out loud. Everyone looked at me. *The worst writer in the class.* How could this be? Some kids could not finish a single work sheet without help, and yet on this they'd done much better. In a flush of anger, I ran out of the room. I never wanted to see a blue test booklet ever again. Everyone would think I was stupid. Maybe I wouldn't make it at college.

I walked around outside for at least ten minutes and then came back into the room. Mr. Doty had put the booklet away with the rest of the tests that had to be sent back to the district. I sank down in my chair with my cheek resting on my fist. Stupid test.

At break I didn't move. I didn't want to talk to anyone. That's when Barbara came over and leaned down so close to me I was compelled to look up and meet her eyes. Then, to my surprise, she smiled and popped a hard lemon candy into my mouth. "When life gives you lemons, make lemonade." Then, without another word, she walked away.

Lemons! I have plenty of lemons.

Barbara had made a bold move, putting candy into my mouth. Not even my mom would have dared try to put anything in my mouth. But Barbara, having no idea how I would react, had given me something she thought I needed. And as the hard lemon candy rolled around in my mouth, I began to think through what had just happened. At break I walked toward Barbara's desk.

"Thanks for the candy," I said to her. "I'm going to be making lots of lemonade."

She agreed and added that she was proud of me. "You don't have it easy, but I see you here every day, making something good of it."

Barbara's directness caught me off guard. "I don't have a choice," I said to her. Lemons were my reality, and even if there had been an easier way for me, I am not sure I would have taken it.

CHAPTER EIGHT

I wore a pink dress to Nana's funeral. Clothes were hard to come by in Coalinga. There was one small store called Beno's, and they had exactly one funeral-appropriate black dress. Sara wanted that one, so I took the pink one.

There was so much about Nana Pauline that I wanted to know after she was gone. I knew some of the stories. She had a breakdown after losing her one-year-old son. Her husband had her committed to an institution, where she had shock treatments and had to hold other women down for their treatments. She was there four years. Her husband abandoned her, while other women raised her two surviving children. It was her mother who rescued her, brought her back into the world, and helped her to sign up for college. She was determined to get her education and a job, so that she wouldn't be dependent on a husband again.

She had graduated from the University of California at Berkeley right out of high school and was now attending Mills College in Oakland for her teaching credential. Once she completed that, she found a job in Stratford, California—what she called "the middle of nowhere"—and there she met Granville Smart. They fell in love, and when his employer, Standard Oil, transferred him to Coalinga, she went with him as his wife.

Around the same time Nana was settling into her life, her sister's husband walked out, throwing her into a tailspin that left her incapable of raising five children, so Nana and Granville adopted two of them—one of them, my mother, was five; her little sister Selene was four.

In her later years, when Nana was diagnosed with cancer, we moved from Lancaster to Coalinga to be closer to her. She'd planted a tree on the side of her yard—I have such clear memories of her tending to it, watering it, making sure it survived through the hot, arid summers. The day she died, she went outside to water it again, and my little brother Jacob came to bring her a glass of water. There was something about her appearance or voice that concerned him; he wasn't sure just what. "Do you need any help?" he asked. "Do you want me to call Mom?"

"No, honey," she said. "Thank you for the water."

Jacob left as Nana sipped the cool water. Moments later, instead of watering her tree, she sat down Indian style and leaned her back against the large trunk. That's how Steve found her later. "She looked like she was praying," he told Mom.

While she lived, Nana gave generously to everyone while trying to be prudent, saving enough to pay for her own burial. But her hard-won thousand dollars barely made a dent in the thousands more that the service and funeral home cost, and Mom needed to borrow the money from Emily. They had the viewing in nearby Avenal, because it was cheaper. They had a headstone made, and it had the wrong date of death. They had a second one made and kept the mistake in the garage for years, reluctant to throw out something that had cost so much. Their saving the botched headstone made me distance myself from my parents even more than I already had.

The services took place at Pleasant Valley Cemetery, just outside Coalinga, where Nana would be buried next to Granville. There was a small tent at the graveside and chairs for the family to sit close to one another. As I walked toward the tent, I held my dress down and suddenly realized how out of place I looked and felt in pink. Everyone was sad and sulking—there were tensions between Nana's biological and adopted children and between Steve and everybody under the age of eighteen. I didn't want any part of the sadness and didn't feel like being bullied, either. I chose to sit alone, to smile, and to remember Nana as she was: kind, generous, and loving.

When Emily took the podium to speak, I could barely pay attention. I wished that I'd worn shorts under this silly pink dress. The breeze kept flipping my skirt up. The morning had been chaotic, everybody getting dressed to leave the house, doors slamming, people yelling. I hadn't had any clean underwear, hadn't wanted to borrow any, and had decided that instead of making a big deal about it I just wouldn't wear any.

When everyone stood up, I realized why underwear was important—especially under a dress. I wanted to hide; anywhere would do. I was planning my exit when the ladies came toward me. One by one, slightly bent over in their floral dresses, Nana's old friends spoke to me in soft, kind voices that made my heart ache for Nana. The first one took my hand in hers. I looked at her nervously.

"I'm so happy to meet you." Behind "happy to meet you" came the next woman, and then the next. I was stiff and unyielding in their embraces, trying to keep my arms down at my sides, my hands holding my dress down. "We all prayed for you," said the last one, smiling and looking into my eyes. "We all prayed for you with your grandmother."

My heart sank. Nana's friends prayed for me. I struggled to smile back, remembering what Ron had taught me. "Thank you. Thank you for praying for me, and for telling me." I relaxed and put my arms around her. She hugged me back the same way Nana would have. I could have stayed in her arms another five minutes, but it was time to go, to put on normal clothes, to collect flowers, plants, enchiladas, and doughnuts that had been delivered to my grandmother's tiny blue house.

For Nana, life's rules were simple: "Love your mother." "Love God." "Embrace the Holy Spirit." She wanted me to love God. Love Mom. As if love and faith would simply make everything better. If Nana knew about Icey, it wasn't from me. I knew she wouldn't like what he had said about God. I couldn't have defined what faith was, I didn't know anything about a spiritual core, but I knew for sure that Nana held God close.

I told Mom about the ladies, but she didn't seem to get it. I wrote out my thoughts in a journal entry that night. *Those prayers saved me when I was on the streets.*

■ ■ ■

One morning, before a long weekend, Barbara appeared in class with her arm in a sling. She had fallen off a horse the day before and cracked two ribs. Because she couldn't move around easily, she asked a few of us at Cambridge if we wanted to help her around her house for an hour or two. "Nothing too tough," she said. "I'll pay you for your time." When we heard "pay you," my friend Cammy and I looked at each other and quickly said that we'd do it.

Cammy and I had shared a babysitting job at her church, so working together was easy. We met up at her house before going to Barbara's. Cammy looked neat and clean in her ironed shirt, and she let me borrow a brush and a scrunchie to straighten my hair, which still went its own way. I did my best to look as put together as she did.

Barbara lived in one of Coalinga's best neighborhoods, a far cry from the burned lawns and poorly constructed homes in my neighborhood. Almost every single-story tract home on her street had a tidy cement walkway in front that cut through a green yard. Each looked freshly painted in varied shades of beige, brown, or tan, with coordinating painted shutters. The well-manicured lawns seemed to reflect well-manicured lives, good homes, good families—a message to outsiders that they were doing things right. When Barbara greeted us at the door, I was surprised by how happy she looked, smiling even though her arm was in a sling.

"Does it hurt?" I asked.

"No. I'm still a little bruised, but it hurts less every day. The toughest thing is not being able to do my routine—but that's why you're here."

We stepped inside, and I looked around, instantly confused. "There's nothing to clean," I said to Barbara. No clothes tossed across the couch, no dust on the furniture or crumbs on the floor. The hallway carpet was spotless, and every picture frame was straight. Ninety-degree angles everywhere, and not a single dirty dish.

"That's very nice of you," Barbara said, laughing, "but it's got to be vacuumed, swept, mopped, and dusted." Mystified but willing, I followed Cammy around, mimicking her moves, dusting dustless cabinets and washing spotless countertops. In less than an hour we were done with Barbara's list. "This must be how clean houses stay clean," I said to Cammy.

"That's right," Barbara said. "I can't thank you girls enough. "That was so helpful. Are you thirsty or hungry? Do you have time for a snack?"

We sat at the kitchen counter while Barbara placed tiny individual plates and bowls in front of us. She filled them with celery, apples, chips, and nuts. I would have had a hard time sitting still without the snacks. Reaching for them kept me busy, kept my mouth full, and ultimately kept me anchored. I listened as Cammy and Barbara talked about what seemed like nothing at all. Cammy lived in the same neighborhood; they knew the same people. I didn't have anything to add.

"Where do you live, Carissa?" Barbara asked, trying to get me into the conversation.

"Over by Olsen Park," I said, knowing that my neighborhood was a dead giveaway of the way I lived. I wondered what Barbara would think of my house. How do you clean tattered wallpaper or get the black off a moldy shower or vacuum shredded carpets? The better answer would have been "I have no home." I was fifteen, the age Emily had been when she emancipated herself and the age my mother was when she decided she would marry our dad. "Sometimes I sleep at my sister's apartment, other times at friends' houses."

"That must be hard," Barbara said with concern, "never knowing where your stuff is."

I didn't tell her that I had no stuff to worry about.

■ ■ ■

I was often late to school, too late, really, but for a while it didn't stop me from going. Then, one morning, I'd made it about halfway there when I began to think about the night before. I'd done drugs, hard stuff, with a friend's dad and wasn't feeling great about it in the cold light of morning. The guilt made it easier to skip class than to go in late. And then, fearing I'd need a legitimate excuse, I skipped the next day, and the one after that, never imagining that anyone would miss me. I wasn't home when Mom answered a knock on the door to find Barbara outside.

"I'm a teacher's assistant at Cambridge," she told my mother. "I'm concerned because we haven't seen Carissa at school for a few days." Barbara expected to find out that I was sick or maybe, knowing my history, that I had disappeared again. She accepted Mom's invitation to come inside. Only ten days earlier I had been sitting in her kitchen, and now she was standing in mine.

"I'm sorry to bother you," she said, "but . . . Carissa. Will she be returning to school?"

Mom responded in her customary soft voice, with an impassive expression on her face. "I'm not sure where she is. Maybe at her sister's?" When Barbara realized that my mother had no idea where I was, and seemingly no interest in finding out, she set out to find another way to bring me back to Cambridge—through my friends.

A day or two later, after hearing from classmates at Cambridge that Barbara was asking where I was, I decided to go back, thinking, *If she's mad at me, if she's mean to me, I'll split.* Barbara was grading work sheets at the desk and looked up at me as calmly as though I'd been there all along.

"How are your college classes going?" she asked.

"Pretty good." A lie. "I still like math the best." The truth.

I finished the greeting fast, avoiding any chance for a lecture. Barbara smiled and left me alone until I got comfortable. About an hour into class, she approached me. "Can I talk to you for a minute?"

I followed her back to her desk, worried about what she'd say. "I'm happy to hear that you're doing well, but I was wondering . . . Would you like to come over to my house to do homework some afternoons?" Before I could answer, she went on. "It will be quiet there, so you can study."

I only had to think about it for a second. "Sure." I said it, even though I was anything but.

"Wonderful!" she said. "How about this week? You can ride home with me from here on one of the days you don't go to West Hills."

And like that, it was settled. On the appointed day I pled with Cammy to join me, but she had to babysit. "I'm so glad you're here!" Barbara said, after she'd pulled her spotless Cadillac into her garage. We made our way into the house. "The kitchen table should be comfortable for you to get set up." She handed me a brand-new, sharpened pencil.

I hadn't said more than two words to Barbara on the drive from school, and with no one to mimic or take cues from, I felt completely out of place. I anchored myself to the table and opened a book, wishing that I could literally jump into it. Barbara did her best to make me comfortable, providing a steady stream of water and snacks, but we didn't say much. "Do you have everything you need?"

"Yes, I'm fine. Thank you." I wanted to keep it short and polite. I wanted to be invited back.

Only once did she peer over my shoulder. "You're amazing with those math problems," she said.

I came back the following week on Tuesday and Thursday. The week after that was the same. We established a rhythm—I'd ride home with her or arrive on my own and put my books on the dining room table.

I had set paths in the house—table to stool, table to guest restroom, guest restroom to table. I knew where I belonged, and the rest of the house was in the background. At the counter we had our best talks. We mostly talked about big things as Barbara prepared dinner for herself and her husband, Doug.

Barbara's house, always quiet and orderly, with everything in exactly the same place, made me feel like I needed to be clean. I'd ask to use the guest bathroom to wash up. Soft, clean towels hung over the towel bar, and a designer bottle of liquid hand soap sat next to the sink. I held my hands under the warm water, slipping the soft suds gently through my fingers. After I dried my hands, I squirted a dollop of lotion into my palms, then another. I rubbed the cream all the way up my arms, over my elbows, and right to the edge of my shirt. Before leaving, I checked myself in the mirror a few times, pushing my hair behind my ears to look more presentable. I smiled back at my image; I was ready for more.

"Would you like to stay for dinner?" Barbara asked one night.

"Sure." I wasn't hungry, but I had nowhere else to be. I watched her as she went to the phone that hung on the wall. She picked up the receiver and held it out to me. "What's your home number?" she said, fingers waiting to dial.

"Why?" I asked.

"You need to call your mom, so she'll know where you are."

I almost laughed. "She doesn't care." I hadn't been home in several days. Mom would probably be more worried that something was wrong if I called than if I didn't.

"Well, let's just make sure," she said, still holding the receiver. I gave her the number.

"Grand Central Station," my stepbrother answered the phone.

"Hey, can you get Mom?"

"Who's this?" he asked.

"Carissa."

"This phone never stops ringing, and half the time it's your friends. Will you tell them to stop calling? You don't even live here."

"Just get Mom, please." Normally I would have screamed at him, but I tried to be nice in front of Barbara.

"Sharol!" he yelled. "Your daughter is on the phone!"

"Which one?" Mom said as I heard her getting closer to the receiver.

"The bad one," he replied.

"Carissa," Mom said.

"Hi, I'm at Barbara's," I said.

"Who's Barbara?"

"You know, I told you—the teacher's assistant from Cambridge.

I do my homework here sometimes? Anyway, I'm staying here for dinner. I told her you wouldn't mind, but she wanted me to call you so you knew where I was."

"Oh, that was nice of her. We're just having pizza tonight, and the boys can always eat more. Are you coming home tonight?"

"I'm not sure, Mom." I wanted to hang up the phone before I lost it with her.

"Well, it would be nice if you could let us know, because your cousin is here and was going to sleep in your bed."

"Okay, bye, then," I said. With my heart racing, I placed the receiver gently back in its cradle, fighting the urge to slam it.

"Everything okay?" Barbara asked.

"Yes. Do you want me to help with anything?" I needed a quick distraction from what just happened.

Barbara had a place for everything. "The place mats are in this drawer here, and silverware and napkins." She pointed everything out. I tried to remember—was it fork-knife-spoon or fork-spoon-knife? Did we even need spoons? Where did I put the napkins, and what about the glasses?

"Thanks for joining us for dinner," Barbara said as she placed a bowl of mashed potatoes on the table. Next, a plate of veggies and a platter of chicken breasts, each on special heat-resistant pads to protect the table's finish. I watched as though she were painting a picture.

"Thanks for inviting me," I said.

"Oh, you're welcome here anytime." I believed her. "Later, I'll give you a ride home," Barbara said. "It will be dark, and it's getting cold." Her concern surprised me. Walking through Coalinga at all hours in any kind of weather was nothing unusual for me. Besides,

I didn't even know for sure where I'd be sleeping, though my sister's house seemed most likely.

Over dinner, Barbara asked Doug questions about his day at work, and Doug asked me a little more about my college courses. After we finished eating, I did my best to help Barbara clean up and put away the leftovers, but she was happier with me just watching and talking to her.

"Do you stay in touch with your counselor, the one from juvenile hall?" she asked.

"Ron? Not really anymore. He's moved to LA and he's married. The last time he wrote, it was about his son being born." Ron would've liked to read a letter about my time with Barbara, I thought, about dinner with her and Doug.

"It's great that he cares about you so much," Barbara said, "and he's right about your potential. You've just got to stick with your education. It's something that no one can ever take away from you."

I wanted to believe her, but I'd never managed to hold on to anything—how could an education be any different?

When Barbara was done drying the last dish, she grabbed her keys and I followed her through the garage out to where her car was parked. We climbed in, and I told her where my sister lived.

"I'll always be here if you need a ride," she said. "I'd rather come get you in the middle of the night than think of you walking around out here by yourself."

For the rest of the semester, Barbara's ordered, deliberate life became mine for a few hours a week. She fed me physically, while giving me the calm to settle down emotionally. Across her kitchen counter, as comfortable as though I'd been sitting there since childhood, I heard Barbara tell her own story. "I was only ten credits short of graduating from college," she said. "If I had continued my education, I would've become a school counselor, maybe even a police officer." It was easy to imagine Barbara as an officer, in charge.

Finally one night I got up the courage to ask why she had never returned to school to get her degree. "It's not my time anymore," she said. "That time has passed."

"What do you mean, 'not your time'?" I asked. "You want it."

"When Doug got out of the service, he got this great job working for PG&E, so we came to Coalinga." She lowered her voice to a whisper so he wouldn't hear her. "I've always been happy in my marriage, but not so happy in Coalinga. It's flat, and I was raised in the foothills. I always thought that someday he'd be transferred, but now it's been thirty years. I raised my daughters here."

"Are you going to move away?" I was concerned that I'd lose her.

"To tell you the truth, I never felt at home here until I started working at Cambridge. That's where I found my place. I feel at home now, and I have no plans to leave."

She'd found her place at Cambridge—maybe I could too.

■ ■ ■

By now I knew some of Barbara's history, and her life had not been as easy as I'd thought. That perfect home had not been preordained. As a girl, she and her sister shared a small wood house with their parents and grandmother. The nearest neighbor was a mile away. Barbara's father worked as a bulldozer operator on logging roads between the forest and the mill, and her mother stayed home, taking care of the girls. Barbara inherited her mother's affection for horses; by the sixth grade, she felt more at home on a horse than anyplace else. "Horses saved me," she said. "Taking care of them gave me a purpose." Barbara learned that all she had to do was give horses love. She didn't apply pressure to get her horse to do something she wanted her to do. "A horse will run away if she doesn't understand what you expect from her."

Barbara approached all students the same way she approached her horses, with respect and generosity of spirit. She knew her students partly through academic files, but she didn't judge us by our past or use it to justify our behavior. She understood that most of us weren't at Cambridge because we were stupid or lazy. We'd ended up in that trailer because of stuff going on that was out of our control, stuff she could not even fathom. She knew she couldn't take away the reasons we were there, but by sitting with us, being patient, being accepting, she was confident that she could help us find another way to be.

The day Barbara announced that Cambridge was replacing her, there was not a dry eye in the trailer. *"Why?"* It was the question we repeated all day. The reason—that someone more senior in the school system wanted the job—didn't make sense to any of us. Barbara was ours, and we were hers. How could that end because of seniority?

Finally Barbara came up with another answer. "Everyone needs a place to be, when everything else goes bad. I was at Cambridge when both my parents died. Being here helped me through that. Maybe this new teacher needs help through something herself. She needs this experience, and I've already had it."

I loved Barbara's attitude, but the thought of her being replaced, of someone else at her desk, made me angry. Why was someone making this choice? Why didn't her students have any say in it?

That night, I went to her house, not to do homework but to talk about finding another way. "I think we should write a letter to the superintendent or somebody," I said. "We'd all sign it. I'm sure that Mr. Doty would too."

Barbara took her time to reply. "That's so sweet, but there's nothing I can do about it. It's the rules. She has a choice and she made it."

Transfering to another position in the district was not B's choice. She wanted to stay with us.

■ ■ ■

My second year at Cambridge, I loaded my schedule with eighteen college units' worth of courses. I knew it was a lot, but if I passed them, no matter the grade, it would equate to completing almost a full year of high school, putting me an entire semester ahead of the sixth-grade class I had left behind. That fall was my junior year; in addition to the three hours I spent at Cambridge, I was taking Spanish, English, trigonometry, health, piano, and interpersonal communications. I'd signed up for more West Hills courses than anyone else at our school and, I was told, more than any student in the school's history. In the trailer and at West Hills, I was surprising everyone, leaving the label of "failure" behind. I was not even seventeen and I'd completed more college courses than 90 percent of the people in Coalinga.

As the number of credits increased, the time I spent at Barbara and Doug's decreased. I missed them—their calmness was a life raft I could cling to when everything else moved too fast. "It's been a while since you've had dinner here," Barbara said late one afternoon when I dropped in unannounced and planted myself at the counter. "Doug and I have something we'd like to talk to you about."

After dinner we settled into the living room, Doug and Barbara on two oversized leather chairs, me directly across from them on the gigantic and pristine matching couch. Were they sitting me down to tell me some kind of news? Was one of them sick?

"Carissa," Barbara began, "Doug and I realize that you don't have a regular place to stay." She looked at him, then back at me. "We've discussed your situation and how much we enjoy having you over. We'd like you to consider living with us. We have the space, and you can have your own room."

Her offer caught me by surprise. I'd stayed at other people's houses as a guest, I'd even stayed here before, but no one had ever officially asked me to move in. Barbara and Doug wanted to give me a room of my own, with a dresser and a closet where I could put my things. I could see how serious they were, and I suspected I wouldn't get another chance at what they were offering. But instead of being overjoyed, all I felt was fear and pressure. If I lived with them, I'd have to follow their rules. They'd want to know where I was going and when I'd be home. Like the group homes, they'd expect me to be good all the time, and I knew I wasn't. There was a part of my life—the side where I was still testing my limits, with boys, with drugs and alcohol—that I didn't want them to know about.

"There would be only two rules." Barbara spoke very carefully. "You'd have to be in every night by eight P.M., and ten on the weekends. And you could not have friends over, girls or boys, until Doug and I got to know them." I was relieved—she'd just given me the out I needed.

I took a deep breath, knowing I was about to disappoint both of them. "Thank you so much, but I have to think about it. I don't know that I'd be able to follow the rules." I already knew I wouldn't move in. It wasn't worth ruining everything we'd built. The risk was too much for me.

"Well," Barbara asked, "where are you sleeping tonight?"

"At Tara's." A friend Barbara knew from Cambridge.

"You could stay here instead, sleep on it before you decide."

I agreed, as a form of compromise. At least I would not have to say no to them in person. I slept comfortably, as I always did at Barbara's, but the next morning I made my way out before she or Doug woke up. Consciously, I was choosing a life that made sense only to me, instead of choosing something that would give me refuge. Freedom versus safety—there seemed no way to have both.

■ ■ ■

After that night, I avoided Barbara and her house. Ashamed, I didn't even call to say hi. How could I when I had refused her offer to take me in? All she had wanted was for me to stay.

But I couldn't, and during the next month I lived the life that I was afraid to let her see, which is how I ended up with my cousin Joey at a party at his boss's house. Joey was a few years older, and we'd been partying since I was twelve, when he'd given me my first hit of marijuana and laughed when I choked on it. The best thing about being with Joey was that he didn't expect anything from me, no money, no sex; he just handed me the pipe. Only now he was handing me a straw. I watched carefully as he tilted his head back and wiped his nose. "It's strong stuff," Joey warned me. "Uncut."

Leaning over, I wiped the straw's end and put it into my nose; the other end went over a line of methamphetamine. I sucked the substance up through my right nostril, and I tilted my head back just as he had. I thought I must look like a pro. The drip down the back of my throat tasted awful, then the numbness set in. First in my mouth, then all over my body. For the next couple of hours, we did line after line, trying to pace our high and stay up all night. As the sun came up, he and his boss had to leave for work. "Can she stay here?" Joey asked his boss.

"Yeah, no problem. She can sleep on the couch," the guy said, and then he laughed. "If she sleeps at all."

Meth goes by many names, but in Coalinga we called it crank, and I was convinced I could handle it. I told myself I only "dabbled" in drugs and only did it in groups when we were partying. Addicts smoked crack every day, and on their own. Addicts drank all alone. Addicts stopped eating and couldn't function in daily life. But that wasn't me. I wasn't alone. Sitting on my right was the drug dealer's wife.

I'd been up all night before, but this was something else. My mind was racing fast. I was losing weight just sitting still. In an effort to focus, I went for my schoolbooks, which I'd brought with me. I was in no shape to go to a lecture, but the books were an anchor. As long as I had them, I wasn't lost. West Hills was only a block away, but the time for my classes came and went. Before I knew it, another day slipped by. I had not slept or eaten.

At some point the phone rang, startling us, but we let it go for two more rings before the dealer's wife picked up. I couldn't make out what she was saying. She hung up. "Oh, shit!"

"Who was it?" I asked.

"He was arrested. He's in jail." After being pulled over by the cops for speeding, her husband, our dealer, was off to jail on an outstanding warrant.

Within minutes, we were lining up more crank. "Maybe we should smoke it. Like my brother does, to get a better high," she said. Using a hollowed-out pen, I breathed in the white curls that rose from the yellow rocks we'd heated with a lighter. Inside my lungs the chemicals unleashed euphoria unlike any high I'd experienced. Amped up, my heart rate soared. All I wanted to do was talk and move. I had forgotten about my books. There was no place to work here anyway. The small kitchen table was full of old food wrappers, mirrors, and aluminum foil, and there was a wet diaper on the chair.

Speeding and delusional, I thought that this woman and I were becoming friends. She let me borrow a shirt when I sweat through my clothes. *How many days have I been up? How many days have I been in these clothes?* Then the drugs ran out.

"I'm going to the store," she announced. Before I could ask any questions, she was out the door with her three-year-old daughter, leaving the baby boy behind. He was just starting to take his first steps and cried when his mother left. *Oh, shit!* I thought. A wave of paranoia washed over me, and I started making sure there was nothing bad he could get into. I took all the cleaning products from under the counter and put them where he couldn't reach. With the boy in my arms, it took me about ten minutes to make the house baby safe. An hour passed, then two, then more.

I hadn't slept in days. I was scared. *How can I care for a baby in this condition?* I had washed his bottles. Given him fresh milk, changed his diaper . . . Where was she? Was she ever coming back? Had she been arrested? I was lost. The baby slept soundly, but every minute I'd walk toward him to make sure his tummy was moving up and down with gentle breaths.

I knew I needed to crash. After the crank was gone, I popped vitamins like they were M&M's, hoping to come down a little easier. The high was over, but the drug wouldn't let me rest. When the baby woke up and began crying, I couldn't take much more.

Finally the front door opened. His mom was back. "Where the fuck have you been!" I screamed.

"I had to get more shit!" she screamed back at me.

I marched toward the door. "You're a fucking bitch for leaving me here alone with your baby," I said. "I'm out of here!"

"Give me back my T-shirt, you whore!" she demanded.

I whipped off the oversized green V-neck and threw it at her. Storming out, I was shirtless, braless, and, for that moment, fearless. Arms crossed over my bare chest, I walked across the Coaling Station B apartment complex, looking for a place to go. I remembered that some boys from my West Hills classes lived in one of the units nearby. I rushed to their place and knocked on the door with the side of my fist. A big guy from the basketball team opened the door, and I darted past him, arms still covering my chest. In the living room, a few guys from West Hills were sitting on a couch watching a basketball game. They barely glanced back at me as I ducked into the narrow kitchen.

And then I came to rest, curled up on the linoleum floor, against the sink and facing the refrigerator. I hadn't showered for days, and as awkward as I felt, I couldn't find the will or energy to move from that spot. After a few moments I heard whispers as the television went silent. One of the guys tossed me a large T-shirt and I slipped it over my head, letting it fall loose around my body. Someone else handed me the phone. "Is there someone you can call?"

When my friend Melisa answered her phone, I blurted what little I knew to be true: I'd been up at least a few days, on crank for the last five. I'd been smoking it but didn't know how much. I was at a Coaling Station B apartment but didn't know which one. I was weak and sick, wearing someone else's shirt and needing a bra.

She didn't have a car. "Who can I call to come and get you?"

Of the list of names that passed through my mind in that moment, only one made sense. "Barbara." She'd said she would always be there to give me a ride, anytime, anyplace, no matter what. I'd never wanted her to see this part of me, but I was sick and helpless, and I knew it. Covering my eyes with one hand, I handed the phone to my classmate so he could explain to Melisa where the apartment was.

By the time I heard Barbara's voice, she was already kneeling in front of me on the boys' tiny kitchen floor. She smelled like floral soap, sweet and clean. She put her arm around me with just enough pressure that I knew she wasn't angry but taking control. I wanted her to wrap her arms around me and hold me tight. I buried my head in her sweater as she stroked my matted hair.

"Everything's going to be okay." I believed her, but I couldn't bring myself to look up at her as she led me out of the apartment to the parking lot where she had parked her truck. I crawled into the passenger seat and we drove away. She was quiet and so was I, drifting slightly in the warmth of the cab.

Back in her living room, Barbara turned her couch into a cozy bed and covered me with sheets and a blanket. She placed a warm washcloth on my forehead, sat down on the rug, and held my hand as my body twitched until my limbs relaxed, my heartbeat slowed, and I fell into something resembling deep sleep. Later she told me she had debated whether to call for help but feared I would be arrested. "That's the last thing she needs," she whispered to herself, and in her mind she wondered if I would make it through the night.

The next day, washing the sleep from my eyes and the sweat of drugs off my body in her shower, I knew I'd lost too much ground too fast. I tried to reassure Barbara that I'd learned my lesson, but she wouldn't hear it. "Your mother needs to know what's going on," she insisted. "I need your permission to call her and tell her, to meet with her in person and talk to her about this."

"Okay," I said. "But I don't know what she can do." Barbara had done her own research while I slept. She'd found a rehab center in Fresno, but she couldn't take me there on her own; I was still a minor and needed to have a parent sign me in.

That evening, after calling my mom to let her know we were coming, Barbara and I walked into my house together. As we sat with my mother around the kitchen table, still wet from being wiped clean, Barbara explained what had happened. Mom seemed confused about the whole thing. "She looks fine to me," she said.

But Barbara would not stand down. "She wasn't okay last night. She was in serious trouble. And I believe Carissa needs serious help." She handed over a piece of paper with the telephone number and address for the rehab center in Fresno. "Please check this out," she told my mother. "They're waiting to hear from you."

Barbara had not made a request. She was giving Mom only one option. Sitting at the rehab with Mom was reminiscent of my suicide attempt; there was the same surreal sense of an emergency that had passed and all we were doing was waiting for someone to render a verdict. Once again we waited for my name to be called; once again we walked back into an office. It wasn't a doctor's office, more of a professional office with a desk separating the admissions counselor from Mom and me.

This was a white guy, with white clothes and a white job. He was comfortable behind his desk, about to make a big decision about my life based only on a sheet of questions in front of him. He didn't know me. He asked about drugs as though he were consulting a shopping list, but he didn't ask about my life or anything that might have put my behavior in some kind of context. I wanted to tell him about what I'd been trying to achieve, about who I wanted to be, but his body language and tight facial expression told me he wasn't interested in any of that. He wanted to know about the drugs, and he wanted me to be specific. I was tired, and I trusted Barbara that there were not going to be police involved. We flew through his questions. I didn't calculate. I didn't care what the outcome was. I told him everything.

"What's the hardest drug you've ever used?" he asked.

"I guess acid," I replied. "I did a lot of acid in Florida."

The interview took about twenty minutes, then he asked if I'd return to the waiting room. He needed to speak to my mother about the details.

Within ten minutes, Mom emerged from the office down the hall. "Let's go," she said, her mouth set in a firm line.

"I don't have a drug problem?" I asked.

"We'll talk about it in the car," Mom responded.

Once she was behind the wheel, she looked at me. "They were going to lock you up, and I said no. They think you do have a problem, and they didn't think you'd stay there without being locked up."

He'd given her the option of tricking me into staying—we would go on a tour of the facility, then he would have me locked in a room to detox. Mom had refused. She shook her head, a haunted look on her face. "I didn't want you locked up like Nana was," she said. "No more locking up. Plus, it's five thousand dollars. Even if you had the chance to agree to it, we can't afford it."

I think now that if she'd had the money, she might have pressed me to stay. And I think I might have said yes. Wakefield had been safe and productive for me; this would have been more of the same.

When I told Barbara the outcome, she wasn't angry or disappointed; instead, she seemed calm and satisfied. She had done what she could do. Attention had been paid, she'd told both me and Mom what she thought, we'd followed through on the intake visit, and that was as far as it would go for now. Without money, without insurance, it could not go any further. And so the conversation went no further as well.

I continued to use when the occasion presented itself, but I made some rules. Only on weekends. Never when little kids were around. Only with people my own age. Never with adults who used more or were dealers or were prone to violence. It was for fun, I thought. It was also a way to keep from facing the truth: I could not manage my life. Even success was impossible under the pressure of my past. Drugs and alcohol were a way to manage the stress, loneliness, and unpredictability of my life—a drug, a beer, a boy, a fast car ride, a lost weekend, a lost week. It was a fight between the girl who knew what was right and good and the girl who often just couldn't give a shit.

I recovered physically quite quickly; school was another matter. I had missed whole days, assignments, exams. I still had a small window of time remaining to drop classes without having to take failing grades, which I did. I saved my textbooks for the following semester, determined to go back and finish.

Less than a year later, with a mix of excitement and disbelief, I put on my first cap and gown. Cambridge graduation was held in the elementary school auditorium, on the same stage I had walked on—hobbled on, with crutches—in fifth grade when I received my math award and a letter signed by President Ronald Reagan. This time there was no acknowledgment from the president, but the accomplishment was greater. I had completed high school on time.

Barbara had said she wanted her students to know how it felt to be "safe" and to "belong." "No child should ever feel unsafe or unwanted," she often said. This was the belief that had carried her into my life with no hesitation, no fear. At graduation I asked her why she kept giving to me, even when I messed up. "Because you let me," she said. "It was always up to you."

Part II

THE PEOPLE IN THE SNOW GLOBE

CHAPTER NINE

∎

"Isn't everything we do in life a way to be loved a little more?"
—CELINE IN THE MOVIE *BEFORE SUNRISE*

For years, whenever I looked into a mirror, I didn't trust what I saw: a pretty girl, a confident girl, a girl who knew where she was supposed to be. The coping skills I had used to survive my teens—to survive the streets, juvy, and high school—were not good enough now that I was moving on to college. I wanted to see potential and possibility, but all I saw were scars reflecting back at me. My smile, my makeup, my styled hair, my brushed-on confidence—these were the only things that kept me from hiding. I was accumulating victories, but I could not help but feel the image looking back at me was false. I didn't know the young woman in the mirror. I didn't love her, and I had a hard time believing anyone else did or ever would.

■ ■ ■

When kids from Coalinga left high school, their options ranged from the oil fields to the Ivy League. One person a class ahead of me had gone to Yale; many others were accepted into smaller liberal arts colleges. But it took a steady record of achievement to get there, and my living situation, my uncertainties, and my constant self-doubt made me feel like a reject before I even applied. With an academic record that looked like a seismograph charting Coalinga's fault line—from all Fs to an early graduation, from being in AP calculus to being unable to find a pair of closed-toe shoes for chemistry lab—anything that required an explanation to strangers felt overwhelming.

With the Ivy League and four-year colleges out of my reach, reality and comfort dictated a community college. California was full of them, and they offered a road to four-year schools by offering courses that would fulfill the first two years of undergraduate requirements. I briefly considered West Hills but almost immediately rejected staying in Coalinga. I needed to get away. A friend was going to go to Cuesta College, a two-year college in San Luis Obispo, a beautiful coastal town a little over an hour away. I completed the paperwork with ease, found a job at a coffee shop downtown, and started a new life there in the fall.

San Luis was new, unmarked by bad memories. The peaceful, swept sidewalks, window boxes full of flowers, and tidy trash cans into which people actually deposited trash all reflected a kind of order that I wanted in my life. I was determined to be a new Carissa in this environment, to become that familiar yet unknowable stranger looking back at me in the mirror.

The transition was awkward at first. My courses required a different kind of brain work than I'd done in Wakefield or Cambridge, and it took every bit of concentration I had to keep up. I couldn't do small talk, couldn't hear a question without wondering about the questioner's motive—I could barely respond to "How was your weekend?" In a college-success class, a professor introduced an exercise with these words: "This is to illustrate the many masks we wear. Throughout the day and throughout our lives. We are students. We are mothers. We are siblings. We are friends. We are employees . . ." The list seemed endless. *The masks we wear.* Maybe that's why I didn't know the girl in the mirror: She was wearing masks, layers of them. Some days, just showing up to class was more than I could do; I'd call in sick to work or just disappear. How could anyone possibly miss me when I didn't even know me?

In that same college-success class, we were given a personality profile test—I scored ten out of ten on the introvert scale. As the teacher explained how rare it was to see extreme scores and what a life challenge such a condition presented, I got scared. "Did anyone get a ten out of ten?" she asked. I slowly raised my hand and looked around the room. I was the only one. The look on her face wasn't very comforting.

I approached my newly discovered introversion with the logic I used in solving math problems. After class I looked at the questions on the personality test and then at my answers. All I needed to do was the opposite of what I had put down. Answer the phone on the first ring! Be on time! Expect the best from people!

I started with work at the coffee shop. The effort to get to my shift on time seemed enormous. Punctuality just wasn't a habit I'd ever learned, and it felt like I was trying to write with the wrong hand. Every day, I shaved off a couple of minutes. Fortunately, I liked the job. I liked the way it felt to work a shift, be efficient, put a smile on people's faces. It was also a good place to people watch. I noted body language, the way young men and women interacted, the casualness, the clothes, how girls carried their books, how they walked through the room without self-consciousness. *Do I fit in here?* A little at a time, I did. Hours at work began to pass quickly, and when a customer said "Thank you," it grew easier to say "You're welcome" and mean it.

■ ■ ■

Francisco Curiel was from Santa Maria, a first-generation college student who went on to become a college basketball coach at St. Joseph's in Indiana and St. Louis in Missouri. He had returned to California as the new director of Extended Opportunity Program and Services (EOPS), a state-funded program meant to help students access resources in college. Franky didn't need to share his struggles with those of us who made it into his office. He'd overcome adversity, and the students he connected with knew it. His implicit acceptance and understanding gave me permission to drop at least one mask, maybe more. Franky had an open-door policy, and through him I met a small group of Cuesta students interested in exploring four-year schools—private, public, religious, and secular, all sizes. We each wanted to take that next step, but we had no idea how to do it. Franky didn't just provide one road map; he gave us many. The first hurdle was a practical one: application fees, which potentially could be hundreds of dollars for the schools I hoped to apply to after Cuesta. Franky had the fee waivers ready to go for up to three University of California campuses and most of the California State University campuses. The next step, declaring a major, was less straightforward.

I started with what I knew for sure. "I'd like to earn a degree that will allow me to help people."

"Who do you want to help?" Franky asked. We'd had many

conversations about my background, but I had not told him everything; I worried he'd change his opinion of me. Yet I instinctively recognized that we were similar—we each had hard beginnings, we each had taken some hits, and the odds were against us.

"People like us," I answered. "People who need help. People starting out with nothing or with very little. Maybe I could be a lawyer. I want to change things, fight for justice."

"Law school," he said slowly. Then he nodded. "That means you can major in anything in undergraduate school. You can do prelaw, but you don't have to." Instead of narrowing them down, our conversation expanded my options.

Instead of choosing one major at one school, I decided to increase the odds of finding a good fit: I'd choose a different major at each school I applied to, then go to the best one that accepted me. If I got into Cal Poly, it would be applied psychology; at UCSD, neuropsychology; at UCLA, social psychology; and at UC Berkeley—Nana's legacy—it would be social welfare.

With a big assist from Wite-Out tape and a borrowed electric typewriter, I finally got the application essay done and called my sister Sophie in Los Angeles to read it to her. A few changes, one more rewrite, and the applications were mailed minutes before the deadline.

Three months later my top choice won—or rather, I won. I was going to Berkeley.

■ ■ ■

When I graduated from Cuesta, my entire family showed up, as did Barbara and Mr. Doty. "I have some news," I announced over nachos and ice water. "I've been hired by a tutoring company in Colorado, just for the summer." They cheered, seeing it as a good lead-in to my start at Berkeley. No one knew that I had a new boyfriend, a relationship that put everything I had gained at risk.

Chase was not a college kid—he was in the army, training to be a tank mechanic in Kentucky and afterward on his way to the Fourth Infantry Division in Colorado Springs. He'd joined because his life had been a mess, he told me, and his family and a judge thought this was a way to get straightened out. The day I met him, on a train between San Francisco and San Luis Obispo, he was on leave, in his street clothes going to visit his brother in Lompoc. We talked for the next hour, as though we'd known each other for a long time. He was sarcastic and funny. We got off the train and said good-bye. He had my phone number. I knew he would call.

A week later, I received my first letter from him, but soon his letters weren't enough for me; we planned a visit. I flew to Kentucky before he left training. The night I arrived in Louisville was chaotic. It had been eight weeks since we'd sat so close on that train, and now he wasn't there to meet me at the airport as planned. He didn't miss me. Did I miss him? Did I know him? After checking into my hotel, I unloaded my backpack, spreading his letters out on the bed, deciphering each page and studying the one picture I had of him. What was I doing in Kentucky meeting a stranger?

He arrived hours later with another enlisted guy and two young girls—and the girls promised to come back for him in two days, when he'd have to report back to his squadron. I packed up his letters and squashed my suspicions; I wanted this romantic weekend together. I needed the possibility of a family of my own, someone to share in all the excitement of my future.

The next day we explored downtown Louisville, eating and drinking and wandering around, casually getting lost while looking for bus stops that would take us to our next destination. The city seemed quiet, but I was reminded of the uncertainty of new places when a fight broke out right in front of us: two homeless men, both drunk, swinging wildly at each other over some insult and missing as many punches as they threw. Chase grabbed my hand and deftly steered us around the ugly scene. I was no longer the scared little girl who might have been at the center of that fight—I was someone valuable, someone worth protecting.

When Chase left on our third day together, it was hard to let him go. I knew it would be months before we would be together again, which is why I had taken this summer job in Colorado. When I settled into Denver, I was less than two hours from his division headquarters in Colorado Springs. As busy as each day was at my new job, as beautiful as the surroundings were, I waited impatiently every afternoon for the mail and the sound of the telephone announcing his call. I'd had my nose to the grindstone, focused on what was next, but when I was calm enough to feel my loneliness, there he was, ready to fill my void.

By the end of the summer, Chase and I had physically seen each other only a half dozen times—nothing to build a life on, yet I insisted to myself that it was enough. My expectations and my fantasy of domestic bliss sent him off in the opposite direction—he was having fun raising hell with his army buddies, and I wasn't interested or old enough to barhop with him. The closer the time came to head to Berkeley that fall, the more panicky I felt; how could I leave? We were already strained. How would things be with two states and over a thousand miles between us? What if we made a commitment? Thoughts of marriage consumed me.

The day before I left, we sat together in my place and I listened as he laughed off my concerns. "You're going to Berkeley!" he said. "You'll find someone else."

"No, I won't," I insisted. All I could think was *Right now or never*. I wanted it official, I wanted it in writing, and I didn't want to go back to California without it. Something inside me told me that all the best men in the world went to the best women, and that this man was not the best, but he was the right one for me.

If it had been a movie and I'd seen a character do this, I'd have yelled at the screen. "No, no, stay out of that old abandoned house!" *Stupid girl*. But I didn't think I was that stupid girl; I thought I was smart. I'd added everything up—marriage meant consistency and security when I was going to an unknown place. He would be my person in the world and I would be his. I wouldn't be alone at Berkeley; I would go there as someone's wife. Plus there was the practical aspect, and that I was *not* stupid about: I would be on his insurance, and we could manage the distance with visits he could pay for with the extra pay he'd receive each month.

By that afternoon, we were married. It was easier than when I got my driver's license—a couple of signatures and we were done. I never met his family; he never met mine. And I entered Berkeley a married woman. If anyone asked about our honeymoon, I just said we'd do it later, maybe over the following summer. No one would ever need to know that I wore my best dress to the courthouse or that after the certificate was signed his friend drove us to Wendy's for burgers, fries, and a Frosty.

■ ■ ■

My sister Sophie was at the airport in Oakland to pick me up and take me to Berkeley. She had driven up from LA to get me situated and make sure that I didn't freak out due to the overwhelming amount of administrative detail that needed to be covered on day one.

While in Colorado, I'd answered an ad, writing to a family who was renting a room. A Chilean dad, an American mom, and their son and two daughters welcomed me in their home for the first few days, and we agreed that if I liked it, I could stay on.

The mom was a political activist and avid gardener. The dad was head chef in a Berkeley restaurant and luckily, he liked to cook at home too. Since my rent included his meals, I was soon spending my evenings around the family table, trying to hold my own in passionate discussions about world affairs and politics. *This is what a family is. This is what a family does.* Often I'd find my mind drifting to my husband. I didn't know what he thought about some of these issues. I didn't know much about his family, their traditions, what his dreams for the future might've been before I entered his life. One night I called Chase to tell him what we were discussing and to describe the incredible meal we'd shared.

"Oh, that sounds cool," he said. "I've got to go now. I'm running out of time on this calling card."

None of it had landed with him. "Okay, well, call me later," I said, trying to hide my disappointment. "In the morning, whenever."

It was a sign of what would come. As quickly as my marriage had happened, it came unraveled. The romance had evaporated, and it turned out that in addition to having difficult pasts, we both had explosive tempers, careless mouths, and many unresolved issues. The relationship was complicated. Hope dissolved quickly under the weight of mounting expenses, unmet commitments, and mutual infidelity. We'd joked the day we were married that we were starting from zero. Now zero was all there was.

When we separated, I felt relieved. It had been a mistake; now it was over. We walked away as if it hadn't happened and turned our attention back to what mattered most to each of us. School and work were once again the glue that held me together.

■ ■ ■

The problem with trying to be in two places at once is that you end up being no place. The months before my relationship with Chase self-destructed, I was distracted, nervous, and behind in my class-work. I studied on the bus to and from school and stayed on campus during breaks, playing catch-up. I'd never used Excel before, and instead of getting help, I spent hours in the computer lab, trying to figure it out for myself, correcting error after error. Even tougher than the technical aspects of being a student was the actual content: The classes for my major were too close to my real life. During one "getting to know you" exercise, when we were asked to discuss our social and cultural histories, I stammered as I selectively edited my responses for the starry-eyed college girl sitting next to me. *Where did you grow up?* It was a simple question that sent me into an uncon-trollable tremor. We watched videos in class—one of children being exploited, street kids, abandoned kids, sent on trains across the United States to work in brothels, in restaurants, in fields. I tried to sit still, to watch the young faces flying past on the screen, but with one image quickly replacing another, it was too much. Each of those kids had a story not unlike my own. I left class sick to my stomach.

Luckily, there was an escape at home. Dinner and interesting people waiting for me to join them—living there was the best decision—until their genuine interest in my life made it impossible for me to hide my setbacks. "How was class?" someone would inevitably ask. It was a simple question with no simple answer.

One day, instead of agonizing in the computer lab, I decided to sit in on a calculus class. The room was packed, so I sat just outside the open double doors, pretending I was waiting for someone. I watched in amazement as the professor spent nearly an hour solving one problem on four different blackboards. I was with him through almost all of it. Watching him find the derivative of a function, dx/dy into dx'/dy left me reeling with excitement because I understood! When I heard the familiar terminology—numbers, intervals, real and imaginary solutions to the unknowns—a wave of longing swept over me, something similar to homesickness. *That's my language.*

I needed to find the adviser for my department. "I'd like to change my major," I began, but before I could arrive at my reasons, he cut me off.

"I don't do that here," he briskly responded. "But we can talk about it. What are you changing to?" He opened a catalog.

"Math or engineering, but not social welfare or psychology." I explained that I wanted to be a lawyer, so I could major in anything.

Looking through the catalog, he found the mathematics requirements. I followed his pointy finger moving down the page. "Do you have two semesters of calculus? Or any physics?"

"One semester of calculus. I got a *B* in it, but my professor said it wasn't because I couldn't do better. She said it was because I took such a heavy load." The explanation landed in dead air; he didn't even look up.

"There are prerequisites for math and engineering, and you don't have them," he said. "You need to withdraw before the midsemester deadline and tell the registrar that you'll be back when you've got the prerequisites."

Withdraw? Leave Berkeley? It wasn't an option I'd considered, but once it was on the table—or rather, the adviser's desk—it was the only option I saw. It wasn't as though I was being kicked out. It was a mutual understanding. I was going to leave with an open door. In my head, I was not fully letting the Berkeley family legacy go.

■ ■ ■

I met Jake, a Southern boy from Grand Isle, Louisiana, in a bar on a naval base in Lemoore, California. His slow drawl, accompanied by a slow-breaking smile, gave away his Southern roots immediately. I was holding a pitcher in each hand, taking them back to my friends at our table, when he asked me if I needed another beer.

I smiled. "Has anyone ever told you that you look like Ben Affleck?"

"Well, no. Has anyone ever told you that you look like Sandra Bullock?" In that moment we connected. I started talking about the movie I'd just seen with the two of them in it. "Have you seen it?" I asked.

"Not yet," he answered. "Do they end up together?"

"No," I said, grinning. "But it's still a good movie."

Later we went to Denny's. Over mozzarella sticks and dip, he told stories about back home. About his small graduating class, only twelve students, about his accomplishments, about his time at LSU and joining a fraternity. He looked at me. "Your eyes are beautiful."

I was completely, utterly charmed. We laughed and laughed; the physical relationship was everything I could've hoped for. I felt like a woman, and he was a spectacular man. Funny, smart, handsome, he made me feel on track again. I felt whole when we were together. I didn't want to return to Berkeley if it meant leaving him.

Jake took me home to Grand Isle, but not for the usual boy-introduces-girl-to-family; his father was dying. We went to Mass there, and I was moved and honored and sad to be included in something so intimate, part of a family's tradition, the place they went for prayer and comfort. I'd only been to a Catholic Mass once before, with a friend in Coalinga. I didn't understand any of it, but Jake trusted me to not disrespect it. He shared it with me. By the time we returned to California, Jake's daddy had died, and he was devastated.

"You don't understand what it's like to lose a parent," he said.

How could I? I've been living without a dad and with only part of a mom my whole life. For the next hour we didn't say anything else. When he was ready to talk again, we decided we were going to move in together.

Jake was with me when I turned in the paperwork to enroll at Fresno State. I did it all right over the counter. No essays. No hassles. I checked a box and declared mathematics as my new major. My classes were Monday, Wednesday, and Friday, and every night I was home in time for dinner. We shared everything. Our struggles, our stories, our pasts. His were mostly fun, inventive; mine were rougher, on the edge. But he hadn't had an easy time, either; his dad had been an alcoholic, and his mom was basically a single mom who juggled lots of different jobs, from housekeeper to cook. Her work ethic was inspiring, and every holiday we spent together in Grand Isle was like a movie about being home for the holidays. It was more than anything I could have dreamed of. I fell in love with Jake's entire family. Eating gumbo, making homemade pies, and playing Bourré, a French Louisiana card game, I got to know them as intimately as I'd known anyone. His momma, his sisters, his aunts, and his uncles embraced me one at a time. They were warm, nonjudgmental people, and the facts of my life were revealed slowly, as naturally as they possibly could be. This was the family I wanted, and everything they did gave me the feeling that they wanted me back.

"This one, she's going places," his aunt proclaimed of me. *This is a reason for someone to love me,* I thought. *I am going places.*

Jake and I settled into a two-bedroom duplex apartment, declaring our intention that we would always have room for our families to visit, anytime, and stay as long as they wanted. We ordered household things out of catalogs and made each choice—a picture, a candle, a book, the furniture—with deliberation and care. We had our own washer and dryer, and there were clean matching towels and designer soap dispensers in each bathroom. Our dishes were a set, our silverware was complete, and we had a welcome mat at the door. The tile countertop was never cluttered and always gleamed, and there was rarely a dirty dish in the sink. I thought of Barbara every time I sponged the counter or folded the laundry. Our life was a page out of *Better Homes and Gardens* magazine. We lived on a quiet street in a small town. I never looked nervously over my shoulder, never worried about what I'd see in my rearview mirror.

I signed up for yoga and for aerobics and was up for anything physical, including dancing with Jake at any hour of the day or night. I cooked for us, and he did the cleaning and the decorating. He decorated for every holiday, every change of season. Before we'd moved in together, he'd even decorated his navy barracks room at Christmas.

The first Thanksgiving I ever cooked, I had a "to do" list as long as my arm. The precleaning, the postcleaning, the shopping list, the knives, forks, napkins, and candleholders, the perfect tablecloth, the perfect flowers, the perfect centerpiece, the coasters, the scented candles—there was nothing we didn't consider, and we worked together like a well-ordered team of two.

Our guests arrived on time, to be greeted with a generous spread of traditional finger foods and starters. My mom, stepdad, siblings, stepsiblings, nieces, and nephews and Jake's friends from the base were comfortable from the moment they walked in.

We'd rented a large table, and everyone sat together around it, like a scene from *It's a Wonderful Life* or from my imagination. And just as in a movie, everyone laughed on cue at Jake's silly stories and jokes.

It was the height of our applying the Golden Rule—treat others as you want to be treated. If we spoiled them, if we were nice to them, if we fed them and nurtured them, then they would do the same for us. The evening ended early with everyone saying good-bye except the one faithful sailor friend of Jake's who stayed behind to help with cleanup. There had been no fighting, no kids crying, no one leaving hungry. I'd made three times as much food as we could possibly eat and bought plastic containers so that each person could take some of their favorites with them. *This is a normal family,* I thought.

■ ■ ■

At Fresno State linear algebra, math history, number theory, and solving unsolved problems all had their own energy, keeping me focused and pulling me forward. My favorite exercise each semester was to browse through a complicated math book and lose myself in the pages of new material, as excited about what I'd learn in the weeks ahead as some people are about new cookbooks or travel brochures. I aced all my courses. We had new friends. I had a closet full of clothes that were all my own. I had a flexible job working as a tutor for the children of two prominent doctors in town. I was happy.

Around this same time, I stumbled upon talk radio—all political persuasions, plus public radio and progressive talk out of the Bay Area and LA. My commute to and from Fresno State was forty minutes each way. Most mornings, especially the foggy ones, the familiar radio voices were a comfort, like chatting with an old friend. But some days what I heard filled me with so much sadness that I had to pull off to the side of the road and just cry. Children—children throwing rocks at tanks, children victims of their parents' choices, children survivors of labor trafficking, of sex trafficking. I'd never thought of myself as one of those children, but each time news of children being harmed or abused came over the radio, I felt frantic. As a social welfare major, I'd turned away from these images, afraid to be graded on stories that resembled my own. Now, as a math major, I felt a safe distance. This wasn't class; this was life. *Once I finish up, complete my education, that's when I'll fight. When I'm a lawyer, that's when I'll be able to do something.*

The second year, Jake joined me on the forty-minute commute. He'd been able to get a night shift at the base so that he could take classes during the day. Always interested in politics and considering some kind of political future, he chose history as his major, with a plan to go to graduate school after college. We had our goals, our separate ones and our "together" ones, and our days were full and busy. Then came the attacks of September 11, 2001, and we paused, suddenly part of a bigger, sadder world. Jake was attached to the USS *Lincoln*, which was not scheduled for another workup until after his detachment date. The war pushed deployment forward, and it was with utter relief that I learned he'd be separated before the cutoff day that would have sent him into the war.

All the time I'd been with him, through long nights of deep and personal conversation or discussions about politics and current events, we'd somehow avoided talking about God. Now I was praying again, the way I had when I was a child. I needed a community, a place to belong, a house that would shelter my soul as our home sheltered my body. It was easy to lean into Jake's Catholic traditions and the solemn, deeply moving rituals. We'd gone to Mass in Grand Isle; now we began attending together on the base. The ceremonies were ageless and somehow reassuring. *This has lasted,* I thought. *This is certain.*

■ ■ ■

As my graduation from Fresno State approached, I wanted desperately to find Ron and ask him to be there. It had been almost ten years since we'd been in touch. I knew from our last letters that he had a job in Southern California at a youth prison. He was the first adult who had inspired me to pick myself up every time I fell and to go after my education no matter what else happened. And now I was graduating from his alma mater. In my gratitude and excitement, I wanted him to know that he had been with me all along. Still, I found myself nervous about reaching out to him. I rehearsed the plan several times before I actually searched the Internet for phone numbers of California Youth Authority facilities in the Los Angeles area. The list of five numbers sat on my desk for a few days before I finally had the courage to dial. The first call was a failure. "There's no one here by that name." I apologized, hung up, and took a deep breath before I punched in the second number. "He's left for the day," said the voice on the other end of the line. I was ecstatic. I had found him! I double-checked.

"You mean Ron Jenkins, right? Ronald Q. Jenkins?" I asked excitedly, remembering that rare middle initial from his famous signature on my journal pages.

"Yes," she said. "Would you like to leave him a message?"

Ron called me back the next day, as soon as he was at work.

"Carissa!" he exclaimed. "Where have you been?" He'd been searching for me too. "I called your old numbers. I looked for your mom. I couldn't find you anywhere. I can't believe you're calling me! What have you been up to?"

"Well, you told me I had potential. . . ." I filled him in on everything, right up to Fresno State. "I want to invite you to my graduation at the end of May."

"Sweetheart, I'm so proud of you! I never dreamed you'd be doing all of that. It's amazing everything you've done, but seriously, you know, you could have called me from prison and I would have been happy to hear your voice." He went on to explain how every year a couple of times he'd check the prison rosters in the state to see if my name would turn up, always hoping it wouldn't but desperately wanting to connect with me no matter where I was.

"I'm gonna see about your graduation," he said. "You know I'm gonna try to be there." I believed he'd be there if he could, but I also knew that he had a wife, children, and other responsibilities.

"Whatever you can do," I told him. "But even if you don't get here for my graduation, we're going to need to connect, meet up in person." I was beyond excited—our thirty minutes on the phone seemed to have gone by in less than five.

"Well, I'm at work, but I have your number, and here's mine." Ron gave me his home number and we hung up.

Jake came into the room and gave me a big hug. He'd heard bits of the conversation from the other end of our apartment. As I hugged him back, I felt the joy from deep inside beaming its way out. "Jake, I would not have all this without you."

Jake disagreed. "This is all yours, Carissa. You've earned every bit of it." I knew he meant the achievement, the degree, the success, the goals we were reaching together. But I also knew he meant my happiness, so hard won. After three years, Jake knew my past almost as well as I did. He knew that healing came only a few small steps at a time, and joy was always fragile.

■ ■ ■

I graduated with a perfect 4.0 in math and spent the summer filling out job applications and going on interviews. I wanted to teach high school math for a year so I could save money while I applied to law school and Jake finished up his degree at Fresno State. On the side, I had my own little freelance tutoring business, working with teenagers on SAT prep and college applications. The first teaching-job interview was the most challenging—I still hadn't become accustomed to or comfortable with someone I didn't know asking me questions. Wasn't everything they needed to know on the application? One principal, sensing my discomfort, explained the interview process. "Off the record, this is what they want to hear from you," he said, as he let me in on all the kinds of answers that would lead to job offers. I landed every job after that, with five good offers at high schools around the Central Valley, one of them in Coalinga. I didn't take it—the one I did choose, Hanford High, was only fifteen minutes from where Jake and I lived.

As it was, Hanford wasn't a slam dunk. I taught ninth and eleventh grades, Algebra 1 and Algebra 2. There were many kids in those classes who never should've gotten that far, not because they were failed students but because they'd had failed teachers. They saw math as a punishment to them, a drudge, a place where they were just doing time. I was determined to make them like it, and, like all missionaries, I got a little overzealous. "You can't smile; they'll see your weakness" was bad advice I took from a fellow teacher.

Under the pressures of time and state standards, I became the superstrict teacher. But my version of showing them I was totally committed to them didn't work. I'd come home each night frustrated. "Math was my lifeline," I'd tell Jake. "Why can't I get them to see that it could be theirs too?"

I had finely tuned radar for the students who were most like me at their age—the runaways, the sexually promiscuous, and the otherwise left behind. Once, in the teachers' lounge, I heard teachers talking about a girl who'd been caught under the bleachers with a boy. They were laughing and joking about it, and it made me want to scream. "Did anybody talk to her about it?" I asked.

They looked at me like I was crazy. "Talk to her? About what? That's just the kind of girl she is."

"How do you know that?" I asked.

"Because she's in my class," the other teacher said. "She's probably going to drop out."

I thought about this for a minute, remembering the people who had made an extra effort for me. The girl's math teacher was one of my closest friends at school, and together we managed to get the girl moved into my class. Another student, a chronic runaway, was living couch to couch and trying his best to keep up appearances. He was always clean but would skip days of class and return in the same clothes two or three days later. Still, he aced all the quizzes and tests he was present for—math was an instinct for him as much as it had been for me. "You've got potential," I told him. "The class misses you when you're not here." When I hadn't seen him for one week, I called his house, and his mother's response was not unlike my mother's had been: "I'm not sure where he is."

I went to a couple of his friends. "Tell him when you see him that it's okay to come to my class. If he's on the run, he can still come here. I won't turn him in, and I won't even mark him on the roll if that's a problem. I just want him to know that he's got a place here."

The next week he was back in my class. It was only for a few days, but it was enough for me to know that I'd reached him. "You made a difference," said Jake.

A few weeks after I applied to law school at UCLA, I drove through the campus to get a feel of what it might be like to go there. I parked on a side street but stayed in my car, not comfortable with crossing into territory that didn't belong to me, a club that hadn't yet asked me to be a member. I imagined that each brick in each building represented the energy and time that had been spent on making it a great institution. If I could only be part of it, be able to do things, change things. Growing up in Central California, in an area deemed the Appalachia of the West, I had idolized the great change agents who had sacrificed their lives for a more just world: Malcolm X, Helen Keller, Cesar Chavez, and Gandhi. I believed that with my past I had a unique perspective. I'd learned things—surely there was something I could add, some value I could bring to the fight that wouldn't be there if I didn't show up. I couldn't save everybody—but maybe one at a time?

■ ■ ■

Taking care of my students left less time for taking care of myself. I'd been running almost every day, plus taking aerobics classes and yoga, but there began to be days when I skipped exercising or couldn't find the energy to finish a run. I shortened my route, eventually just trying to get through one mile, and ended up walking much of the way home. Soon I was sleeping through the alarm clock in the morning, and all I wanted to do when I got home was go to bed. For months I'd been losing weight; now suddenly I was gaining it. I felt bloated and slow, like I was trying to walk in mud.

"What's going on with you?" Jake asked. At first he was concerned, but after a few weeks he got grumpy. Now he wasn't just making observations; he was criticizing. "Your clothes are looking tight, aren't they?" The word "lazy" came up in the conversation. We fought, badly, for the first time in the three years we'd been together, repeating the same argument every few days.

"I've been a little busy, in case you haven't noticed," I said. "Get off my back."

"Maybe you should try getting off the couch," he said. I'd never heard him be mean before.

If it had just been weight, my vanity might've done the trick—limit myself to salad and water until it fell away. But this was something else. I felt like crap all the time. My periods were either overwhelming or nonexistent. My gut hurt, my back ached, and standing up in class got harder every day. Plus there was some kind of lacy rash on my face, like a little child with a constant fever. This went on for weeks, the first time in years that the sheer force of my own will was not enough to attack and solve a problem. When I'd finally had enough, I took myself to a doctor.

A series of lab tests revealed there wasn't much that *wasn't* wrong with me. First, I had a serious thyroid problem—I needed surgery to remove the thyroid gland or radioactive-iodine treatment. There were complications in other areas as well. Further testing led to Serious Diagnosis Number Two: pelvic inflammatory disease (PID), the same thing that had caused me to pass out in a group home with a temp of 104. There had been no treatment back then other than a handful of antibiotics (which I probably didn't finish taking), and now I was faced with the results: My fallopian tubes, cervix, and ovaries were badly scarred, and my liver was damaged as well. I had to have surgery to remove the scar tissue, and even then my chances of conceiving or carrying a child to term were not good.

"Removing the scars surgically won't end the problem," said the surgeon. "The likelihood is, they'll continue to form. If you're considering pregnancy, right after surgery might be the best time. But I can't promise anything."

Sexually transmitted diseases, the legacy of Icey and the streets— and all this time, while I'd been pushing myself to move forward into a different life, the scars inside had been growing. No wonder I'd never gotten pregnant. Maybe this doctor saw this kind of PID all the time. Nevertheless, I felt compelled to explain. "I was raped, repeatedly," I said, weeping. "I didn't know about this part of it; no one ever explained. I never had an examination. Nobody warned me. I thought I was past it, that it was over."

"We can cut out the physical scars," she said very gently, "but not the memories. I need to warn you, with this kind of surgery and what it will do to your hormones for a while—it won't be an easy recovery. It will bring up a lot of stuff. You're going to have a bad emotional reaction to this; all rape victims do. Have you ever heard of posttraumatic stress disorder, PTSD? Rape victims and sex-abuse survivors suffer from it."

I thought PTSD was a disease from war. "Yes, I know it, but do you think . . . ?" Before I could finish, she added, "Rape can change the way your brain works. It is a form of survival."

The third diagnosis almost seemed trivial in comparison: parvovirus, likely caught from the kids at school and complicated by a weak immune system. That explained the weird rash and the exhaustion. Antibiotics and rest. More time on the couch. More time to feel worthless again, and sad, and angry. I'd worked so hard to rebuild, and now, with my health going downhill, I felt disoriented.

It couldn't help but spill over with Jake. That Easter, he once again decorated our home as he had every holiday. Hearts at Valentine's, Santas at Christmas, jack-o'-lanterns at Halloween. This time the cutesy decorations annoyed the hell out of me. These things didn't matter. Why couldn't he see that? We were not living in a department-store window. "This is all so artificial," I said. I wasn't sure if I was picking a fight or just resuming one. "It's crap. It's fake, it's not real. Why do you act like we're perfect?"

I knew I had crossed a line. Maybe I wasn't perfect, but Jake was, at least in his own playbook, and now I was challenging that. He picked up a big wooden Easter bunny, looked at it square in its painted-on eyes, and hurled it at the sliding glass door that went out to the back porch; it hit with a terrible "whap!" and broke into two pieces. Jake calmed down within the next few minutes, though, and the following day the bunny was glued together and back at the bottom of the bookcase.

The news that I'd actually been accepted to law school—to UCLA—came when I most needed it, and it came in a phone call. The woman on the line delivered the pro forma announcement in a rehearsed, measured tone, but she might as well have been a visitor from Publishers Clearing House standing at the front door with a big check. I hollered, "Thank you! Thank you!" over and over into the phone. I may have deafened her. *Now my life's really going to change*, I thought—as though it hadn't been changing all along.

■ ■ ■

Jake had always given me wonderful gifts: a promise ring for Christmas, two dozen roses on my birthday, a violin on Valentine's Day.

For months I'd been stashing away money to give him a gift for his graduation from Fresno State and his own acceptance to grad school. We'd accomplished so much in our time together; I wanted there to be peace between us. The moment I told him about the graduation gift—a trip to Europe—all the dissatisfaction we had built up over the past few months disappeared. We'd done everything we'd set out to do, and now, here was our reward. "Rome!" he said. "There's so much history there! I can't believe we're going!"

It was a thrill for us both to get that first passport stamp, and the trip itself was beautiful. In Rome the weather was perfect, and the Vatican was amazing, but we were in two separate worlds. I knew nothing about Europe, so while Jake went through his mini-lectures, I absorbed the place, the feeling, the bit of chaos, and the flood of culture.

In Paris we moved at a faster pace. "Let's dress up for the Moulin Rouge tonight," Jake said. "We'll stop at the Eiffel Tower on the way." I was so tired, but Jake wasn't going to let me slow down. "We have to go tonight," he insisted. "There's no other time." We left the hotel with just enough time to make a train.

At the top of the tower, we were both struck by the beauty of the evening skyline. The City of Lights was everything I'd ever dreamed, with postcard images coming to life before my eyes. As we walked from one side to the other on the highest platform, he dropped down to one knee, pulled a ring box out of his pocket, and opened it. He struggled to get the words out. My eyes went from his face to the diamond and back to his face. My breath stuck in my chest. I was terrified—wrought-iron gates, nowhere to run, nearly a thousand feet in the air, and I couldn't even get close enough to the edge to jump. *Oh, my God*, I thought, *help me*—and it really was a prayer. *What do I do? What do I do?* I didn't realize how much time had passed since he asked. We were the show, as everyone on the top of the tower turned away from the Paris skyline and toward us. This was the way Jake wanted it, but I secretly wished it could have been more intimate, in a setting where I was agreeing because I wanted to, and not because of the overwhelming magnificence of it all.

"Yes," I managed to say. "I will." People I didn't know began cheering, and flash cameras were going off. Even now, we are probably in a photo album somewhere on the other side of the world.

On the flight home, as we approached LAX, I started to sneeze. First one big sneeze, then another, then another, and a fourth, and a fifth. Soon I couldn't control it. I was having an allergy attack. My face started to get hot, and as we deplaned it got worse and worse. I rushed to the airport bathroom to look in the mirror for the first time—my face was completely swollen. The sneezing wasn't stopping, either. By the time we went through customs in LAX, where we made a stop, and into our car, my face was as puffy as a basketball and it felt like fire. I'd asked God for help. If this was the help, I was in very big trouble.

We drove through Los Angeles looking for a walk-in clinic, me gasping and wanting desperately to scratch and dig at my skin and Jake looking wild-eyed and grim. We found a clinic and rushed in, and while I did the intake paperwork, Jake didn't leave my side. Weirdly, my blood pressure was normal, and so was my temperature. The only shock was that I had gained eight pounds since we'd left for Europe. Eight pounds in only two weeks! Of course, we'd eaten cheese and chocolate and bread and butter and we drank a lot as well, and walking miles every day didn't come close to burning off what we were taking in. Still, I thought it was a few pounds to burn off. When I told the doctor about the thyroid surgery, he nodded. "Your metabolism isn't where it should be yet," he said. "It might be that the synthetic hormone levels need to be adjusted."

Jake barely said a word at the doctor's office. Initially, he'd been worried; once we'd been reassured and I'd been sent out the door with a couple of prescriptions, he was upset. I hoped it was about the way our trip had ended, but suddenly I knew it was about the scale. When he parked the car in the Rite Aid parking lot, I said, "What's the matter?" He looked at me and then at my ring.

"I can't do it, Carissa." I heard guilt in his voice, and regret, and even fear.

"What do you mean, you can't do it?" I asked.

"I can't marry someone who is overweight. You're fat."

I could not believe what I was hearing. I felt ugly—how could I have looked otherwise with my red face puffed up like the Elephant Man's, my clothes wrinkled and sweaty, my hands swollen so big the engagement ring felt like a small vise on my finger? Right at that moment, I didn't want to marry him, either, but I didn't want him to dump me, not here, not under these circumstances. I started to cry. "Can you just pick up my prescription, so I don't have to go in like this?"

"Sure." He opened the car door and disappeared inside the pharmacy. I cried until he came back to the car. We drove to my sister's, where we'd planned to stay until we found an apartment near the law school. "I'm sick," I told her, and went straight to bed.

The next morning he apologized, and I cried again, this time in relief. We both admitted that it had been a bad scene, that we were exhausted, that so much was changing so fast—once we were settled into our new home and our new routine, back in school and focused on the future, everything would be back to normal. Everything would be just fine.

CHAPTER TEN

Emily was at least as excited as I was that I got into UCLA's top-tier law school. "My baby sister is going to law school!" Proudly, she paraded me around her office at the California Public Utilities Commission, introducing me to colleagues. As we approached the chief lawyer's office, she said, "I really respect him. He's brilliant in hearings and depositions." When I extended my hand, he took it, looked into my eyes, and said, "Is there any way that I can convince you to do something more meaningful with your future?" He saw the surprise on my face and smiled ruefully. "Sorry. I don't expect you to understand until you're done, but by then, it will be too late."

As my routine stabilized and I heard classmates making plans for summer internships and clerkships and specializations and career directions after law school, I sensed that there was a code, an unwritten book of rules, that I still wasn't understanding. My professors were inundated and busy, and so were my classmates. I realized that what I needed was a guide, an interpreter or translator of this culture. I needed a mentor.

The annual UCLA Public Interest Law Fund auction was (and still is) one of the biggest events of the year. It was said that the specialty of public interest law gives the greatest satisfaction for the least pay. This was a job my friends would take, I thought, but I simply couldn't afford it. At the very least, attending and bidding at the silent auction would support them. Plus, it just looked like fun, free wine and beer, and a chance to score some nice gifts: auction items I otherwise couldn't afford, like high-priced haircuts, manicures, lunches, and dinners. Some of the faculty were putting themselves on the block. One professor would prepare a home-cooked dinner for six; another donated a week at his vacation home. But one offering in particular caught my eye: lunch with Sky Moore, a UCLA alum and adjunct professor in both the law school and Anderson School of Management. In addition to lunch, he offered a chance to review all his class and study notes from his student days and a $250 refund on the winning bid. Free time with a professor named Sky was better than a haircut, and just what I needed.

The bidding started at $300. There were at least four bidders. It went up to $400, then $500. I stayed in. At $550, lunch was mine; with the refund, I'd have $300 on the credit card—more than I'd planned to spend, but with any luck, worth every penny. We exchanged e-mails to set up the lunch meeting for the following week, and I rehearsed my half of the conversation.

We met at an Asian fusion restaurant near Sky's office in Century City, and he asked all the usual questions: What aspect of law was I exploring? How were classes going? How did I get to UCLA? "I'm looking for a mentor," I said, with my usual discomfort with small talk. "I need some guidance about where to go from here and how to put it all together. Do you think you could help me?"

"You seem pretty sure of yourself," he said, smiling. "I can't imagine that you need much help."

I shook my head and took a deep breath. "Well, it's complicated. I didn't exactly take the direct route to get here," I said. "In fact, I spent some time on the wrong side of the courtroom as a kid. I was a runaway when I was twelve, I was homeless, and I was locked up in juvy."

He sat straight up in his chair. "Did somebody set this up?" he asked. "Why did you bid on me?"

"Nobody set this up," I said, a little confused about his reaction. "I bid on you because your name is Sky, same as my sister. I thought it was some kind of sign."

"Well," he said, relaxing into his chair, "this *is* a trip. Because I'm more like you than anyone knows. I had a similar past as a kid, one that I'm not returning to, ever." He mentioned having a sibling still on the streets. We were both amazed at the coincidence. Sky put his notebook and all the stuff about succeeding in law school to the side. "Okay, so how *did* you get here?" After I gave him the short version, he willingly took on the role of my first mentor at law school.

The jobs my fellow students all seemed to want were in corporate law. Sky warned me about the big firms and what they expected from new associates in exchange for high salaries—long days, late nights, lost weekends, and bad burnout. I had reason to believe him—one alum I'd met was only a year out and had deep, dark circles under her eyes. She'd left a high-end firm a month earlier and was looking to catch up on sleep before finding something new. I checked out her picture in the law school face book; she'd easily aged ten years since graduation. Other alums I spoke with were wearing elegant designer suits but confessed to buying them bigger every few months—no time to exercise, no time for vacation, and pounding down carbs or booze to counter the stress. I wondered about home lives, about spouses and children. The final straw was when a partner at a large firm warned me directly, "Any big firm will bleed you dry!"

■ ■ ■

About two weeks before an exam in criminology class, I was in a small-group study session analyzing a rape case. The husband had raped the wife. Was it rape? My hands started to itch and swell. The night before, I'd seen a small red welt the size of a nickel on my waistline, but I'd ignored it. *Go away, go away.* Now, looking at my hands, I stopped typing, closed my laptop, and walked out of the room. I couldn't deny what was happening, and I knew if I stayed, it would only get worse. By the time finals came around, I looked like I had a bad case of the measles.

When I went to the doctor at the UCLA student health center, we tried to figure out the best mix of antihistamines and steroids to combat what was going on inside me. Many of these drugs I'd already tried; a couple were so strong they made me sleepy, the last thing I needed in law school, where students pride themselves on working the same number of sleepless hours that med students do.

"I think it's caused by stress," the doctor said. "Have you ever considered talking to a therapist?"

I had a hard enough time talking to people I knew well. Talking to Jake about the things that kept me off balance or uncertain upset him; we were on a path forward, and he didn't want to hear about doubts that might set us back. Talking to Sky about the past was different. It wasn't personal and felt more like an investment, a way to gain perspective. Classmates I spoke to were helpful but didn't really know how to respond, and even this talk with a doctor in her exam room made me jumpy. Still, I'd gotten something out of talking to therapists in the past, so it didn't seem totally off the wall. This was law school, not junior high—I had earned my way here, and no matter what I had to do, I was not going to drop out or let this sickness take me down. "Yes, I'll make an appointment," I said. "I have to do something."

My doctor wrote down the names of three therapists who might possibly be willing to see me on a sliding scale, for a fee I could afford. I left messages with all three. Only one of them was taking new patients, and she scheduled an appointment immediately and gave me some of her background. Her name was Ceth, and she had worked with adolescents, specifically with teen girls, but was now in a much broader practice. "The first appointment will be free," she said. "It's an initial meeting, just to see how we can work together."

The building Ceth's office was in was not the sterile, intimidating medical space I expected; it was a prominent financial building on Wilshire Boulevard. I didn't wait long on the couch in the waiting room, and the first thing I did when I walked into her office was let out a deep breath, relieved to be in a safe, confidential space. The office was clean, not cluttered. The lighting was low and warm, not institutional; it was simple and modern. I felt comfortable.

As Ceth and I began exchanging information, I found myself wanting to tell her everything, and soon I did—about my past, about my current life, about my fiancé, about law school classmates, and about ambitions.

My physical response to therapy came almost immediately—as soon as I was able to speak openly, the hives went away. Allowing a professional, a woman schooled in the intricate workings of the mind, to know my truth was like a child turning the light on in a dark room and realizing that the monster is just a chair. "But why can't I forget these things, these images?" I asked. "Why do they come up in my dreams and trigger hives and night sweats? It's been so many years, and I'm building a different life now—why isn't that enough?"

"No one forgets that kind of trauma," she said. "And it can't simply be filed away. People deny it or medicate it, but ultimately it has to be faced. You spend so much energy holding it down that you barely have enough left over for anything else. It works for a while, but eventually your body revolts with hives, chronic colds, arthritis, asthma, even cancer." These were all common in my family.

"It's like I'm not even at home in my own body," I said. I told her how awful I felt about not being able to have children, being scarred, and winding up covered in hives, all because of these things that happened to me when I was a kid.

"Do you want children?" she asked.

"I don't know, but I want to be able to choose and not have to pay to make it happen." Jake and I had never discussed children more than to say that if the doctors couldn't make it happen when we were ready, then we'd adopt.

She nodded. "Your body's reaction is telling you something. The triggers, like talking about rape and your recent surgery, are just that—triggers. What you've got to deal with is what's underneath." I thought back to my first therapy session when I was attending Cuesta.

"Imagine those memories are like a beach ball. And you are holding that beach ball underwater in a large pool. How much energy does it take? How much does it want to come up?"

I responded to Ceth, "My beach ball needs to come to the surface." And then I told her the story of my first therapy session. "I was nineteen then, and not ready to let anything up. My therapist had warned me that if I chose to bring things out we'd do it slowly, together, and in the safety of her office."

"And if you let it up too fast? What are you afraid of?" Ceth asked.

"I'm afraid of the splash," I replied. "It's like I'm in the water and I'm afraid I'll get drenched."

"Soaking wet or hives?" Ceth had a way of pointing out the obvious. I was strong enough to handle these memories and begin the process of allowing them to surface.

"What about the way I feel about my life right now? Is this really all about the past, or is it just the current stress of exams, law school, and normal life pressures?" I asked.

"It's both."

I thought about the selective way I'd controlled the various revelations to different people. My deductive math brain had kept the past locked up tight. The equations looked like this:

The past: rape + crime + prostitution + incarceration = rejection + failure

The future: education + work + growth + freedom =
acceptance + success

I never shared anything that didn't add up to positivity. When
I thought about it honestly, I wasn't even sure I'd ever told Jake
my entire story. It was easy to say that I'd been kidnapped, that sex had
been forced on me. But to admit that I'd gone back out on the streets,
that I'd had sex with strangers, even after Icey was gone, even after
I was back in school? That carried stigma and judgment. *Hooker. Ho.*
I didn't want those labels anywhere near me. I never felt or believed
that's what I was. I'd been a hostage to someone or something more
powerful than I was, and I'd survived that. I was not a teen prostitute;
I was a survivor, a graduate student, a fiancée, someone whose intention was to save kids like me. The beach ball came halfway up, and
instinctively I quickly pushed it back down again.

"I wonder how you'd feel about bringing Jake in one day," she
asked.

"I wonder how *he'd* feel about it," I said.

"Why don't you ask him, and let me know how it goes. If he's
willing, we'll all talk together."

He was willing, but it took some time, and meanwhile the underlying tension and core fragility of the relationship that had revealed
itself on the return trip from Europe lingered. It was as though we
had been injured somehow and weren't recovering. Nitpicky argu-
ments blew up into full-on fights. One fight fueled another, and we
didn't spare the insults. "We have to separate," he said. *No, I'm not
leaving, I'm not leaving. We can fix this!*

Jake and I wanted to be seen as those peaceful, orderly, pretty people that everyone wanted to be. We wanted to *be* those people. But we were both having trouble keeping up with our own expectations of ourselves. We were not the couple in the upscale catalogs or the Sunday "styles" section of the newspaper; every move we made to prop up that image was followed by a fight that tore it down. What had for so long felt like progress to me began to feel like a charade. *The masks we wear*, the Cuesta professor had said. As focused and organized as my academic life had become, I still spent too long in front of the closet every day, pulling out items of clothing, putting them on, taking them off—and topping any outfit I chose with the diamond engagement ring from a man I knew I was not fit to marry.

When Jake at last came to therapy with me, I opened the door to my heart and told him everything about my past. It was a scene of such large emotion for me, I was so caught up in it, that I didn't monitor his reactions too closely. I think I was too afraid of my own—that I would break out in hives, that I would lose control of my own words, that I would race out of the room and into the streets. When none of that happened, I looked at him, and what I saw told me the truth: He was alarmed, he was upset, he was flushed, he was quiet, and he was suddenly very, very distant. If the room had been any bigger, he would've been just that much farther away from me. Five and a half years gone. He was gone. In one therapy session, the snow-globe life we had created was shattered into pieces. The little man and woman inside, and all their little things—revealed to the world as lifeless miniatures of the real thing. We were ending our lie.

For safety, I went back to Barbara. She invited me to stay with her for a few days, and I burst through her door sobbing. "It's broken," I said. "It's all over. It's all broken!"

She knew exactly what to do. Pulling me close, she wrapped her arms around me. "You can begin again," she said quietly. "The past is over. Now we start again." She held me until my eyes were dry.

Jake had been my faithful cheerleader for years, and for a very long time after our breakup I could not figure out why he had used my past against me. As it turned out, he hadn't. He was just as confused and trapped as I was.

Shattering our life together was his only way out of something that in some respects had always been a lie.

The tears rolled again when Jake told me the real reason for our breakup. He knew all along that he was gay. I wondered if he would have loved me if I were the opposite sex, but I didn't have the courage to ask.

Part III

TRUE SELF

CHAPTER ELEVEN

On my own, I was free to do what I wanted and make decisions for a future I would construct. When I was admitted to law school, I'd received a new-admit packet highlighting the career opportunities I'd have. There were a number of joint programs on campus, including a master's in business through UCLA's Anderson School of Management. Most of the politically progressive people I knew were anticorporate, but my research revealed many examples of for-profit business models I liked, companies that not only offered good wages but also did good in the world. These companies had started out as thoughts and grown into major businesses serving employees, communities, *and* the bottom line.

The more I learned about social entrepreneurship, the more I saw that everything kept circling back to money—knowing where it came from, how to make it, how to use it to make an impact. It wasn't just shipping kids out to work on farms, like we saw in our social welfare videos, but building them up, revealing their energy, excitement, and insight to solve problems in their own communities.

I needed to learn more about money—where it came from and how it existed—and an MBA could provide that and more. It was problem solving to the nth power. Getting my business and law degrees together would give me tools to build a bridge between the kids who needed help and those able to provide it. I applied to add the MBA and was accepted into UCLA's Anderson School of Management with scholarships.

About a month after being accepted, I went to a recruiting event for community advocacy jobs. "You've joined the dark side," said one interviewer when I told her about my business-school plans. I contemplated telling her in detail what darkness really was and then thought better of it.

"I can't change the world without knowing how it works," I said. "Just think of it as letting light into dark places." But for me business had the potential to represent the light.

Letting light into dark places turned out to be my new full-time job. During the sadness of the breakup with Jake—and the loss of our well-constructed little world—I grew more determined to stay focused on my studies. The determination paid off, as I did the best I would ever do on my law school finals. It gave me a boost of confidence. I was once again full of potential and ready to take on the world.

■ ■ ■

MBA classes officially began in the fall. That's when I met David Sauvage, a fellow business student in my small study group of five and an aspiring filmmaker. It was a fortuitous connection, and well timed. The idea of making a documentary film about revisiting the streets where I'd met Natara and Icey had been playing out in my mind for a long time. Scene by scene, I could see how the movie would unfold.

"You should make a documentary about my life," I said to David after we'd gotten to know each other a little better.

"What about your life?" he asked.

"About my life, my past, on the streets." I said it with confidence.

"Well, unless you were a child prostitute, it's all been told before," he said. David's tossed-off use of that word—"prostitute"—hit me like lightning. My story, the short version of my time with Icey, had always been: "When I was twelve, I was kidnapped by a pimp." I never thought of myself as the prostitute in that version of the story.

There were a number of possible responses to David's remark, but I wasn't ready to make any of them. I was unsure if I could tell David the whole story, but knew that if I could get enough of it across, we'd have a deal.

Later that same night, David and I met classmates for drinks at a local spot on Wilshire Boulevard. I had taken off my professional armor, swapping my suit for snug jeans and a thin top. I didn't bring up the idea of making the film until he and I were alone, outside the restaurant, away from anyone who might overhear what I was about to say. "There was a pimp. His name was Icey." I felt a pound of pressure jump from my chest. I had said it; it was out there.

"It's a start," he said, and I could see him thinking. "But do you know if it happens to other runaways? How many? Where? Are there still girls there? Twelve–year-olds on Motel Drive?" I didn't know the answers to any of David's questions. For years I'd thought it had been my issue alone, even as I watched similar stories play out in the videos in my social welfare classes. But now I had to face it: If it had happened to me, it happened to others. It was probably happening right at that very moment.

■ ■ ■

I was one of only seven students in the combined JD/MBA program at UCLA. This instantly enhanced my credibility and virtue in the eyes of my classmates and professors. I was wearing a tag of promise, and I was predestined for success. What no one told me, and what few of us realized, was that JD/MBA was not a ticket to a happy and fulfilled life. We were seven different people with seven different paths and seven entirely different ways we would use or not use our degrees.

I knew I was different, not just because of the trauma of my past but because of what I wanted out of my degree. I was not interested in money for the sake of money; I wanted it for one reason: to provide opportunity and decrease suffering. Not just my own, but others' as well. Each time I took on a new challenge or climbed another rung on the ladder, however graceful it may have looked to anyone watching, it was always a fight for me to remain steady. So just as law school and my search for a mentor had led me to Sky Moore, I knew that business school required another mentor, someone who could understand what I wanted to do. Someone who himself had been able to provide access to capital.

Marx Cazenave, a member of the school's entrepreneurial board, had an extraordinary reputation and was reported to be a riveting speaker. His eclectic background—a former Black Panther, a presidential appointee to the Small Business Administration under President Jimmy Carter, and the chairman of his own investment firm, which he had developed in part to open up the world of finance to minorities—seemed to be a perfect fit for me. Marx was disciplined and actively engaged with students. The genuineness of his connections in the finance and business world was beyond question, and he was one of the key reasons people took out big tuition loans and came to Anderson School of Management.

I learned about Marx the day before he was going to be on campus for an entrepreneurial event. He was there to meet students, and I was told there was one spot left in a group course he was leading; if I wanted it, I could find him at the reception and introduce myself. After that it would be up to him.

Entering the banquet room late, I slipped into the empty seat next to Marx as though I belonged there. He was already in conversation with the other students, all of them propped like seals around the table waiting to hear what he had to say. What we heard was not what we expected.

"I made my life hard with drugs and alcohol," he began, as casually as if he were ordering from a menu. "I started drinking when I was fifteen." Suddenly, our full wineglasses at the table became eight feet tall. "I've been through three marriages and two bankruptcies, and at forty-seven I was pumping gas for five dollars an hour. I almost died drinking myself to death, but I've been sober since September 4, 1987."

There was more, and even though his story wasn't the worst I'd ever heard, the pronounced difference between the depths of his past and his present success astounded me. How did he manage his authenticity in a world of business and finance? Did facing his past have something to do with how much he had been able to achieve?

I started to wonder if telling my story the way he had told his could help me be better at what I wanted to do.

Marx asked each of us to introduce ourselves to the group, and I could feel my pulse racing. The guy to his left began the personal-bio parade: He'd worked at a failed Internet start-up. The one who followed was an overworked banker interested in venture capital; after that came someone who hoped to land a job at a hedge fund. Slowly it came around to me.

I knew I could spout my résumé like everyone else had—worked as a high school teacher for a year after college and halfway through law school decided to get an MBA. Or I could follow Marx's example and tell everyone how I had really come to be at this table, in this room, at this time and place in my life. But that meant opening up face-to-face with people I didn't know. In a documentary I could be on the screen but not in the room, but here in the flesh I faced confrontation and possible rejection.

I looked at Marx—he had extraordinary posture. I sat up a little straighter in my chair. I was about to tell a table of men a story I had told only to my closest female friends.

"My name is Carissa Phelps." I focused on a half-full glass of water across the table, and then I let it go. "I grew up in a small town in Central California with eleven brothers and sisters. When I was twelve, my mom told me to pack a suitcase. Then she drove me to juvenile hall and left me in the lobby." *Keep talking.* "I was sent to group homes, but I ran away. I spent the next two years as a junior-high dropout living on and off the streets." *More. You're almost done.* "I was raped more times than I can count. I was arrested and spent six months locked up in juvenile hall, all before I was fourteen."

I paused for a breath, waiting for the ceiling to fall in. It didn't. No one spoke; no one moved.

"I taught myself math," I continued. "I stayed in school and went on to college and graduated summa cum laude with a degree in mathematics. I was a high school teacher for a year before starting law school. I decided to get my MBA too, because without a real understanding of business, I don't think I can make much of a difference in the world." That's all for now, I thought. My shoulders relaxed a little. I think I smiled.

All the details I left out didn't matter, sitting at that table next to Marx. The beach ball was up and bobbing away on an open sea.

Someone announced over a microphone that it was time for students to rotate tables and meet other members of the Price Center's entrepreneurial association's advisory board. Before I stood all the way up, Marx leaned over and quietly said, "Your story is amazing. Find me later."

Flooded with something halfway between joy and relief, I went to the next table, surprised to discover what business school could be— full of human beings with flaws and stories. Could it really be this easy? The faculty member at the next table was Dean Al Osborne, a professor renowned in entrepreneurship—warm, approachable, and kind. He noticed a student next to him was shaking his leg nervously, making the whole table jiggle a little, rattling a glass or two. "You gotta stop doing that," Al said in his deep voice. "It's going to hold you back in life." Slightly embarrassed for my classmate, I thought, *Man, we are just going to come clean in biz school.*

As the evening drew to a close, students flocked around Marx as he handed out and collected business cards. I waited on the sidelines like a benchwarmer, hoping he hadn't forgotten that he'd asked me to stay. Finally he untangled himself from the crowd and walked over to me.

"I get you," he said very matter-of-factly. "And I know you because I know myself. You'll need help understanding how things work outside business school, and I'll help with that." He didn't stop there, and his brown eyes looked directly into mine. "I've been coming to UCLA for over a decade, and now I believe the reason was to meet you. I am here now to be here for you, and I have no doubt that you were meant to be here for me. To remind me why I survived."

■ ■ ■

When Marx first invited me for coffee, I knew I would go, but I wasn't sure what to do when I got there. *Do I valet park? What are we going to talk about? Isn't he so much more important than me?* I felt unsure of myself, but I masked my lack of confidence with a sharp outfit. Before getting out of my car, I rechecked my hair and makeup. At least I could look the part.

I called Marx on his cell phone. "I'm here," I said.

"I'll be right down."

We were to meet in a hotel lobby. I knew that he didn't drink alcohol, so I figured we'd have sparkling water, maybe cranberry juice. I sat down on a couch near the bar; Marx showed up a couple of minutes later, and when I stood and put out my hand, he reached out his arms and gave me a great big hug. We were strangers but somehow so familiar to each other. By the time we sat down, I knew he was my friend.

Marx told me more about his story. It turned out that what I'd heard at the networking event was only the first layer. In the seventies, he'd had a wealthy friend who became his business partner. His friend's family disapproved of Marx because he was African American. Under the mounting stress, his business partner committed suicide. It broke Marx's heart, and he always wondered if there had been something he might have said or done to have prevented the tragedy.

Marx was later appointed by President Carter to be the regional head of the Small Business Administration and White House adviser on small business and minorities. As his dependency on drugs and alcohol increased, his personal life fell into shambles and he lost sight of what mattered most. He ultimately lost his position, and the only job he could get was pumping gas. Then, one day at a time, he started to rebuild.

I was so into his testimony that I forgot we were in a public place until a gentleman approached us. "Excuse me," he said.

The man was in his early forties, he was Korean, and he looked like he was at the upscale Santa Monica hotel on business. I thought for a moment he was going to ask us to move; maybe we were taking up too much space in the room. This guy probably needed to accommodate an important business meeting. I was ready to stand up and move to a small table nearby. "I don't want to interrupt," he said, "but I have to ask—are you Marx Cazenave?"

"Yes, I am." Marx was on his feet now.

"Well, I had to thank you for everything you've done for minorities managing capital." He looked to me. "This man changed things."

By now I was standing behind Marx, who had taken two short steps toward the man. Marx reached out for a handshake and patted the guy on the back. He was comfortable with strangers, open and welcoming. "Let me introduce you to the next generation," he said, gesturing to me, "a joint law and MBA student at UCLA."

The man reached out to acknowledge me. *Firm shake,* I thought. In that moment, it was clear why Marx was a leader. When we returned to our seats, our conversation continued. I wanted to know more—*Is there any room at all in your group?*

He assured me that if I was serious I was in, and for the rest of my time at business school, one Friday morning every month, Marx was my mentor and guide not just in the world of entrepreneurship but in Life in General. He never sugarcoated an opinion or shaded his advice and counsel to shield me. I knew that no matter what he said, no matter whether I liked or didn't like what I heard, it would be his truth. Authenticity was how Marx thrived, and I longed for an opportunity to do the same.

■ ■ ■

In 2005, three years after a Fresno newspaper dubbed juvenile hall's "overcrowded maze of crumbling cells and dingy dorms" a hall of shame, the county decided to shut it down. The news came just as David and I were planning our first trip to Fresno to film there. I'd always imagined that the first time I would tell my story publicly would be at Wakefield, where I'd met Ron. I could picture him there by my side, a group of young girls sitting with us, gaining hope as they realized that I had once been in their place. The brand-new, sprawling, $144 million, state-of-the-art Juvenile Justice Campus would be opening in just a few months, which gave David and me a short window to set everything up.

To speed things along, Ron suggested we call an old friend of his, Elaine Robles, an administrative assistant who knew the system well. Elaine walked us through everything we'd need to do to film in the facility, and just beforehand she surprised me with some news.

"There will be a special opening reception for the new juvenile hall. It will be a fund-raiser to bring programs into the facility," she told me. "The planning committee has asked that you speak at the dinner."

I almost didn't believe her. "They want me to share my story?"

"Yes!" Elaine was excited to be the one to ask me.

"Of course." I hesitated for a moment. "But before I do that, can I speak with the girls? I've never told my story publicly, and it's always been my dream that the first time would be with them, and Ron would be there too."

Elaine said she had to clear it higher up, but if that was my request, she thought she could make it work. And she did.

Before the grand-opening reception, a hundred-dollar-a-plate dinner, I gave my first public speech to a group of girls at the soon-to-be-closed old juvy. Ron sat behind me with a group of staff and administrators, some of whom had been there when I was locked up.

The girls, about fifty of them, in oversized orange sweatshirts and yellow plastic wristband IDs, filed quietly into the gym in a straight line, their hair neatly combed, their hands clasped at waist level. There, in the same space where Mom and I had once spent our visiting hours desperately trying to connect, I stood at a lectern, while David and his crew rolled the cameras.

As the girls settled into their chairs, slumping a little, looking at their feet, I thought, *I know these girls.* I had a truth to share with them. I had been working on my presentation for months with a speaking coach. I'd prepared for every possible response—booing, cussing, even blank stares. I was ready for anything but still started off a little shaky, nervous about how they'd react.

"I was first locked up when I was twelve years old," I said. "I was you." Their faces lifted. As I told my story, one by one they leaned forward, and the air in the room seemed to lighten. School, I emphasized. Potential and possibility.

After I spoke, I walked over to each girl and hugged her, hoping that in me she might somehow see her own future. "Half the people like it in here because they don't have a home to go to," said one of the regulars. "It's kind of like a relief when they come in here—they have a bed to sleep in every night, food to eat."

At the back of the gym, there were cookies for the girls to eat before they filed back to their unit—they stood in line for their share of treats. I knew they'd remember the day, just as I had remembered my family's visits. When it came time for me to leave, I said good-bye to the girls with tears in my eyes and said good-bye forever to the cement halls that held so many memories and ghosts.

That night, in the crowded gymnasium of the new juvenile center, the scent of fresh paint hovered over the tables at the black-tie dinner. So many people I loved had come to celebrate and support me that we needed two tables for everyone. Ron came, as did my sister Sky, along with other friends and family and the documentary crew. I had asked someone who worked at juvenile hall to help locate Mrs. W, but no one could find any trace of her.

When I was introduced, the clanking of knives and forks subsided. People clapped as I removed my napkin from my lap, stood up, and walked to the stage in my new dress. Standing at the podium, with an arc of white and sky blue balloons behind me, I looked at the people in front of me, so many of them with the power to change the fates of children on the streets or behind bars. I leaned in to the microphone and, for the second time that day, told my story. As I finished my remarks, I lifted my chest and stood tall. I did not want or expect anyone to feel sorry for me; I wanted them to *hear* me. "Stay committed," I pleaded. "Reach out. Make sure that each one of these girls, each one of these boys, reaches their potential and becomes a doctor, a lawyer, businessmen, businesswomen, executives. So that someday, when I'm walking at UCLA, one of my homegirls will be there with me."

Back at my table, I was dizzy with the rush of my first standing ovation. As I caught my breath, an older man came up to me, pointed to his name tag—"Henry Wegermann"—and asked, "Do you recognize the name?" I searched his face, trying to match it with the name. Was he a probation officer? A teacher? There was something, but I just couldn't place it. "Well, then, do you recognize this?" he asked, pulling a small envelope out of his pocket. It was addressed in pencil to "Mrs. W." *Wegermann,* I thought. *Mrs. Wegermann!*

"Where is she?" I exclaimed, clasping my hands together in something halfway between a clap and a prayer. Mrs. W had found me. She'd noticed in the newspaper that I'd be among the speakers. "This is my girl!" she'd hollered at Henry, who immediately went out and bought the tickets—a pricey dinner for them, a priceless gift to me. As he led me to Mrs. W, I could feel the tears coming. When Mrs. W and I hugged each other, it was for the very first time; there had been no hugging at Wakefield.

During the sixteen years since we'd parted ways, Mrs. W had kept my letter in her Bible, she told me. She took it out when she felt frustrated or burned out by teaching. When students overwhelmed her, when the bureaucracy set her off, when she doubted she was making a difference in the school or in the world, she reread my handwritten words—"Above learning math in your class . . . I learned that I could do things," and she believed again that, yes, she mattered. In spite of the obstacles and challenges, in spite of discouragement and setbacks, she didn't quit. She continued opening that door for others just as she'd done for me. "I was very lonely as a kid," she explained. "And because I understood that kind of loneliness, I think it made me reach out to kids like you who did not feel connected. A math teacher may be a poor substitute for a best friend, but for some kids, that's all they get."

CHAPTER TWELVE

David and I were both proud of the film footage that was captured in Fresno, and we decided it was time to start screening a short clip. Robert introduced himself to me after one of our screenings, as a volunteer for InsideOUT Writers, a program that conducts regular writing classes in Los Angeles County's juvenile justice system. The program's volunteers are artists, poets, screenwriters, journalists, and teachers who work with the kids, as Ron did with me, to write about their lives and help them, in the organization's words, to "decide how they will write the next chapter." The writing happens on the page; the mentoring happens in the groups. Robert had been working with the girls at a local juvenile detention facility at least once a week. "Would you be interested in coming with me, as a guest, if I can get it cleared with the staff there?" he asked. Seeing the ray of hope I'd provided for the girls of juvy had lit a spark in me, and I readily agreed.

When I went to the facility, I brought along a twelve-minute rough cut of footage from the documentary, which we'd initially shown to potential supporters. I had no idea how big a group would be waiting or, given how difficult it was for these girls to trust, how eager they'd be to have another stranger in their midst.

When I arrived, there were three young women (the youngest was twelve, the oldest I guessed about seventeen) in a small room; a TV had been rolled in on a cart. While the video ran, I paid close attention to their reactions, grateful when they laughed at the few humorous parts, worried when they were obviously emotional or moved. Afterward we moved to a metal table, sitting in chairs that were bolted to the cement floor. Robert introduced everyone, and as we began to talk, a staff member brought in another young woman. "She'd like to join your group."

I wasn't so sure that she *wanted* to join us; she was visibly upset, kept her head down, and didn't make eye contact. She listened silently for a few moments as the other girls and I talked, but the further I got into my story, the more upset she became. Finally she started to cry.

"Are you okay?" I asked.

She nodded, wiping the tears with one hand. "Your story is my story," she said. "I think you were sent here for me. "My name is Carissa, too. I just spell it with a 'K.'" Her eyes were dark and haunted, and in spite of the tears, she held her body slightly away from the others, telegraphing "do not touch me."

I wasn't trained or prepared for someone else's tears, and the coincidence of our names and stories was beyond explanation. "I'm so glad to meet you, K," I said with a gentle smile. "If it's okay with the supervisor, maybe we can sit together for a while after this meeting?" K agreed and chose to stay with us. She stopped crying, although she kept her head down and didn't say another word. When the others in the group had left, K and I started to talk. I realized I might be the first one to ask her what had happened to her. Ron's "How did you get here?" echoed in my head.

K's earliest memory was of her mother's boyfriend raping her while her mother watched. She was five. When she was eleven, she ran away and fell immediately into the clutches of a pimp. She didn't realize there was money involved; she just thought guys were coming in the room to have sex with her. She ran from him, and soon she met pimp number two.

K had been in and out of so many group homes, throughout California and even out of state, that she couldn't even guess how many. She was repeatedly arrested for prostitution but only charged as a minor three times, because she'd learned to give a fake name (which wasn't in anybody's system) and a fake age, just as I had done.

She had a prominent scar over her eye, not unlike Natara's scar; when she was fourteen, a pimp beat her up while she was taking a shower and smashed her face into the shower door. He took her to a local hospital, where the emergency-room docs stitched her up and allowed her to leave the hospital with him. Now she was locked up after having been targeted in a sting operation and trying to run from the police.

"I lost my name out there someplace," she said. "Nobody calls me Carissa anymore. I give everybody a fake name, and my pimp just calls me 'bitch.'" She stood up, lifted her gray sweatshirt, and showed me her back—her pimp had branded her with his initials. "I belong to him," she said, "but I'm not a criminal. I don't belong in here. I didn't hurt nobody." I understood and agreed.

"Will you talk to someone?" I asked.

"I only want to talk to you," she said. "Because you know. You understand." And then she said, "I think something's wrong with me. I'm in a lot of pain. It's been hurting me for a few months, but I didn't know who to tell."

We immediately made a trip to the medical trailer together. The nurse on duty was surprised to see that the girl had an adult in tow. "Who are you?" she asked.

"I'm a law student and K's advocate," I said. "She has some serious health issues but hasn't been able to tell anyone, because it's private, and she's embarrassed. But now she's in real pain. Can you help?"

The woman looked at K. "What's going on?"

K stared at her blankly. She didn't like questions from grown-ups any more than I had. "I think I can explain," I said, and as I did, the nurse's face softened.

"Okay, K, can I take a look?" she asked—asking the required permission. K nodded. I breathed a sigh of relief, having feared that she'd resist being physically examined.

"I'll be right out here if you need me," I said, closing the door between us.

Within minutes the nurse called me in to the exam room. "She needs to be seen at the hospital right away," she said. "We can't help her here."

K was transported to the ER that night for further exams and to address her pain, which was related to genital mutilation and PID, both signs of the abuse she'd suffered on the streets. The hospital was nearby and I was given permission to meet her there. The ER doctor explained to K that she could designate an adult to stay with her, to speak for her. K designated me.

When she was released from the hospital the following day, I started calling everyone I could about getting her out of the hall and into a program.

Good news soon followed. "There's a program created just for youth involved in or harmed by prostitution," I told K. "I didn't have something like this when I was on the streets. It might have made a big difference. They're not like regular group homes. They know about the streets, how tough it's been for you. It's not like jail, either. You do fun things and you're in a special school, right there in the same building where you live. What do you think?"

"Yes," she said, nodding. "I'll go if you say so." The guard allowed us to use a phone to call the 800 number and start K through the intake process. I didn't get home from the hospital until two o'clock in the morning.

Working to help K began to consume me. This was not a case study or a lab experiment or a video or TV screen full of young faces I would never know. This was a real girl who had suffered real damage. I wanted to be everyone she needed—or if not everyone, *someone* she needed. An advocate, a friend, an actual lawyer who could use laws and policy to begin a process of helping her move out of the hell that was her life. *Please, God,* I prayed, *I'm not asking this for me. I'm asking this for her.*

The next day I made more calls to the public defender's office. I wanted her attorney to know as much about K as I did. I also wanted to let them know she'd agreed to go into Children of the Night, that she was sick and needed monitoring—ultimately, I wanted the public defender to get the prostitution charges dropped. *This is a kid, a homeless, exploited, frightened, sick kid!* I knew that being outraged, angry, or pushy was only going to work against me, so I concentrated on being polite, civilized, and logical. I couldn't convince her attorney to budge, so I went straight to the top. The head of Los

Angeles County's public defender's office was more receptive. He suggested that K's hearing date be moved up and helped me get permission to visit her in the facility every day until then.

The day of the hearing itself, I went to the courthouse but was told by the local supervising public defender that I would not be permitted into the courtroom. This didn't make sense. I needed to be there. I'd promised K that new clothes were coming, that she'd have them when she was released. I'd brought them all in a new UCLA backpack, and I stood in complete shock as the supervisor insisted that he would not accept the clothing.

"Why not?" I asked. "Why can't I give her these things, so she'll fit in better when she gets there?"

From the angry look in his eyes, I could tell he didn't like that I'd gone over his head to get K out of juvenile hall early. "Don't you see that nobody wants you here?" he said briskly.

I took a long breath and stated the obvious. "K wants me here." I said it as calmly as possible. "Can't we do something right for her? She's been in the system since she was five and we haven't done anything for her. Can't you at least give her these clothes so she has something clean to wear?"

He didn't even answer. He turned and walked away down the hall, leaving me holding the backpack full of a girl's new start.

I went home completely burned out. I'd been visiting her every day, documenting every detail of her life and her treatment, and banging on every door in the system, trying to dig her out. I was also trying to dig myself out—graduate, complete group projects, manage my own life and work. At night I collapsed on the couch, thinking of this child being alone and scared, probably not getting any real comfort or help.

Maybe I could adopt her, I thought. That thought stuck for all of ten seconds, while I pictured myself being a single mom, scratching out a living while raising a wounded, defensive street kid of fifteen. What qualifications did I have for that job? Exactly none.

Later that night, the call came. "She ran." It was somebody from the program who knew how hard I'd been working with K. "She ran." The words echoed over the phone, and as they did, I felt a stabbing pain in my chest.

I put down the phone, started to cry, and didn't stop for hours.

I'd told Ron all about K when I met her, so when I finally finished crying, I called him with the news. "She ran," I reported.

"Pray about it," he said gently.

"What has God done for her so far?" I snapped back at him. I'd already gone to God and gotten a big "no." I didn't want to hear a talk about God and God's strength; I couldn't handle it. Why had God brought K into my life, just so she could run and be back out there in danger? So I could feel this loss or be humbled by it? Ron was gently suggesting something that came naturally to him, to pray, but after my response he backed off.

"You made a difference for her. You'll see." He went back to the concrete, the logical side of my brain.

"Maybe, but not enough. She needs so much more." By now I was crying again and needed to hang up the phone.

■ ■ ■

Ron had been working when he met me. Like Mrs. W, Barbara, and Mr. Doty, each of whom had some other sort of mission that I became a part of. I thought about what Marx said: "I was sent here for you." That's what K had made me feel. Now that she had walked away, what would I do? Losing her, Marx assured me, was only the first of many lessons I'd have to learn. Helping K was never about what I wanted; it was only about what she and kids like her needed and what I could give—no strings attached.

A few weeks later I completed my first lengthy legal paper on the criminalization of juvenile victims of prostitution and graduated from UCLA School of Law. As I walked the lawn with the other graduates, I saw Ron's face, the huge smile, the look of shared joy in his eyes. I hugged him so hard, my eyes squeezed shut. He handed me a bouquet of roses. "Well done!" he said.

"Well done to *you*," I said. He'd put my feet on the path, and I'd followed it.

■ ■ ■

In all, making the documentary with David took two years from beginning to end—my American Express served as the line of credit that funded our first Fresno trip. We needed a van, tapes, equipment, gas, hotels, and food. David interviewed grad students from UCLA's film school for the position of cinematographer. There were a few requirements: talent, access to equipment, and the ability to work for free. None of the crew was paid, and as David hoped, most of the equipment was donated, including editing equipment on loan from our UCLA Apple rep.

To this day, I have not seen all the footage. Some of the Carissa I saw on film appeared more confident than I'd felt at the time. David pointed out the small things I did when I was nervous—like scratching my head when I didn't want to talk to people and often positioning myself close to the red exit signs near doors. I was critical of weight, of skin, of hair, of the choices I'd made for what to wear, of how I strung my words together, of where I didn't make the point I'd hoped to.

Standing near the row of motels again, where I had first met Natara and Icey, and walking in the yard of the old house where I'd lived with my family, I was tripped up by grief and memories and sorrow for the girl I was never able to be. Learning to accept, to love, to trust, to rebuild relationships, and to forgive would take me twice as long as it did to make a film. Still, opening up to the truth through the film gave me a reason to search for my own meaning, for my own purpose, and for a way to give—no strings.

■ ■ ■

The documentary premiered at "DocuWeek" in August 2008, in both Los Angeles and New York City. Once the press coverage began, I couldn't stop it. "Be careful," Marx had cautioned me. "Be prepared." I'm not sure now that there is any way I could have been.

Predictably, the film created even more tension within my family, and more second-guessing ambivalence in my heart. I knew that no interview in the world could portray Mom as she truly was. I was not surprised by anything she had said, but viewers were angry at her. "How could she have done that to you?" I knew more than they did. I knew that before the interview, she'd asked my sister Sky what to do or say if she could not remember something during David's interview. Sky told her that if she didn't remember, just say that. So when asked about leaving me at juvy, Mom says she "can't remember"— not because she's cold but because she truly did not remember, and she says it firmly (without apology) because she didn't want to look like she was struggling (or stupid) on camera.

Meeting with my real dad on film could not have been more false. It was only happening for the documentary. To make us both feel more at ease, I suggested to Dad that we spend some time hanging out around New York City. I was there on a scholarship, for exposure to a career in finance. Dad loved having the cameras on him. He was the heaviest I'd ever seen him, but he was still forcing exuberance and confidence. With the cameras rolling, he acknowledged me as his daughter, and I acknowledged him as Dad, but deep inside, something else was going on.

We started out walking around Times Square near the hotel. I didn't talk to him about the other reason I was in New York, to explore a career in finance. We stuck to the past, and he, like Mom, claimed to not know or remember much of it. I asked him a simple question: "Do you know our birthdays?" referring to his six children with Mom. He looked at me, confused. No, he did not know one birthday. The next day, when David asked him about when I was born, he stumbled again. "Carissa was born . . . during an Oakland Raiders game."

When I saw the scene in the documentary, I looked at him through the eyes of the child I had been; then, through my tears, I looked again and saw him through the eyes of the woman I'd fought to become. And I knew I had to find a way, at long last, to let go of what we never had.

CHAPTER THIRTEEN

■

"When it's meant to be, it will all be easy."

—MARYANNE, MY SEVENTY-YEAR-OLD FRIEND WHO SURVIVED

FIVE YEARS IN A JAPANESE INTERNMENT CAMP IN INDONESIA

graduated with the MBA portion of my degree a month after law school ended. This degree was less about status and more about gaining access to a world of finance and business that puzzled me. How could profit be above people? Ever? My MBA led to enough confidence and understanding of "business speak" to hope that I'd be able to convince colleagues that business, including finance, could be used for good.

Marx helped me to focus on a career in private equity. When a position at the Los Angeles County Employees Retirement Association became available, he encouraged me to apply. Going to work for a multibillion-dollar fund seemed like the dream job for any JD/MBA student, and with his encouragement I took the job seriously and sat for an interview.

Two weeks later I was offered the position and accepted. The first few weeks on the job I was high on the achievement—a six-figure salary, smart coworkers, and constant interaction with power players all around the world. But as the realities of the position set in, I began to feel ill at ease, uncomfortable about the lack of self-determination. I was gaining access, but it came at a price I would not pay: conformity. It was like taking an exit too soon when you know there are still a thousand miles to go.

I tried an "introduction to improv" class at night with some friends, to keep my mind and self busy and to loosen up a little. We laughed and played in the class, but once class was over, I was back where I'd started, feeling stuck. Something had fired up in me during the documentary shooting in Fresno, and I was flat and uninspired at work—a lightbulb in a basket waiting for something else, something I was meant to do. "Give it a year," a coworker advised. But I knew my boss wanted three years, and I just could not commit to that. I felt like a cog in a wheel; money was not the same as math, and whatever it was I needed, or needed to do, I could not find it in an office. If I had known it would be as difficult to build income on my own, or what was going to happen to the economy—well, hindsight is always twenty-twenty. I didn't want to knock the opportunity or let Marx down or make him regret investing time in me. But I did not want to stay in that job. I wasn't sure where my place was—all I knew was, it wasn't there.

Perhaps Marx might've understood better if we'd known each other during my second year in law school, when I had discovered community economic development. The premise of CED is that exploited, impoverished, challenged individuals can be organized into a community and create economies on their own. For example, a group of women in a poor neighborhood, urban or rural, form a co-op to make and market a particular product—soap made from fresh herbs and flowers, say, or homemade marinara sauce. They prepare a small business plan and borrow seed money from a reputable microlender, such as Women's World Banking or Kiva's Opportunity Fund.

"Regular" banks rarely grant business loans under fifty thousand dollars—a debt a small business owner usually doesn't want or need—but a microlender might lend as little as twenty dollars to someone in a third-world country, allowing the borrower to pay it back sooner, then return for more; the goal is not profit per se but economic development. The lenders stay in close touch with borrowers, sometimes teaching them management skills, keeping an eye on how the books are balanced, and ensuring that the money loaned and spent stays circulating in the community.

One of my favorite examples of CED, Homeboy Industries and Homegirl Café in Los Angeles, started in the late 1980s when Father Greg Boyle, a Jesuit priest, simply got tired of burying kids. It started as a jobs program to benefit at-risk kids who were trying to get free of gangs or who'd been in jail and couldn't get a second chance; it's now grown to include a popular restaurant, state-of-the-art bakery, catering kitchen, and silk-screen business, all teaching work and life skills to kids who otherwise might've been lost. The jobs they do, the products they sell, the dollars they earn and generate—that energy stays in their community and radiates hope as well as autonomy and dignity.

So here I was, for the first time ever, with security, a solid paycheck, and the possibility of success and advancement. And I was desperate for a purpose. I was not a priest or a nun or anything even close, yet I wanted the same impossible challenges that they had. Convinced I could start an economic-development project from scratch, I fell to my knees, squeezed my hands together tightly, and asked God out loud if He could please help me to do whatever He had planned for me next.

The words of a local politician came back to me: "Every community needs a place where you can buy drugs and sex." I wanted to scream when I heard it, but I said nothing. *Does every community need a place where children are sold for sex or introduced to drugs?* If so I needed to be a part of getting rid of these places. It seemed almost too big an idea to contemplate, but if I did nothing I risked being lost, undone, and incomplete. To be fair to myself and to honor my past, I needed to try.

I gave my notice, left finance, and returned to Fresno, on a mission to bulldoze the motel that had become, for me and so many other children, a place that never needed to exist.

■ ■ ■

I was borne back to Fresno on wings of hope, but not surprisingly, trying to raise a multimillion-dollar redevelopment fund when I had no experience, less money, and only a handful of contacts proved to be more complicated than I'd anticipated. The community that surrounded the Villa Motel was made up of grandmothers, aunts, uncles, and cousins of children who had been lost to the ruthless economies of sex and drugs that had plagued the neighborhood for years. They supported the idea of acquiring the sleazy and abandoned motels, bulldozing them, and starting over with businesses that might offer real jobs and real futures for their families. Longtime residents met with new residents at a local veterans' association, and together they started talking about the change they wanted to see in their neighborhood. Elaine, Ron's friend from juvenile hall, had spent her childhood on a street just behind the motels. She spoke movingly about the many friends she'd lost to pimps. Her mother still owned a home there, but it was gated and locked up, an attempt to keep danger out. Time and again I heard the same story: "Before the freeway, this used to be a safe place. Children could ride their bikes and walk to the zoo."

Elaine became a key organizer within the community. She scheduled meetings and brought in her neighbors and friends, as I did the research and planning. We spent hours with her family canvassing residential streets. Everyone we spoke to was ready for something, some kind of new development that might begin to transform the community, bringing jobs, as well as safe places to shop, eat, and gather. The proximity to the freeway and zoo, I thought, could be a bonus. The zoo was anticipating an eighty-million-dollar renovation, and having a nice place to stop on Highway 99, halfway between Los Angeles and Sacramento, seemed like a no-brainer to me. It was an easy sell to the community and, I thought, an easy sell to investors.

After one of our initial meetings, Elaine called me. "Did you see the *Fresno Bee*?" I had seen the newspaper story she was referring to. A facility had been proposed at the site of one of the longtime vacant motels near the neighborhood. "It's a prison, Carissa!" The planning department had approved a four-hundred-bed community-based prison for the neighborhood. When we protested, the prison developers started positioning themselves politically.

As an organized community, we faced off with the developers in heated meetings, in public debates, and finally with a direct request to the mayor, who was the only person with the ability to stop, or at least slow down, the project. Ultimately the prison became a smaller facility that offered housing and drug rehabilitation for women and their children. The idea of placing desperate women in a community swarming with pimps and drug dealers still haunts me. The facility was dramatically reduced in size, but I knew from here on out we'd have an uphill battle convincing investors that the street was commercially viable.

On the surface it was a small victory—the community's support and activism, along with some legal research and persistence, had paid off. Elaine served as a community liaison with the facility operators, working closely with them to welcome their residents, women who were homeless, on parole, or recovering from drug and alcohol addictions. Still, I could not help but feel our "win" was somehow a defeat. A respite for women and children in the midst of sex and drug trafficking? Where children were still being bought and sold every day? I wanted to go further; I wanted to stop this type of haphazard development altogether, but in order to do that, I needed to sit for the bar.

I went back to the books. It was going to take me every waking second over the next three months to learn how to pass this exam. Contracts, evidence, civil procedure—it was time to put it all back together. As I took the practice tests, I watched from a distance as the stock market went to hell. It was 2008, and all over the country almost every financial entity I'd studied in business school—and perhaps could've been working in—was collapsing like an untended bridge or tunnel.

I passed the June 2008 California bar exam but still was not earning any money, and after my bouts with the city and the planning commission, I'd earned a reputation for being "difficult"—and, as a result, unemployable in Fresno. I tried to reconnect in Los Angeles, in New York, anywhere but could not pick up the momentum I'd felt around the documentary, in the outreach, and especially within finance and private equity. The stock market had crashed; the banks were in meltdown, the country was heading into a full-blown recession, and despair was spreading like mold.

On the surface, the world looked the same as it had before I disappeared into the books, but everything was different. "He's no longer at this office," I was told several times. E-mails were rarely returned, unless they were regrets. "Sorry, we can't help you now." Desperation was setting in everywhere. Defeated and down, on my way to a community meeting, I got a flat tire. I had fifty dollars in the bank and wasn't sure if it was enough to cover a flat. I went to my trunk for the tiny spare tire, jack, and tire iron that had come with the car. They looked like toys.

It was nearly dark when a couple in a truck pulled up behind me. "Need some help?" the man asked.

"That would be wonderful," I said, right back on that long-ago Sarasota beach, stuck and relying on a sweet couple who went out of their way for me. Just then, my cell phone rang. I reached into the car to see who it was—probably another call about my student loans coming out of deferment, I thought. I apologized to the Good Samaritan for needing to take the call. "That's okay," he said. "I'm going to get some things from my garage, but don't worry, I'll be right back."

By the time the man returned with the large jack, it was dark, but I was lighter inside. Not only was he going to change the tire, but the phone call I'd received was about a job opportunity. I'd be flying to Utah in the next few weeks to train with an organization that had a formula for motivating and engaging all types of learners. The company, WhyTry, seemed like my only option. And it was.

WhyTry was created to work on dropout, violence, and drug and alcohol prevention in schools. In some ways, it was like my little tutoring businesses had been; the pay would be based on the business I built as an educational consultant, but starting out, I had no business. I put my student loans on hold again and negotiated to have my work-related expenses covered up front. I could once again move around the country and the world.

The job was a catalyst. I began learning the product I was going to sell, applying the WhyTry exercises and trainings to my own life. The material worked to build up my confidence and convinced me that it could do the same for younger students. This formula for hope was the breath of air I needed.

On the road, late at night, I started to write again. I had mostly questions, and few clear answers. "What am I supposed to be doing?" I cried to Marx. I liked this work, but it wasn't what I'd gone to school for. Was the structure of the company itself somehow getting in my way? Or was I doing it to myself?

I was at a conference in upstate New York—a local agency was screening the documentary, and I was speaking to help them raise funds for a small home for runaways. Kyra Braxton, a friend from the world of finance, had joined me, and on our train ride from New York City to Saratoga, all we talked about was building a program to rescue girls. My interest in community economic development remained strong, but with the market still in shambles, the short-term prognosis was bleak. Looking out our train windows into darkness, I had no idea where we were, and I didn't like the way that felt; I was misplaced. *How can I get back on track? How can I make the experience and degrees I have count?*

I once again went back to prayer, slowly and methodically speaking directly to God in a low voice, back to the routine I'd practiced as a child: lying in bed, flat on my stomach, propped on my elbows, hands folded, head down on my knuckles and eyes closed, with legs crossed. In the world I was loud, outspoken, and demanding, a witness, a voice for the voiceless. It was only in the presence of God that I made myself quiet and small. I trusted Him.

Memories, from my first fistfight to Icey to solitary nights on the street, had all caught up to me again, and I had no choice but to trust that it was all happening for a reason. I knew, because I'd been here before, that in addition to being given grace time after time, I'd also been given resilience. When sorrow and crisis are dished out, it is not academic degrees or designer suits that help even the odds; it's hope. My messengers—a helpful man in a pickup truck, a fortuitous call from a job prospect, my friend Kyra from New York—all let me know that I'd be okay.

■ ■ ■

My first-ever talk to a group of incarcerated boys was at Camp David Gonzales, a juvenile detention facility just outside Malibu. Carol Biondi, a true friend and dedicated youth activist, was on a mission to redefine the camp as a sort of pilot project in the probation system. One of the newest offerings at Gonzales was a newspaper class; the teacher was helping the boys write a real newspaper, teaching them to observe, to ask questions, to report about what they learned to the other boys, the staff, and anyone who would listen. Carol spent every Saturday there and asked if I'd come with her and share my story with the boys in the class. She believed my story and my presence would be valuable to them.

I had some concerns each time I went into a juvenile facility to talk to girls, but I'd never dreamed of being in front of a group of incarcerated boys. My personal experience with teenage boys had been pretty bad, and I wasn't sure what to expect. My biggest fear was that I was going to be boring—talking about money in exchange for flesh, about being raped, about living on the streets and spending time in juvy, all experiences I guessed most of them were familiar with. Every possible outcome ran through my mind except what actually transpired when I got there: They listened attentively, they spoke respectfully, even gently, and we had a real conversation, one that I would value maybe even more than they would.

I stood at one end of their newspaper room, in front of, not behind, a long desk. They faced me, their backs to the door, in the standard-issue uniform of white T-shirts, jeans, and laceless shoes. I started as I always did: "When I was twelve . . ." Not one of them wiggled or shifted in his seat; no one rolled his eyes or made a face of disgust or shock at the boy sitting next to him. Faces upturned, their eyes steady and attentive, just like real journalists, they listened. Slowly I relaxed.

At the end of my remarks, when I asked if anyone had any questions, the one that came was a big surprise. "Have you forgiven your mother for dropping you off and leaving you that day?"

My heart sank. "No one has ever asked me that before," I replied, hearing the catch in my voice. The boy was perhaps fifteen, and his question was so matter-of-fact, so calm, it was as though we'd known each other and talked like this for a long time.

"Well, that's been the thing *I* needed to do," he went on. "Forgive my brother, my mother, my father, in order to be okay." He then repeated the question. "So, did you forgive her?" The word "forgive" seemed suspended in the space between us.

I answered the only way I could. "I haven't," I said. "And I don't know if I can or will be able to."

I left that day with the question running in my head, and it stayed with me. *What does forgiveness even mean, and can I do it?* I asked my sisters, my friends, and my therapist to tell me what they thought about forgiveness. "Forgive and forget" was the most common response. *Forget?* "You just can't hang on to stuff or it will get you down."

Another friend admitted, "I don't know what to tell you. I've never had to forgive anything that big or life changing." Sky explained how Steve had apologized to her for "hurting" her and "making a lot of mistakes." He was in tears, and although he did not list his wrongs, Sky understood they included his attempt to sell or purchase her virginity. In his brief moment of vulnerability my sister found out something about herself. She could forgive him. I didn't get it exactly. How could Sky forgive our stepdad for something he did to her, but I couldn't? The father-daughter type of relationship that came out of this one talk was not something I envied or desired. To this day I continue to avoid Steve. My heart remains distant but confused because I believe he is proud of me, that he loves me, and that if he could he would take back all his mistakes and be a better father.

Did forgiveness come in different shapes and sizes, then? Big forgiveness for big crimes; small forgiveness for petty ones? After that day I searched my heart, my brain, and the Internet. I read books on the philosophy of forgiveness, the self-help of forgiveness, the empathy of forgiveness, the getting-stuckness of *not* forgiving. *Can I do this? Should I do this? What will happen if I don't do this?* I gave myself a mantra: *Forgive. Forgive. Forgive.* As if I could will myself to do it. If only I could just say it and make it true—"I forgive!" I tried it for a few days, but I was no different in feeling or conviction. There was something standing between me and forgiveness, and there was no way around it.

For as long as I could remember, I had tried to organize my days as though they were math problems—linear, controlled, with a formula that imposed order on process. Imposed control. Or what I thought was control. I held on to grievances, real and imagined, and allowed friends and lovers in my life only for a short time; my relationships were genuine but not too close. I was always packing, always with my eye on the door, as though preparing for a long journey, a kind of war, from which I might or might not return. When I grew tired, I tried to dig in, make a real home, an actual place to unpack and be safe, but I consistently chose relationships that had an underlying shakiness—the wrong people under the wrong circumstances and at the wrong time.

The need I had to love and be loved was tangled up in the need to believe I was lovable at all—that *I* could be forgiven. I'd lost years of my life—some stolen, some gambled. I'd been shut out, locked up, and told over and over that I was untrustworthy. I'd been introduced to sex not in a way that enhanced or confirmed my essential womanly self but rather by situations that degraded me, interfered with the development of my brain and my character, and even threatened my life. It made every "normal" life situation look and feel like a threat, a fight, a danger. I'd gone through school focused on math and math and math, then on lawyer lawyer lawyer, in a kind of forced march toward goals that kept me moving forward while my subconscious self was mired in the past. It's simple physics: If you put one foot on the gas and put the other foot on the brake, you will destroy the car.

After graduating from Fresno State, I'd seen Thich Nhat Hanh's book *Anger: Wisdom for Cooling the Flames* in the bookstore. I liked the title, bought the paperback, but couldn't "stay" in the reading of it. I'd read a page or two at a time, then I'd put it down to rush on to other things, deadline things, classroom or Real Life things. I carried the book from apartment to apartment, trying to understand the words but not ready to know what they meant. The pages were beginning to turn dark, and the corners of the cover curled up a little. It was not until I knew I needed to grapple with the question of forgiveness that I picked up the book again and realized that across all the miles and all the years, this Vietnamese Buddhist monk had sent me a message: "If your house is on fire," he wrote, "the most urgent thing to do is to go back and try to put out the fire, not to run after the person you believe to be the arsonist." My problem was not forgiveness; my problem was, I was on fire.

I had been so deeply afraid of my own anger at myself and at others that I could not look at it. It stood between me and my reflection in the mirror; it stood between me and the people I wanted to love and trust. It stopped me from being able to forgive my mother; it stopped me from even *wanting* to. Before I could forgive her—or anyone—I had to come to terms with how angry I was about my own decisions and choices. I had to see clearly the chaos in which I'd lived, the circumstances in which I'd been harmed, and admit that all the progress I'd made in the intervening years did not erase the monster emotion that had burrowed under my skin the day my mother walked away. Anger was consuming me like flames that could not be put out.

When I had this realization, instead of feeling daunted or overwhelmed, I felt as happy as the lucky person who finds the baby in the king cake at Mardi Gras. Everybody knows the little plastic baby's in there, but only one person at the table will get it. To some it represents Jesus; to others it represents good luck for the following year. To me, it was the aha moment, and it had been there all along, waiting for me to be ready. I needed to put out my own fire. How it started didn't matter anymore.

At seventeen, eighteen, nineteen, even at thirty, with degrees and accomplishments and honors, I was not okay. I burned through friendships, drank myself silly, and dated recklessly. My only enemy was a mirage, a shadow from the past, yet there I was, constantly punching, defending myself against something that wasn't there anymore.

I found a mantra—*inner peace, outer calm*—and repeated it, hour by hour, day by day. Slowly my heart settled—not because I solved the question of forgiveness but because anger was something I had real control over. I could let it go or keep it up. I could put out the fire or let it burn. Unlike forgiveness, my own feelings about my own past were entirely up to me. When I realized the power I had, I put it to work a little at a time. As I did, forgiveness flowed in—a sweet result of letting go.

I was afraid, even terrified, when I went to my mother with forgiveness. We had a conversation over the phone, and then, when I thought I had sped through it too quickly to keep it in my memory, again in an e-mail. In making peace not with her but with myself, I made space for a mother who loves me and is proud of all I do.

The boy at Camp Gonzales was younger than I was, less educated, and heading down a path that I'd once been on—yet he was years ahead of me when he asked the question and answered it at the same time. "It's the thing I had to do in order to be okay."

My shield, my defensive patterns had tricked me, but once forgiveness happened with my mom, and I recognized it, it happened again and again. I stopped looking back at Icey with thoughts of how I could hurt him or get even with him or with any of the men who bought the body of a little girl. When Steve approached Sky to seek her forgiveness, she forgave him. They reconciled, but for another decade I would wrestle with the fear and anger that his actions stirred up in me. Letting go of that hurt was the last step in my healing. It unfortunately didn't happen until we lost Travis in a tragic car accident. Only then did I recognize that Steve was human, a man mourning the loss of his son. And it was there in his most vulnerable state that all the things he had done to try to provide for us shone the brightest. When I got the news of Travis's death, I spent the evening with my mom and Steve. I didn't know how else to show my love except by helping with cleaning and making tacos. For that night it was enough just to be there. To stay and not run.

EPILOGUE

∎

"By Coach [John] Wooden's definition, success is peace of mind,
which is a direct result of self-satisfaction in knowing you've done
the best of which you are capable."

–BRIAN D. BIRO, *BEYOND SUCCESS*

That girl in the mirror—she *survived*. And now that I can see her looking back at me, I am able to love her for the first time. She is the child in me who seeks happiness and helps me keep balance in a sometimes crazy and backward world. She's the one who brings me to books like the Dalai Lama's *The Art of Happiness,* which I've read or listened to at least a dozen times. I keep listening because every time I get something new. During a recent five-hour drive, I heard one passage for the twelfth time, but I finally got it: *"When you are aware of your pain and suffering, it helps you to develop your capacity for empathy . . . looking at suffering [this way], our attitude may begin to change, our suffering may not be as worthless and as bad as we think."*

Many of us have so many comforts, we tend to believe that suffering is an aberration, the exception and not the rule; it simply should not be part of our lives. Our entitlement can be so ingrained in us that when we do suffer—from grief, from heartache, from deprivation—it's almost a default position to protest, *Why me? Why am I the only one? Why did God or the universe or the cosmos do this to me?* Which does nothing to lighten the pain and only adds resentment to it.

As I realize the value of my suffering, I see that others feel pain and that they have found ways to muddle through it. The suffering we have in common makes me feel less alone, less singled out, and more in tune with others. Looking for sympathy is "poor me"; Learning empathy is "We're all in this together." One only digs us further into the hole, but the other—the blessed, healing other— sheds the kind of light that will eventually bring us closer to our God-given selves.

Awareness of child sex exploitation and trafficking for too long has been limited to Somewhere Else—far away in Thailand or Cambodia. The U.S. Department of Justice estimates that nearly one million human beings a year are bought and sold over international borders. But it is not a faraway tragedy; it happens here at home as well, fed by (and often shielded by) the Internet, where pedophiles and predators actively search for vulnerable children.

According to recent studies from Shared Hope International and the National Center for Missing & Exploited Children, one in seven American children will run away from home, and within forty-eight hours of running, one out of every three will be asked, as I was, to "take care" of someone in exchange for food, money, clothes and at times just affection. Runaways commonly report that a family conflict led to their departure, but the consequences to them extend beyond the obvious perils of homelessness. In the United States alone, the average age at which children are bought and sold for purposes of sex is between twelve and fourteen; some are as young as five. These children are not prostitutes; what they are engaged in is *not* prostitution. It is rape, abuse, slavery, and torture. The severity and impact of sex trafficking on a victim, especially on young victims, translates into lengthy recovery times with many setbacks.

I have accepted that every survivor is unique. Not all of us love math, or even school. Most of us won't make it out the first time we're offered help. Some of us won't make it out at all. Relapses, whether with drugs, alcohol, or domestic abuse, are destructive methods of coping—but sometimes these crutches are all we know. And "success" is defined differently for each of us: a good night's sleep, the ability to hold a job, to maintain friendships or relationships, to further an education, to be self-sustaining, to trust in people again, to nurture our faith in God—or simply not to harm others in a cycle of violence and abuse that gets perpetuated generation after generation.

Despite all of our differences I find in our similarities my inspiration to continue to do outreach and advocacy. Survivors are the same in that we no longer want to be the victim, and if given the opportunity we will do what it takes to improve our lives. This has been proven thousands of times over in the sexual assault and domestic violence movements, and the same is happening now in our fight against modern-day slavery. We are finding ways to be empowered—through education, mentorship, and most of all through recognizing our own worth by making valuable contributions in our communities.

One program, Girls Educational and Mentoring Services (GEMS), has been working for more than a decade to enhance the lives of young girls who have been disempowered through sexual exploitation. Rachel Lloyd's model of providing opportunities to move from victim to survivor to leader is arguably one of the most successful models in human history.

Though empowerment is the goal, the first step continues to be the most grueling and at times the least rewarding work: rescuing victims from the street and providing for their immediate needs. In the United States no one has been doing this longer than Dr. Lois Lee at Children of the Night. Both Rachel and Lois are available to provide training and opportunities for children escaping prostitution. Lois also provides outreach and housing for boys and has an alumni group that numbers in the thousands. This alumni group, as well as the young women graduating from GEMS and other programs, is paving the way for an international movement to be led by empowered survivors.

The hope I share with many is that the next generation of victims will be met with an informed approach that addresses their actual needs and desires. Continuing the transition from victim to survivor and later to advocate enhances the quality of our services and keeps our efforts in outreach and prevention informed. *How can we know about the greatest harms done in our communities unless we build bridges for those who have lived through them?* Contact information for Dr. Lois Lee and Rachel Lloyd and additional contacts are included in the resource pages at the end of the book. If you are in a rural area or are simply not sure what to do to protect runaways from exploitation in your community, connect with larger agencies that are seeking partners around the world.

For adult survivors searching for an opportunity to give back, browse through all of the resource pages to find something that fits your interests. In my own journey to find my place in this movement

I have made many mistakes, had my setbacks, and changed directions many times. Still Ron, Mrs. W, Barbara, Marx, and my best friends have all stayed on my personal list of resources—which I believe we all need.

■ ■ ■

ROMANS 8:28

And we know that all things work together for good to them
that love God, to them who are the called according to His purpose.

Given enough time and effort, life brings us closer to our true selves. As the years go by, I am better able to accept the flawed nature of who I am. My early experiences created roadblocks to intimacy—hurt, fear, and even regret held me back. I have been close to many people, even loved them, but I could not find a way to stay in these relationships for long. Once fights broke out or disagreements surfaced—sometimes even at the first hint of frustration—I was gone.

Still, I went through the motions, trying my best to carve out meaning in otherwise shallow relationships. I was hopeful that a friend I brought along to share a celebratory dinner with Mrs. W and Henry would become much more. We had been dating for months. He was a good person, with a wonderful daughter, but we both wanted something that I suspected was not there. I tried to push my doubts aside. Leaving the restaurant shoulder to shoulder with Mrs. W, I waited until we were out of earshot, and then I asked her, "What do you think? How is he for me?"

"Oh, sweetie," she said in a low voice, "when will you forgive the men who have hurt you? It's the only way you'll ever be happy."

I was stunned. She must have seen it on my face. The determined-to-be-sure-of-herself woman in me instinctively wanted to scream back, "Never! I will never forgive them!" But I knew better. Her words hit me like a bucket of cold water, as though waking me from a dream. Could it be that I still carried this resentment with me? Was *I* the one who was not ready to be in love yet?

That night as I drove away in my car, alone, my mind still resisted. To be unable to fall in love made me feel like that unworthy, locked-up child who could not be trusted until she learned her lesson. It hurt to hear, but as much as I wanted to dismiss Mrs. W's words, I could not. She recognized what I was capable of when others could not see past my juvy-issued blues and golds. Her belief in me all those years ago had helped me to find my way. Sitting in my car, I let her words of forgiveness wash over me. Maybe I was capable. Maybe I could find a way to forgive those men.

Years have passed since that night, and recently Mrs. W lost her second battle with cancer. But I watched her closely as she lived. She began each day with purpose and gladness, sustained by her companionship with her dearest Henry and her deep faith that God's hand was always on them. Tired moments came, after chemo and lost sleep, yet she still expressed only one thing: gratitude. In the beginning Mrs. W taught me about numbers, the unknowns, the reals, and the imaginaries. Toward the end she taught me how to carry myself in the world, and today her life lived reminds me that only good comes to those who dare to love perfectly.

ACKNOWLEDGMENTS

My mother cared for me in the only ways that she knew how, and as I grew she never once doubted that I could accomplish whatever I set my mind to. My baby brother, my sisters, my nieces, and my nephews have loved me dearly, and life just would not be as good if they weren't a part of it. Ron Jenkins, the dad of all dads, unleashed my potential when he listened to me like no one else did. Ron's family, including Harrel, Rosetta and Dezetta Burnett; his friend Myron Ashley; and his coaches Roddy Hyett, Steve Mooshagian, Chuck Hollis, and Rob Martin made it possible for Ron to be there for me; thank you. Roganne and Henry Wegermann believed in me while Barbara and Doug opened their hearts and their home to me. Marx and Eric Cazenave strive to be the best people they can be and I am grateful they have allowed some of that goodness to rub off on me. Riccardo Baldini, your heart has been able to embrace mine even when we are miles apart; thank you for that and for all your positive energy. I am grateful for Melisa O'Quinn and Rachel Jones, my two best girl friends, who know without constant reminders how important they are in my life. Thanks is a small return to each of you who held me together through the toughest times, then and now.

My literary agent, Stuart Krichevsky, found the perfect home for the book at Viking while Clare Ferraro, the president of Viking, invested in it to make it happen. Joanne Gordon, my first writing partner, created a winning proposal and made contributions to this book's content, but more than that she set a determination in me "to first and foremost be proud of what goes on the shelf when this is done." My editors, Carolyn Carlson and Kevin Doughten, made sure that happened.

I am grateful for all the families who brought me into their homes over the years, especially the Cooke family, for allowing me to move in when I was uncertain about where to go next. And for Patty, Terry, Jim, Jack, Eunice, Joan, Joey, and Alethea for lighting the way toward my new spiritual home in The Old Mission.

Once again, thanks cannot be enough for people like Carol and Frank Biondi, who invest in children who have been thrown out by society. Carol and Judge Jan Levine, Susan Friedman, and Jo Kaplan have gifted me with their friendships as well as their ongoing support. David Sauvage created a short documentary that was the precursor to this

ACKNOWLEDGMENTS

book and many of these friendships. My journey with David back to the streets of Fresno would not have been possible without all the people above, as well as Jamie McCourt, Chad Troutwine, Virgin Mobile's RE*Generation campaign, our classmates at UCLA Anderson School of Management, and the Larry Wolfen Entrepreneurial Spirit Award.

While my attorney, Sky Moore, worried about things so that I did not have to, my writing partner, Larkin Warren, relived these moments with me and continually gave her spirit and her strength for the end product. My gratitude grows daily for Larkin, as it does for all those people in the world who lose themselves in work to protect runaway and exploited youth. Especially Joanna Friedman, Kim Biddle, Marianna Smirnova, Lauren Alon, Michelle Guymon, Hania Cardenas, and Judge Donna Groman, who are fueling with their sacrifice and commitment the change that is taking place in Los Angeles County.

Pat, my closest friend, continues to lend me his strength day after tough day. I am beyond grateful for his focus, reason, and continual reminders that this is not a book, but a calling. It is my hope that in answering this calling, God will find a way to reach runaway children at any moment wherever they are on their journey.

There is more space in my heart than there is room on these pages to hold all of the people, families, and organizations that have helped give my life meaning and purpose. I am grateful for each one of you!

To all the other "Runaway Girls," especially Agnes, Amanda, Ashley, Loretta, Sandra, Shirley, Vanessa, Victoria, R, and K:

You each have the potential to change someone else's world! When we make our peace, close chapters, forgive, let go, and find our paths, we light the way for others. It doesn't take much to make a difference for someone else. The simple words that we take from our hearts serve a great purpose, whether they ever make it onto a page or into a book.

Your stories can shift the thinking about youth, about runaways, about crime, about trauma, and about abuse that happens in houses and on the streets. Each one of you, on your own separate journeys, connects ideas, connects communities, and connects deeply with the spiritual side of life.

When I was no longer afraid, I took trusted others to the places where I hurt the most and let them care for me. This is one way of many that I made sense of the senseless parts of my life. I know that you can do the same, but only you can choose your way. My wishes for you are unending as you find a way to be in this world.

Sincerely,
Carissa
a mentor and friend, for then and now

RESOURCES

Special Thanks

Special thanks to my trusted friend Nicole Hern for her contributions throughout this book and for being a resource to me at times when no one was watching. For the following list of shared resources special thanks go to Kim Biddle, Marianna Smirnova, and Holly Smith, who each contributed to this list. Please visit their respective Web sites for additional resources.

Online Resources

This selection of resources was compiled for the first edition of *Runaway Girl*. It is a partial list and does not represent all of the services that are available for runaway and homeless youth. You can comment on your experience with any of these resources and update the list with additional resources at www.runawaygirl.org.

The following Web sites offer additional resource lists:

Holly Smith's Web site: www.hollyaustinsmith.com

Antonia "Neet" Childs's organization Neet's Sweets has a sweet mission for your next event: www.neetssweets.com

The California Coalition for Youth gathers and strengthens the voice of youth: www.calyouth.org

The Respect Institute is on a mission to institutionalize respect: www.therespectinstitute.org

Girls for a Change is a global organization empowering girls: www.girlsforachange.org

The Polaris Project offers a state-by-state resource guide: www.polarisproject.org/state-map

A Note About Services for "Adults"

Some organizations listed below provide services for women or adults. Typically the age of adulthood is eighteen, but this may be lower in some states and regions. In addition, "adult" services may be available for teens under eighteen who have been legally emancipated from their parents.

NONEMERGENCY 24-HOUR HOTLINES
Dial 9-1-1 for Emergencies

2-1-1

Dial 2-1-1 or visit http://www.211.org to search communities that offer 2-1-1 as a referral service. 2-1-1 is an easy to remember telephone number that, where available, connects people with important community services and volunteer opportunities.

Alcohol and Drug Helpline

800.821.HELP (800.821.4357)

Operated by Highland Ridge Hospital. Provides referrals for drug and alcohol treatment across the United States

California Youth Crisis Line

800.843.5200

Referrals for California–based shelters and services; can refer to crisis lines across the country.

Child Find of America Hotline

800.I.AM.LOST (800.426.5678)

Childfindofamerica.org

Child Help

800.4.A.CHILD (800.422.4453)

To make reports of child abuse. If a child is in immediate danger, please call 9-1-1.

http://www.childhelp.org

Children of the Night

800.551.1300

http://www.childrenofthenight.org

Covenant House Nineline

800.999.9999

Crisis line for youth, teens, and families. Locally based referrals throughout the United States. Help for youth and parents regarding drugs, abuse, homelessness, runaway children, and message relays.

http://www.nineline.org

Domestic Violence Hotline

800.799.SAFE (7233)

800.787.3224 (TTY)

Anonymous, confidential help in English, Spanish, and more than 170 other languages.

http://www.thehotline.org/

Human Trafficking Resources Hotline

888.3737.888

http://www.nhtrc.polarisproject.org

Runaway Hotline

800.RUNAWAY (800.786.2929)

http://www.1800runaway.org/

Rape, Abuse, Incest National Network (RAINN)

800.656.HOPE

http://www.rainn.org/

Suicide Prevention Lifeline

800.273.TALK and 800.SUICIDE

(800.784.2433)

800.799.4TTY (TTY) (800.799.4889)

888.628.9454 (Spanish)
http://www.hopeline.com/

The Salvation Army STOP-IT Program

Chicago, IL
Hotline: 877.606.3158 option 1
stop-it@usc.salvationarmy.org
http://www.sa-stopit.org

The Trevor Project

866.4.U.Trevor (866.488.7386)
Information for lesbian, gay, bisexual, transgender, and questioning youth
866.4.U.Trevor
http://www.thetrevorproject.org

Teen Dating Abuse Helpline

866.331.9473
866.331.8453 (TTY)
http://loveisrespect.org/

Your Life Your Voice

800.448.3000
Crisis hotline. Operated by Boys and Girls Town. Go to Web site to send an e-mail, chat, or find more information for you or a friend.
http://www.yourlifeyourvoice.org

STATE-BY-STATE SHELTERS AND OUTREACH

Alaska

Covenant House
609 F Street
Anchorage, AK 99510-3533
907.272.1255
Youth shelter, crisis intervention, street outreach, transitional housing, health, mental health, and educational services.

Salvation Army
Booth Memorial Home
Anchorage, AL
907.279.0522
Residential and outpatient services as well as emergency stabilization center for girls 12 to 18 years old.

Arizona

Arizonans for the Protection of Exploited Children and Adults (APECA)
Goodyear, AZ
Support activities for teens, life-skills workshops for children and teens, support groups for adult women survivors of childhood sexual trauma.
protectchild.org

Catholic Charities DIGNITY House
Phoenix, AZ
24-Hour Intake Line: 602.486.4973 or 602.434.1100
602.224.5457
http://www.catholiccharitiesaz.org/dignity.aspx

Natalie's House (girls under age 18)
Goodyear, AZ
623.247.6026
(Opening soon—capacity 8 residents)
For more info: jolson@protectchild.org
http://www.protectchild.org

Street Light PHX
Phoenix, AZ
623.435.0900
Housing and more for sexually trafficked girls, ages 11 to 17.
http://www.streetlightphx.com

RESOURCES

Arkansas

Sexual Assault Recovery & Prevention Agency (SARPA)
589 White Rd.
Suite A
Springdale, AR 72762
800.794.4175
http://www.sarpa.us

California

Bilateral Safety Corridor Commission (BSCC)
San Diego, CA
Hotline: 619.666.2757
619. 336.0770
An alliance of over 60 government and non-profit agencies in the United States and Latin America that is convened in and along the U.S.–Mexico border region to combat slavery and human trafficking.
http://www.bsccoalition.org

Center for Young Women's Development (CYWD)
San Francisco, CA
Intake Line: 415.703.8800
415.703.8800
http://www.cywd.org

Children of the Night (ages 11 to 17)
Los Angeles, CA
Hotline: 800.551.1300
818.908.4474
http://www.childrenofthenight.org/home.html

Coalition to Abolish Slavery and Trafficking (CAST)
Los Angeles, CA
888.KEY.2.FRE(EDOM) 888.539.2373
213.365.1906

Social and legal services to trafficking victims; transitional living center for adult victims of trafficking. Specialize in labor trafficking.
info@castla.org
http://www.castla.org

Courage House (6 beds, long term)
Jenny Williamson, founder
916.517.1616
info@c2bu.org
http://www.couragetobeyou.org/courage-houses/

Covenant House
Los Angeles, CA
San Francisco, CA
Multiple locations—national
800.999.9999
http://www.covenanthouse.org/homeless-youth/human-trafficking

FACESS: Faces of Slavery
Phil Ludwig, founder of Teen Rescue www.teenrescue.com
855.690.4860
Capable of caring for up to 150 rescued children. Boarding school model with a family atmosphere that aims to meet the following needs for CSEC survivors: shelter, food, clothing, counseling, education, social/life skills training, medical, liaison to legal services, and extracurricular activities.
info@facesofslavery.org
http://www.facesofslavery.org/

George P. Scotlan Youth and Family Center
Trainer: Nola Brantley, founder of MISSSEY
Oakland, CA
510.832.4546
http://www.acgov.org/icpc/sem/scotlan.htm

Little Tokyo Service Center, a Community
Development Corporation
231 E. Third St.
Suite G-106
Los Angeles, CA 90013
213.473.3030
http://www.ltsc.org

The Mary Magdalene Project
Assistance after escaping or trying to escape
prostitution. Provides a transitional living
center for females 18 and over as well as being a drop-in center.
http://www.mmp.org/

Motivating, Inspiring, Supporting, and
Serving Sexually Exploited Youth
MISSSEY, Inc.
Oakland, CA
510.267.8840
info@missey.org
http://www.misssey.org

My Friend's Place
5850 Hollywood Blvd.
Los Angeles, CA 90028
323.908.0011

888.YOUTH.50
http://www.myfriendsplace.org

San Diego Youth and Community Services
(SDYCS)
San Diego, CA
Hotline: 619.325.3527
866.752.2327

866.PLACE2STAY
619.221.8600
http://www.sdycs.org

Saving Innocence
Kim Biddle, MSW, founder
Los Angeles, CA
Case management and advocacy for domestic child victims of sex trafficking. Train,
equip, and connect front-line workers to
identify victims and provide wraparound
services. Collaborating to create systemic
and policy change.
kim@savinginnocence.org
www.savinginnocence.org

Silver Braid and Voices for Justice
http://thesilverbraid.org
http://www.voicesforjustice.org

Standing Against Global Exploitation (SAGE)
San Francisco, CA
Intake Line for Youth Services (Mon–Fri
9 A.M.–5 P.M.): 415.358.2727
Intake Line for Youth Services (after hours/
weekends): 415.595.5403
415.905.5050
info@sagesf.org
http://www.sagesf.org

Colorado
Polaris Project
Denver, CO
Hotline: 888.229.3339
720.227.0542
http://www.polarisproject.org

Prax(us)
Denver, CO
303.974.2942
http://www.praxus.org

Connecticut
Paul and Lisa Program
Westbrook, CT

RESOURCES

Hotline: 800.518.2238
860.767.7660
contact@paulandlisa.org
http://www.paulandlisa.org

District of Columbia

Covenant House
Washington, D.C.

Polaris Project
Washington, D.C.
Hotline: 888.229.3339
202.745.1008
http://www.polarisproject.org

Restoration Ministries
Washington, D.C.
info@restorationministriesdc.org
http://www.restorationministriesdc.org

Shae's Place (opening soon)
Courtney's House
Washington, D.C., and Virginia
courtneyshouse.org

Florida

Beauty from Ashes
Ft. Myers, FL
Street and strip club outreach.
beautyfromashes.org

Covenant House
Ft. Lauderdale, FL

Florida Abuse Hotline
1.800.96.ABUSE (1.800.962.2873)
Florida Coalition Against Human Trafficking
(FCAHT)
Statewide
Toll-Free: 888.630.3350
Intake Line: 866.446.5600

Naples: 239.390.3350
239.947.2452
Jacksonville: 904.384.0961
Tampa: 727.446.4177 ext. 115
Shalimar: 850.651.2593
Miami: 305.547.1557
Orlando: 321.848.2202
http://www.stophumantrafficking.org

Project Gold Shelter (opening soon)

Kristi House
Trudy Novicki, founder
Miami, FL
305.547.6800
Kristi House provides a healing environment
for all child victims of sexual abuse and their
families, regardless of income, through prevention, treatment, and coordination of services with our community partners.
TNovicki@kristihouse.org
http://www.kristihouse.org

Georgia

Angela's House (girls, 13 to 17)
Juvenile Justice Fund
Atlanta, GA
404.224.4415
info@juvenilejusticefund.org
http://www.juvenilejusticefund.org

Center to End Adolescent Sexual Exploitation
(CEASE)
Juvenile Justice Fund
Atlanta, GA
404.612.4628

Covenant House
2488 Lakewood Ave., S.W.
Atlanta, GA 30315

404.589.0163
http://www.covenanthouse.org

Illinois

Anne's House
Partnership to rescue minors from sexual exploitation (PROMISE)
http://www.sapromise.org/anne.htm

The Salvation Army STOP-IT Program
Chicago, IL
Hotline: 877.606.3158 option 1
stop-it@usc.salvationarmy.org
http://www.sa-stopit.org

Chicago Alliance Against Sexual Exploitation (CAASE)
http://www.caase.org

Chicago Coalition for the Homeless—Prostitution Alternatives Roundtable (PART)
Chicago, IL
312.435.4548
info@chicagohomeless.org
http://www.chicagohomeless.org

International Organization for Adolescents (IOFA)
Chicago, IL
http://www.iofa.org

Young Women's Empowerment Project (YWEP)
Chicago, IL
773.728.0127
Social justice organizing project that is led by and for young people of color who have current or former experience in the sex trade and street economies

http://www.youarepriceless.org
http://ywepchicago.wordpress.com/

Indiana

My Sister's Place
Carol Wellman, MSW, founder and director
My Sister's Place, Inc.
PO Box 24754
Speedway, IN 46224
317.509.1219

Kansas

Veronica's Voice
Magdalene Manor (opening soon)
Kansas City, KS, and servicing Missouri
24-Hour Crisis Hotline: 816.728.0004
816.483.7101
http://www.veronicasvoice.org

Louisiana

Covenant House
611 North Rampart Street
New Orleans, LA 70112-3505
504.584.1111

Maryland

You Are Never Alone (YANA)
Baltimore, MD
Hotline: 410.905.5839
410.566.7973
yanainc@earthlink.net
http://www.yanaplace.com

Massachusetts

Germaine Lawrence (girls, 13 to 18)
ACT Group Home (Acknowledge, Commit, Transform)
Arlington, MA
781.648.6200
http://www.germainelawrence.org

The Home for Little Wanderers
271 Huntington Ave.
Boston, MA 02115
888.HOME.321 (888.4663.321)

Reaching Out to Chelsea Adolescents (ROCA)
Chelsea, MA
617.889.5210
http://www.rocainc.org

My Life My Choice, a program of JRI (Justice Resource Institute)
Boston, MA
617.779.2179
http://www.jri.org/mylife/

Roxbury Youthworks—A Way Back (AWB)
Boston, MA
617.445.5500
http://www.roxburyyouthworks.org

The SEEN (Support to End Exploitation Now) Coalition, a program of the Children's Advocacy Center of Suffolk County
Boston, MA
617.779.2146
http://www.suffolkcac.org/programs/seen/

Michigan
Alternatives for Girls
Detroit, MI
Crisis Line: 888.AFG.3919
313.361.4000
http://www.alternativesforgirls.org

Covenant House
2959 Martin Luther King, Jr., Blvd.
Detroit, MI 48208-2475
313.463.2000

Minnesota
Adults Saving Kids
Minneapolis, MN

612.872.0684
http://www.adultssavingkids.org

Family & Children's Service—Prostitution to Independence, Dignity, and Equality (PRIDE)
Minneapolis, MN
24-Hour Crisis Line: 888.PRIDE.99 or 888.774.3399 or 612.728.2062
612.339.9101
pride@fcsmn.org

Breaking Free
St. Paul, MN
651.645.6557
breakingfree@breakingfree.net
http://www.breakingfree.net

Missouri
Veronica's Voice
Magdalene Manor (opening soon)
Kansas City, KS, and servicing Missouri
24-Hour Crisis Hotline: 816.728.0004
816.483.7101
http://www.veronicasvoice.org

Covenant House
2727 North Kingshighway Blvd.
St. Louis, MO 63113
314.533.2241

Exodus Cry
Grandview, MO
http://www.exoduscry.com

Nevada
Anti Trafficking League Against Slavery (ATLAS) Task Force Crimes Against Youth & Family Bureau—Las Vegas Metro Police Dept.
Las Vegas, NV
702.828.0237

Destiny's House
Annie Lobert, founder
10120 W Flamingo Rd.
Suite 4-506
Las Vegas, NV 89147
702.883.5155
www.hookersforjesus.net
info@hookersforjesus.net
CRISIS: emergency@hookersforjesus.net

Network for Emergency Trafficking
Services—Salvation Army, Family Services
Las Vegas, NV
702.649.8240

Westcare
Las Vegas, NV
Crisis Line: 702.385.3332
702.385.2020
Safe Place Hotline: 866.827.3723
Hotline for Youth Services: 702.385.3332
http://www.westcare.com/slnevada.jsp

New Jersey

180 Turning Lives Around
Hazlet, NJ
Domestic violence shelter for women and
children, transitional housing, counseling,
education, outreach, and advocacy. This
center has provided services to trafficking
survivors. Maximum length of stay at the
shelter is thirty to sixty days.
http://www.180nj.org

Atlantic County Women's Center (ACWC)
Linwood, NJ
Advocacy/support and limited-stay shelter
for victims of human trafficking.
http://www.acwc.org

The Coalition Against Rape and Abuse
(CARA)

Covenant House
330 Washington St.
Newark, NJ 07102-2630
973.621.8705
Provides outreach and services to homeless
youth.

Essex County Rape Care Center (ECRCC)
Montclair, NJ
Trafficking victims would be helped with
temporary shelter as well as outreach en-
abling them to begin healing.

International Institute of New Jersey
1 Journal Square Plaza
4th floor
Jersey City, NJ 07306
Case management and counseling. Multi-
lingual caseworkers and counselors provide
an array of services ranging from seeking pro
bono attorneys for clients for immigration
purposes to providing referrals for concrete
needs (food, shelter, medical, clothing) to
providing in-house psychological counseling.
201.653.3888
http://www.iinj.org

Lutheran Social Ministries of New Jersey
Trenton, NJ
Immigration legal services program to assist with T & U visas.
http://www.ismnj.org

New Jersey Coalition for Battered Women
Trenton, NJ
Provides shelter for adult female victims of
human trafficking.
http://www.njcbw.org

Pathstone Corporation—New Jersey
Hammonton, NJ

800.888.6770

Human trafficking outreach/education services to farmworkers and new immigrant populations, etc.

http://www.pathstone.org/services

Polaris Project NJ
Newark, NJ
Hotline: 888.229.3339
973.624.5454
Case management, crisis intervention, counseling, shelter, legal, and medical referrals.
http://www.polarisproject.org

Providence House
Whiting, NJ
Assists victims of domestic violence.
http://www.catholicharities.org

Salem County Rape Crisis Services
PO Box 125
Salem, NJ 08079
24-Hour Emergency Hotline: 856.935.6655
Office: 856.935.8012
Emergency shelter, case management, counseling, and advocacy for women and children who are victims of domestic violence and sexual assault.
http://www.salemcountywoman.com/help/

Shelter Our Sisters (SOS)
Hackensack, NJ
Shelter for victims of domestic violence/sexual assault. They have worked with trafficking victims in the past when there is a need for shelter and safety.
http://www.shelteroursisters.org

YWCA of Eastern Union County
Cranford, NJ

Westfield, NJ
Elizabeth, NJ
Legal advocacy, representation, counseling, housing program, and emergency shelter.
http://www.ywcaeuc.org

New York

Covenant House
460 West 41st Street
New York, NY 10036-6801
212.613.0300

Safe Horizon's Streetwork Project
New York City, NY
800.708.6600
212.227.3000
Reaches homeless and street-involved youth who are victims of violence and abuse.
http://www.safehorizon.org/streetwork
help@safehorizon.org (allow 72 hours for a response to e-mails)

North Carolina

The Hope House (ages 12 to 17)
The Hope House 2 (ages 18 to 25)
Asheville, NC
877.276.8023 (Mon.–Fri. 9 A.M.–5 P.M.)
877.750.6948 After-hours emergency, someone will return your call.
http://www.hopehousenc.com

Ohio

Second Chance
Toledo, OH
Crisis Line: 888.897.3232
419.244.6050
http://www.secondchancetoledo.org

Wake Up Youth
Toledo, OH
24-Hour Crisis Line: 419.870.4402

RESOURCES

419.244.8911

http://www.wakeupyouthinc.com

Oklahoma

The Salvation Army

Oklahoma City, OK

405.246.1100

www.salvationarmyokcac.org

Oregon

Sexual Assault Resource Center (SARC)

Portland, OR

Hotline: 503.640.5311 or 888.640.5311

http://www.sarcoregon.org

Youth Villages

Lake Oswego, OR

Oregon City, OR

http://www.youthvillages.org

Pennsylvania

Covenant House

31 East Armat Street

Philadelphia, PA 19144

215.951.5411

A Home for Dawn

Philadelphia, PA

Proactively supports women (18 and over) negatively affected by commercial sexual exploitation by providing services to women and raising awareness through education. The nine-bed three- story home was named in honor of a prostituted woman who was murdered in Camden, New Jersey.

http://www.ahomefordawn.org

Project Phoenix

Philadelphia, PA

Support groups, street outreach, and prison outreach for young girls and women.

http://www.projectphoenixwebsite.com

Texas

Letot Center/Catholic Charities of Dallas

Dallas, Texas

214.357.9818

http://www.letotgirlscenter.org

Catholic Charities

214.520.6590

http://www.catholiccharitiesdallas.org

Covenant House

1111 Lovett Blvd.

Houston, TX 77006

713.523.2231

http://www.covenanthousetx.org

Virginia

Courtney's House

Shae's Place (opening soon)

Located in northern Virginia; provides residential services to girls ages 12 to 18 and nonresidential services to boys, girls, and transgender individuals ages 11 to 18. Clients 18 and over receive housing referrals and all other services up to thirty days.

National Center for Missing & Exploited Children (NCMEC)

Alexandria, VA

Hotline: 800.THE.LOST(800.843.5678)

723.274.3900

http://www.missingkids.com

The Gray Haven Project (TGHProject)

Richmond, VA

http://www.thegrayhaven.com

Washington

New Horizon Ministries

Seattle, WA

Hotline: 206.795.1056

206.374.0866
info@nhmin.org
http://www.nhmin.org

Shared Hope International
PO Box 65337
Vancouver, WA 98665
866.HER.LIFE (866.437.5433)
savelives@sharedhope.org
http://www.sharedhope.org

Wisconsin

5-Stones, Appleton and Madison
PO Box 1010
Freedom, WI 54131
920.277.5510
Promoting awareness, support, restoration,
response to sex trafficking
http://www.5-stones.org

A Parent's Guide to Community Resources
in Milwaukee
866.211.3380 for most up-to-date edition

ARC Community Services, Inc.
Including Project RESPECT
2001 West Beltline Hwy.
Suite 102
Madison, WI 53713
608.278.2300
info@arccommserv.com
http://www.arccommserv.com

Rethink Resources
Milwaukee, WI
Young people doing outreach to children and
teens who have been asked to have sex in return for someone's meeting their basic needs.
414.212.5121
http://www.rethinkresources.net
Claudine@rethinkresources.net

Multiple Locations

Covenant House
For runaways, homeless teens, and children
at risk of running away.
24 hours 800.999.9999
http://www.covenanthouse.org/nineline/

Additional Human Trafficking Resources

The Alliance to End Slavery and Trafficking
(ATEST)
http://www.endslaveryandtrafficking.org

Freedom Network
http://www.freedomnetworkusa.org

Human Trafficking Resources Project
Marianna Smirnova, MIPA
http://www.htresourcesproject.com
Marianna@htresourcesproject.com

Migration and Refugee Services, Diocese of
Trenton
Trenton, NJ
Case management services for certified vic-
tims of trafficking.
http://www.diocesesoftrenton.org

Polaris Project
202.745.1001
http://www.polarisproject.org

The HEAAT Foundation
"Turning up the HEAAT on Traffickers"
Support and advocacy for victims and survivors of sex trafficking, forced labor, and
domestic servitude.
theheaatfoundation@gmail.com
http://www.heaatfoundation.org

Women's Investment Network
Shared Hope International

PO Box 65337
Vancouver, WA 98665
866.HER.LIFE (866.437.5433)
Provides internship and leadership opportunities to survivors of child sex trafficking.
savelives@sharedhope.org
http://www.sharedhope.org

FAITH-BASED STREET OUTREACH

Afterhours Ministry
Los Angeles, CA
213.399.0057 or 213.361.7763
http://www.afterhoursministry.com

Night Light International
Los Angeles, CA
la@nightlightinternational.com
Atlanta, GA
atl@nightlightinternational.com
http://www.nightlightinternational.com

Red Light Ministries
Faith-based street outreach, Christian counseling, prison ministry, shelter, food.
http://www.redlightministries.com

Restoration Ministries DC
Washington, D.C.
http://www.restorationministriesdc.org/

PRACTITIONER RESOURCES

American Professional Society on the Abuse of Children
630.941.1235
800.THE.LOST (800.843.5678)
Cyber Tip Line for reporting the exploitation of children
http://www.apsac.org/

The Diane Hall Center for Family Justice
Sandra Day O'Connor College of Law, ASU
http://www.law.asu.edu/dhc/TheDiane-HalleCenterforFamilyJustice

Friends of Battered Women and Their Children
800.603.HELP (800.603.4357)

ECPAT-USA
End Child Prostitution Pornography and Trafficking of Children for Sexual Purposes
718.935.9192
ecpat@ecpatusa.org
http://ecpatusa.org/

Los Angeles Homeless Services Authority
800.548.6047

Los Angeles Emergency Food & Shelter
800.339.6993
Call for information on a wide variety of Los Angeles–area resources for homeless and runaway youth as well as victims of human trafficking.

National Association of Children's Hospitals and Related Institutions (NACHRI)
703.684.1355
Find local children's hospitals child abuse programs under "Directories" at http://www.childrenshospitals.net.

National Children's Alliance
202.548.0090 or 800.239.9950
Contact the alliance to locate children's advocacy centers to provide advocacy and facilitate video testimony of child victims of sexual assault.
nationalchildrensalliance.org/

RESOURCES

National Institute of Mental Health
Information Line: 800.647.2642
Provides information and literature on mental illness by disorder; for professionals and the general public.

National Center for Missing and Exploited Children (NCMEC)
800.THE.LOST (800.843.5678)
missingkids.com

National Mental Health Association
800.969.6642 (Mon.–Fri, 9 A.M.–5 P.M.)
Provides free information on specific disorders, referral directory to mental health providers, national directory of local mental health associations

NAMI (National Alliance for the Mentally Ill) Helpline
800.950.NAMI (800.950.6264)
http://www.nami.org

National Runaway Switchboard
800.621.4000
Information for youth, parents. and providers:
http://www.nrscrisisline.org

SAFE (Self-Abuse Finally Ends)
800.DONT.CUT (800.366.8288)
info@selfinjury.com
http://www.selfinjury.com

Self Reliance Foundation Linea de Ayuda
800.473.3003 (Spanish)
For Spanish-speaking callers in the United States and Puerto Rico.
Provides referrals for health clinics, social services, mental health services, educational programs for adults and youth, employment programs, and legal assistance.
http://www.selfreliancefoundation.org/

PROGRAMS TO MODEL
Children of the Night (COTN)
Los Angeles, CA
Hotline: 800.551.1300
818.908.4474
Dr. Lois Lee founded Children of the Night more than thirty years ago. Her experience in running and growing Children of the Night makes her invaluable to the children and communities she serves. COTN residents and alumni are provided structure and resources as well as individual attention and case management. There is a school on-site and a number of outings that keep the children engaged while fostering a community within the program.
http://www.childrenofthenight.org

Girls Educational and Mentoring Services (GEMS)
New York, NY
212.926.8089
GEMS' mission is to empower girls and young women, ages 12 to 24, who have experienced commercial sexual exploitation and domestic trafficking to leave the commercial sex industry and develop to their full potential. GEMS is committed to ending commercial sexual exploitation and domestic trafficking of children by changing individual lives, transforming public perception, and revolutionizing the systems and policies that affect sexually exploited youth.
info@gems-girls.org
http://www.gems-girls.org

Homegirl Cafe

Homeboy Industries
130 W. Bruno St.
Los Angeles, CA 90012
213.617.0380

Homegirl Cafe grew out of Homeboy Industries. Homeboy offers jobs, life skills, and more to teens and young adults who have been on the streets, in and out of jail, or involved in gangs. Outreach, education, and training are available, along with a wide range of products, including clothing, books, baked goods for resale, a full restaurant, and silk-screening services for large events and conferences.

hgcafe@homeoy-industries.org
http://www.homeboy-industries.org
http://www.homegirlcafe.org

The Runaway Intervention Project (RIP)

A novel, intensive home-visiting intervention for runaway, sexually exploited girls. Program components are available at http://www.ncbi.nlm.nih.gov/pmc/articles/PMC2874576/

The Runaway Intervention Project provides health care, intensive support, and life-skills development for young runaway girls (ages 10 to 15) who have been, or are at risk of being, sexually assaulted or exploited. The aim of the program is to help girls heal from trauma and rebuild self-esteem and connectedness to family and school. The research project has evaluated the program since 2006, conducting a longitudinal of health outcomes for participants and tracking the perspectives of their families and community agencies involved in the program.

Elizabeth Saewyc and Laurel Edinburgh conducted an analysis of the results from the first two years of the intensive services component of tRIP. Findings were published in a peer-reviewed article early in 2010. From 2006 through June 2010, more than 1,300 girls were referred to some aspect of the program, and more than 250 girls received services.

Elizabeth Saewyc and Laurel Edinburgh, "Restoring Healthy Developmental Trajectories for Sexually Exploited Young Runaway Girls: Fostering Protective Factors and Reducing Risk Behaviors," *46 Journal of Adolescent Health* 180–88 (Feb. 2010).

Reentry & Transition Planning Circles for Incarcerated People

Lorena Walker and Rebecca Greening have designed successful reentry and transition tools for prisons and other institutions that confine people. Their recently published handbook is based on evidence of successful reentry and transition processes. The restorative circle practice has promoted desistance from crime while helping to repair damaged relationships. The process has its roots in public health, restorative justice, and solution building.

Lorenn Walker and Rebecca Greening (2011) by Hawai'i Friends of Justice & Civic Education

StreetLight

PO Box 6178
Peoria, AZ 85381
623.435.0900

Streetlight's mission is to eradicate child sex slavery through a three-tier strategy of awareness, prevention, and aftercare. Their

aftercare property is strategically located on five acres and includes one large administrative building, one large enrichment center, a commercial kitchen, a medical examining room, classrooms, and six residential houses arranged in a peaceful neighborhood setting on an enclosed gated campus.
http://streetlightphx.com/
jami@streetlightphx.com

StandUp for Kids

National Headquarters
83 Walton Street
Suite 100
Atlanta, GA 30303
800.365.4KID (800.365.4543)
Operates the Don't Run Away program. Start or join a local chapter to educate and prevent harms that result from running away.
www.standupforkids.org
staff@standupforkids.org
DRA@standupforkids.org

A PERSONAL FAVORITE

There are a number of books on the market, but there is only one that I carry with me almost everywhere I go. My first copy was a gift from a former principal who was my trainer at an AVID Data Analysis Training session. His gift eventually went into the hands of someone else and I purchased another copy for myself. I carry it with me to read and reread and also to pass along to the person who needs it next.

Steve Van Bockern, Larry Brendtro, Martin Brokenleg. *Reclaiming Youth at Risk: Our Hope for the Future.* Bloomington, IN: Solution Tree, 2001).

Submit and gift your favorite books and resources online.
http://www.runawaygirl.org

YOUR JOURNEY YOUR RESOURCES

We all have our own path toward forgiveness, and our needs vary based on our own circumstances. As you journey, the following options may be useful for you and/or someone you love.

Apology Letter

A free program to help people with trauma provided in part by Lorenn Walker, JD, MPH.
lorenn@hawaii.edu
www.lorennwalker.com
www.apologyletter.org

Center for Young Women's Development (CYWD)

San Francisco, CA
415.703.8800
http://www.cywd.org

Esther Fund

702.974.1690 (Michelle)
The Esther Fund connects women who are looking for a way out of pornography or prostitution to educational opportunities, counseling, medical insurance, churches and pastors, mentoring, and financial aid. The fund is established under the XXX church, which provides resources for teens and adults who are addicted to pornography.
http://xxxchurch.com/getinvolved/theindustry/estherfund/index.html
estherfund@xxxchurch.com

RESOURCES

National Center for Victims of Crime

800.FYI.CALL (800.394.2255)

Provides referrals to local resources. Local offices can qualify victims of crime for relocation assistance, security devices for their homes, as well as resources to cope with the feelings of anger and hurt that may result from being victimized.

http://www.ncvc.org

Urban Justice Center (UJC)

123 William St.

16th Floor

New York, NY 10038

646.602.5617

646.602.5600

The UJC delivers a unique combination of direct legal services, systematic advocacy, community education, and organizing for overlooked and turned-away populations. Relevant links available through the UJC main Web page include Community Development, Sex Workers, as well as Homeless Outreach and Prevention.

swp@urbanjustice.org

http://www.urbanjustice.org

Your Own Personal Resources

My own list when I did this the first time included my sister Sky, my godmother Barbara, and my friend Rachel. Initials are fine, especially if you're private and are passing the book along. After you've named your three, handwrite a thank-you note to each of these people for being a helping hand on your journey.

_____

_____

_____

Sample "Thank-You" Note

July 15, 2012

Dear (NAME),

You've done so much for me. (WHAT THEY'VE DONE). How could I ever repay you, but to strive to be more like you?

Thank you for believing in me. I needed it.

Sincerely,

(YOUR NAME)

and how this person sees you

Roganne Wegermann (1950–2011), in honor of her life and legacy, as both continue to inspire!